D0216688

PAYING FOR HEALTH, EDUCATION, AND HOUSING

Paying for Health, Education, and Housing

How Does the Centre Pull the Purse Strings?

HOWARD GLENNERSTER
JOHN HILLS
and
TONY TRAVERS
with
ROSS HENDRY

OXFORD
UNIVERSITY PRESS

OXFORD
UNIVERSITY PRESS

Great Clarendon Street, Oxford OX2 6DP

Oxford University Press is a department of the University of Oxford.
It furthers the University's objective of excellence in research, scholarship,
and education by publishing worldwide in

Oxford New York
Athens Auckland Bangkok Bogotá Buenos Aires Calcutta
Cape Town Chennai Dar es Salaam Delhi Florence Hong Kong Istanbul
Karachi Kuala Lumpur Madrid Melbourne Mexico City Mumbai
Nairobi Paris São Paulo Singapore Taipei Tokyo Toronto Warsaw

and associated companies in Berlin Ibadan

Oxford is a registered trade mark of Oxford University Press
in the UK and certain other countries

Published in the United States
by Oxford University Press Inc., New York

First published 2000

British Library Cataloguing in Publication Data
Data available

Library of Congress Cataloging in Publication Data
Data available

ISBN 0-19-924078-7

1 3 5 7 9 10 8 6 4 2

Typeset by Best-set Typesetter Ltd., Hong Kong
Printed in Great Britain
on acid-free paper by
Biddles Ltd
Guildford and King's Lynn

PREFACE

The research underlying this book was carried out with funding from the Economic and Social Research Council (project R000236610) at the ESRC Research Centre for Analysis of Social Exclusion (CASE) at the London School of Economics. ESRC's financial support for this project and for the Centre as a whole is gratefully acknowledged.

The authors are also very grateful indeed to the many people who have helped us with this project, particularly those involved in service delivery who agreed to be interviewed by us, the results from which are reported in Part III. We also spoke to a range of central and regional officials who greatly helped our understanding of the funding systems as well as agreeing to be interviewed about their views of them. We are especially grateful to those of our interviewees who took part in two seminars at the LSE in September 1997 to discuss our preliminary ideas and in February 1999 to discuss findings from our fieldwork. Their comments saved us from a number of errors and suggested many helpful insights. To preserve our respondents' anonymity we cannot identify them by name (the list of abbreviations below explains the reference system we have used when quoting from interviews), but we are none the less most grateful to them.

This book has been a joint enterprise, but we have each taken the lead in particular parts of it. Howard Glennerster took the lead on issues connected with health funding and with the issues discussed in Chapter 2; he and Ross Hendry led the historical analysis in Chapter 3; Tony Travers led on the education funding issues; John Hills led on housing funding; and Ross Hendry was primarily responsible for the organization and recording of all the interviews. Finally, we are very grateful to all our colleagues at CASE for their help and support throughout the project, and particularly to Rebecca Morris for preparing the manuscript swiftly and efficiently for publication.

CONTENTS

LIST OF FIGURES

LIST OF TABLES

LIST OF ABBREVIATIONS

ACA	Area Cost Adjustment
ACRA	Advisory Committee on Resource Allocation
ADP	Approved Development Programme
AEN	additional educational need
BMA	British Medical Association
CACE	Central Advisory Committee for Education
CFF	common funding formula
CHAC	Central Housing Advisory Committee
DES	Department for Education and Science
DETR	Department of the Environment, Transport, and the Regions
DfEE	Department for Education and Employment
DHA	District Health Authority
DoE	Department of the Environment
DoH	Department of Health
DHSS	Department of Health and Social Security
ERA	Education Reform Act
FAS	Funding Agency for Schools
GB	Great Britain
GCSE	General Certificate of Secondary Education
GDP	Gross Domestic Product
GNI	Generalized Needs Index
GM	grant-maintained (schools)
GP	general practitioner (family doctor)
GRE	Grant Related Expenditure (Assessment)
GRF	Grant Redemption Fund
HAG	housing association grant
HB	housing benefit
HC	Housing Corporation
HCHS	Hospital and Community Health Services
HIP	housing investment programme
HMI	Her Majesty's Inspector (of schools)
HMSO	Her Majesty's Stationery Office
HNI	Housing Needs Index
HRA	housing revenue account

ILEA	Inner London Education Authority
LCC	London County Council
LEA	local education authority
LMS	local management of schools
LSE	London School of Economics
LW	london weighting
M&M	management and maintenance
MFF	market forces factor
MPC	Medical Practices Committee
NHF	National Housing Federation
NHS	National Health Service
NHSE	NHS Executive
OFSTED	Office for Standards in Education
PCG	primary care group
PFI	private finance initiative
PSS	personal social services
RAG	Resource Allocation Group
RAWP	Resource Allocation Working Party
RCCS	Revenue Consequences of Capital Schemes
RDG	Revenue Deficit Grant
RFC	rate fund contribution
RPI	Retail Prices Index
RSG	Revenue Support Grant (previously Rate Support Grant)
RSL	registered social landlord
SHG	social housing grant
SMR	Standardized Mortality Ratio
SRB	single regeneration budget
SSA	Standard Spending Assessment
TAG	Technical Advisory Group
TIC	total indicative cost
USA	United States of America
UK	United Kingdom

LIST OF ABBREVIATIONS USED IN INTERVIEW REFERENCES

Central/Regional organizations

NHSE1/2	NHS Executive
NHSER1/2	NHS Executive Regional Offices
DoH	Department of Health
DETR-LG	Department of the Environment, Transport, and the Regions (local government finance)
DETR-H	DETR (housing finance)
NHF	National Housing Federation
HC	Housing Corporation
HCRO1/2/3	Housing Corporation Regional Offices

Local organizations, area prefixes

IL	Inner London
OL	Outer London
US	Urban Southern
RS	Rural Southern
UN	Urban Northern

Local organizations, suffixes

HEA	district health authority
GP	general practitioner (non-fundholding)
FH	fundholding GP
CE	local authority chief executive
LEA	local education authority
SCH	LEA-funded school
GMS	grant-maintained school
LAH	local authority housing department
BHA	big housing association
SHA	small housing association
TFRHA	transfer housing association
TFRLA	former local authority or transfer housing association

PART I

Introducing and Analysing Formula Funding

1

Introduction

The delivery of public social services in Britain over the last twenty years—and particularly in the 1990s—has been marked by a retreat from the 'command economy' of welfare under which elected or appointed bodies were directly responsible for welfare delivery. This is not just a question of 'privatization', although that has also occurred in different degrees and ways across most welfare services apart from non-pension social security (see Burchardt *et al.* 1999, for a detailed discussion). The reforms have also involved greater devolution of budgets to lower level units within the public sector and in some cases the creation of 'quasi-markets' in which what remain public providers compete with each other (Bartlett and Le Grand 1993; Bartlett *et al.* 1998; Glennerster 1996). In all these cases, central government retains its responsibility for providing the ultimate funding, but is no longer directly in control of those running and providing the service involved.

This kind of development has affected primary health care, through the Conservative government's introduction of 'fundholding' GPs, with control of significant parts of their own budgets, and with important parts of the principles involved retained by the incoming Labour government in establishing 'primary care groups' (albeit at a higher level of aggregation). Some schools were allowed to 'opt out' of local education authority (LEA) control to receive direct central funding as 'grant-maintained' (GM) schools, but others, while still under LEA control, received greatly increased control of devolved budgets under local management of schools (LMS). Within social housing, the importance of voluntary sector non-profit housing associations has increased, while that of directly owned and managed council housing has diminished (although it remains by far the larger of the two).

Yet at the same time, central government has not given up the desire to set priorities and standards. Indeed, the desire to intervene more directly in service rationing, standard-setting and content has grown (Glennerster *et al.* 1991). This can be seen through the introduction of the National Curriculum and increased role of the Audit Commission under the Conservatives, but also through the enhanced importance given to OFSTED in schools and the establishment of the National Institute for Clinical Excellence and Housing Inspectorate under Labour.

This combination presents government with major new dilemmas in what economists call 'principal–agent' relations, especially if it wishes to retain or strengthen the equity goals which still lie close to the heart of social service purposes. Central government has wanted to maximize day-to-day managerial freedom of action, *and* to ensure that agencies produce results which are consistent with political objectives. It wants to retain certain principles of equity of treatment *and* to give users the sanctions of exit and choice. This is made even more difficult where there are separate funding systems for different kinds of agents providing the same service: district health authorities and fundholding GPs; LEA and GM schools; council housing departments and housing associations.

The problem is how the centre can achieve its aims without direct control and employment of those responsible for service delivery. To try to influence outcomes it has two key instruments: regulation and funding. Regulation has been examined in detail in a parallel book (Hood *et al.* 1999). This concluded that regulation in the public sector, including health, education and housing, has increased significantly during recent years. As funding has been devolved to local agencies such as GPs, trusts, grant-maintained schools, and housing associations, so Whitehall has increased the number and extent of auditors and inspectors in an attempt to keep track of the use of public resources. This 'mirror image' regulation has grown up as a direct consequence of reduced control by intermediary bodies such as health authorities and local government. Devolution of funding has required new methods of control and oversight.

This book looks at the other main instrument by which central government attempts to secure its efficiency, performance, and equity goals: funding systems. How these funding formulae have been devised, the financial incentive structures they embody, and what have been their effects are becoming crucial questions both in examining the effectiveness of public services and policy and in understanding the efficiency and equity effects of recent reforms. How Whitehall pulls the purse strings is now one of the central issues in British social policy.

One reason for the importance of this subject is the sheer scale of the sums involved. Table 1.1 shows that total UK government spending on health, education, and housing equalled £92 billion in 1995–6, or 13 per cent of national income. Health spending in particular had grown

TABLE 1.1. *Public Spending on Health, Education, and Housing (£billion; 1995–6 prices; UK)*

	1973–4	1979–80	1995–6
Total NHS spending	18.3	23.6	40.7
Hospital and Community Health Services and Family Health Services (GB)	16.1	21.1	38.5
Total education spending	27.5	27.5	36.1
Current spending on primary and secondary education (GB)	11.9	14.7	18.5
Total public spending on housing	15.7	17.1	15.3
Net subsidies to local authorities (GB)	2.8	5.4	–0.4
Gross capital spending, local authorities (GB)	9.4	7.8	3.6
Gross capital spending, housing associations (GB)	0.6	1.7	2.0

Sources: Glennerster 1998: table 3A.1; Hills 1998: table 5A.1; Le Grand and Vizard 1998: table 4A.1.
Note: UK figures include Northern Ireland; GB figures exclude Northern Ireland.

rapidly over the previous twenty years. The spending items, the distribution of which we examine in this book, made up more than half of this total, over £50 billion.

These funding systems are therefore of great national importance. However, in previous research on housing subsidies, the internal market in the NHS, community care, and education policy, we have been struck by the extent to which new funding mechanisms have evolved in isolation (Hills 1991; Glennerster *et al.* 1994; Lewis and Glennerster 1996; Travers 1993, 1994). Unrelated decisions are being made by individual central government departments or agencies, and even by separate divisions within the same department, often with little or no communication between the relevant decision-makers, despite the similarity of the principles involved. Indeed, when as part of the research reported here, we brought officials from different departments together to discuss our findings, they clearly appreciated an opportunity to compare notes which would not normally have arisen. This segmentation means that in some cases time and effort has been wasted reinventing the same wheel, while in others contradictory formulae have emerged, embodying different incentives and delivering different amounts of money to otherwise similar agents.

In research terms, however, the variety of mechanisms which has evolved, and the rapid changes they have undergone in the last ten years, is an opportunity. By examining how they were designed, what their designers intended their effects to be, what effects might be expected from the formulae a priori, and how those receiving funding have in fact perceived them, it is possible to develop and test policy-relevant theory in this field. In order to achieve this, we look in this book at the ways in which the formulae which determine how much money individual health authorities, doctors, schools, and social landlords receive have evolved and how they operate on the ground.

Arrangements vary in different ways between the territories of the UK within each service. While the National Health Service has been financed in a generally uniform way, arrangements for education have been different in Scotland and Northern Ireland from England and Wales, while housing subsidies have been run in different ways in all four territories. Rather than further complicate the discussion, we concentrate throughout the book on arrangements in England.

We look first, in the next chapter, at the intellectual developments which led to current funding systems, tracing two streams of development from left and right which have both supported moves towards needs-related devolved funding. We also examine the economic theories which discuss the problems around the combination of a unitary, national revenue-raising system and local service delivery. Some of these problems could be resolved by 'fiscal federalism'—locally raised finance for locally provided services—but this is inconsistent with both 'spillover' effects of these kinds of local service, and with an overriding aim of redistribution, which remains an important effect of UK welfare funding and provision (Hills 1997; Sefton 1997). But direct central control is made difficult by asymmetries in information, while local voters lack information about comparative service delivery elsewhere needed to measure and enforce efficiency. Meeting these constraints results in a combination of central funding, regulation of standards, and funding systems which deliver budgets for local control. However, the strong aim of geographical equity in a situation where local needs vary creates a requirement for allocation formulae reflecting those needs. Simply basing funding on actual spending causes efficiency problems, leaving central officials with the problem of finding other ways of measuring needs, or other systems for encouraging efficiency. This is what we examine in the rest of the book.

Chapter 3 describes the historical evolution since the last century in funding systems in the three areas, setting out a three-stage model which summarizes the developments. In the first of these stages the state's concern was to establish a comprehensive, but not necessarily uniform or publicly provided service. In the second (never reached by social housing), extensive public provision was established and the concern became local differences within it. In the third, resource constraints became tighter, leading to even greater pressure for funding to become needs-related. The chapter discusses the factors and constraints which have driven this process.

In Part II the next three chapters set out how the funding systems which apply in England at the end of the 1990s have developed and now operate, looking in turn at: funding for GPs and health authorities in the NHS, including the Weighted Capitation Formula; funding for local education authorities through the general system of Standard Spending Assessments for local authorities, and the ways in which resources reach individual schools, whether LEA-controlled or grant-maintained; and the allocation of social housing subsidies, looking at both council housing and housing associations, including the systems for allocating capital resources as well as recurrent subsidies. Chapter 7 recaps the main features of these systems, and compares and contrasts some of these, including their structures; the incentives they embody (distinguishing between what it describes as positive, passive, and perverse incentives); and the different constraints on their design.

The third part of the book reports the results of a series of more than sixty interviews with actors in central government departments and agencies, intermediate funding bodies, and service providers themselves. These latter interviews were carried out during 1998 in five contrasting parts of England: an inner London borough; an outer London borough; a southern urban area; a southern rural area; and a northern urban area. We spoke to staff from the NHS executive; senior staff in district health authorities; fundholding and non-fundholding GPs; local authority chief executives; senior LEA staff; headteachers and school financial administrators in both LEA-funded and grant-maintained schools; senior staff in council housing departments, and those responsible for the council's 'enabling' role as well as its landlord functions; housing corporation regional offices; and chief executives and finance directors in housing associations, including one 'transfer association', whose stock had previously belonged to a local authority. The codes we have used to identify the interviews quoted here are explained in the list of abbreviations at the front of the book.

In each case we were interested in the perceptions of those people at the 'receiving end' of the funding formulae, particularly in terms of the equity effects and incentives they saw them as embodying. As the four chapters describe, these perceptions varied greatly between the different sectors, but there was a high degree of consistency within each sector. In some cases these perceptions accorded with those at the centre; in others they clearly did not, and the messages the formulae were intended to convey were not being received or accepted on the ground.

The final part of the book draws lessons from the study of the 'transmission mechanism' between top and bottom for this important part of the delivery of social policy. Chapter 12 pulls together the common and contrasting themes from the interviews. We draw out the contrast between health services, where the equity objectives of the funding system are understood and accepted (even if the details of funding are not fully understood) from top to bottom of the system, and the other two sectors where they are less well accepted (although those at school level had few complaints). We contrast the relative sophistication of the way in which the health funding formula has evolved with the more politicized process in education and the inconsistencies within housing. Issues around incentives also differ greatly between housing, where they dominate discussion, and the other two services (where efficiency pressures from fixed budgets are more hidden). We also report on the—overwhelmingly favourable—reaction to the originally controversial Conservative reforms of the late 1980s which devolved budgetary responsibility in a number of areas.

The book concludes in Chapter 13 with a brief summary of our findings, linking them to the theoretical discussion at the start of the book. We then look at how funding systems might develop in each sector in future. Readers who want to avoid the detail of funding systems in each sector in the earlier part of the book may want to concentrate on the summaries in Chapters 7, 12, and 13. Others interested in a particular service may want to concentrate only on the relevant detailed chapters, along with the general discussion in the last part of the book.

2

Political Principles and Economic Theories

The intellectual origins of the funding mechanisms we are discussing in this book stem from two concerns. How are we to ensure that all citizens are able to have access to a standard of life compatible with their identity as fellow human beings and citizens of the same nation? How can we ensure that our social institutions function efficiently, responsive to the concerns of those citizens?

The allocation of resources to schools in deprived areas, for instance, regardless of their performance, is something neither the present government nor its Victorian predecessors were willing to countenance. The efficiency with which central resources are used, matters not just to the taxpayers who provide them, but to those who are meant to benefit. Principles of equity have to be merged with those of efficiency and they can pull in different directions.

Distributional Equity

We consider first the question of how we are to ensure that all citizens of a nation state enjoy access to a minimum standard of life. This is a question that came to be posed in that form only towards the end of the nineteenth century. The long tradition of social policy in Britain had been to rely on local administration. The needs for poor relief were judged locally by local magistrates in local parishes before the Poor Law Reform of the early nineteenth century. The Poor Law itself had been inherited from the city-states of continental Europe. Its tradition of local administration was passed on to the old colonies and the new United States. The Elizabethan nation state tried to limit vagrancy but it did so by making local areas responsible for their own poor.

The fear that such devolved responsibility was being abused with misplaced charity led to the Poor Law Amendment Act of 1834. Excessive welfare payments, the political economists of their day feared, undermined the work ethic and led to overpopulation. The national regulation of the new Poor Law Guardians under that Act did not, in practice, lead to anything like the uniform treatment of the poor. But it did lead to a national debate about the rules being imposed from the centre, for example in Robert Brenton Seeley's *The Perils of the Nation* (1843). As Jose Harris (1999) has recently reminded us, such reactions profoundly influenced many Victorians—not least John Ruskin, who in his turn influenced both Sir John Simon and Sidney Webb amongst many others. If the return to a medieval, pre-urban world was to prove impracticable, how could the principles of mutual responsibility for the nation's citizens be translated into practical policy?

The extremes of social deprivation that the new industrial economy brought to some areas of England could no longer be thought of as wholly local responsibilities. If there was a national responsibility to the poor and to the nation's citizens exactly what was it? For Sidney Webb the guiding principle of the twentieth century would be that of the National Minimum. 'The higgling of the market', as the Webbs (1897) put it, produced such degradation in some areas that the nation state was put in danger and its effective operation undermined: 'No one who has not himself lived among the poor in London or Glasgow, Liverpool or Manchester, can form an adequate idea of the unseen and unmeasured injury to national character wrought by the social contamination to which this misery inevitably leads' (Webb and Webb 1897: 766; 1920 edn.). The only practical way to prevent this contamination was to put a floor under the whole population 'below which the individual, whether he likes it or not, cannot in the interests of the well being of the whole, ever be allowed to fall' (Webb 1911). The authoritarian ring is pure Sidney and Beatrice!

Since many of the local authorities who would be called upon to provide most of the services that would constitute the minimum would not be in a position to do so adequately, they should receive a grant from central government which was enough to enable them to provide such a minimum. A figure should be set for grant aid, 'Taking something like the minimum which experience shows to be anywhere necessary for efficiency' (Webb 1920: 104). If a standard local revenue, an equal tax burden in each area, could not sustain that level of spending, local resources should be supplemented by national government. We see here the essential principles on which later local government grant aid was to be based.

R. H. Tawney, the LSE academic and Labour Party adviser in the 1920s–1940s, set his ideals in terms of equality rather than a national minimum. Tawney's influence on Labour social policy is probably without parallel (Shaw 1996). By the 1930s he had already drafted

Labour's education policy, *Secondary Education for All*, and then one of its main policy documents, *Labour and the Nation*. He founded the strand of thought within the party recently referred to as 'qualitative socialism' (Ellison 1994). In a passage to which we shall return later in this book, Tawney draws out the distinction between equal provision, equal outcome, and need: 'equality of provision is not identity of provision'. To achieve equality of outcome and adequately meet individual needs meant that it was important to devote 'equal care to ensuring that [needs] are met in different ways most appropriate to them' (Ellison 1994). It was one of Tawney's intellectual successors at the LSE who put 'need' at the centre of modern social policy and one of his staff who gave 'territorial need' a practical definition.

The Debate about Relative Needs

'All collectively provided services are deliberately designed to meet certain socially recognised needs': this statement forms part of Richard Titmuss's classic definition of modern social policy to be found in his seminal lecture 'The Social Division of Welfare' (1958: 39). Need as a concept has both Marxist and Christian origins that many others have explored. Marx's classic definition of a socialist society is to be found in his *Critique of the Gotha Programme* (1875):'In a socialist society goods and services would be distributed according to the principle from each according to his ability to each according to his needs'. The Christian formulation is: 'Neither was their among them any that lacked, for as many as were possessors of lands or houses sold them and brought the prices of the things that were sold and laid them down at the apostle's feet and distribution was made unto every man according as he had need' (Acts 4: 34). Yet, there in the last phrase, is the rub. Who and how is the decision to be made about every man's need? For Ruskin the answer was 'pastoral "bishops", responsible for knowing personally the needs, characters, and circumstances of the families under their care' (Harris 1999). The more recent philosophical arguments about whether there are such things as basic human needs, and what kinds of resources they require, have been long and erudite (Culyer *et al.* 1971; Doyal and Gough 1991; Gough 1994; Plant 1985; Smith 1980; Stewart 1985; Ware and Goodin 1990; Weale 1978). What none of these generalized discussions do, however, is to answer the central questions: how much, where, to whom, and decided by whom?

It was one of Titmuss' young lecturers who had the quantitative capacity to take the generalized proposition further. Bleddyn Davies's *Social Needs and Resources in Local Services* (1968) was one of those truly path-breaking pieces of work that affect policy and practice for decades.

Davies produced statistical indicators that could plausibly be said to suggest that one area had greater needs for services than other areas. The age structure of the population, family composition, and correlates of family breakdown suggested a relatively high need for children's services, he argued. The size and age composition of the school age population and deprivation factors did the same for education. He was able to demonstrate that spending by local authorities was not highly correlated with these measures of relative need. He not only showed there was a problem but that there was a way forward. These needs indicators could be refined and used to allocate local authority grants. Much the same approach came to be adopted by health economists in the 1970s. There is, therefore, an intellectual lineage from Webb's national minimum through Tawney and Titmuss to Davies and the formula funding systems we have today. We trace the practical developments in the next chapter.

There is another legacy. This time the driving logic is not achieving a national minimum or equality but targeting national tax resources and the maintenance of local government independence. Here the key figure is the Conservative politician, later Prime Minister, Lord Balfour. Balfour's concern was predominantly with ensuring local authority independence, combined with a capacity to ensure minimum standards throughout the country. Central government should not dictate to local councils but enable them to provide minimum levels of service. In his minority report to the Royal Commission on Local Taxation (1901) he argued that local authorities should be free to provide what they wished if local electors were prepared to pay. Central government had no business subsidizing any level of local spending that local politicians wished to undertake (or giving matching grants, as Americans would describe them). Local councils should receive an allocation which would enable them to provide an acceptable standard of service throughout the country. Help should be targeted on authorities in most need. The grant should be based on population as a measure of need to spend, multiplied by some minimum sum. It was a principle that appealed to Conservative governments and to the Treasury in the 1920s. Indeed, it was to be essentially what the Conservative government was to achieve in various reforms to the local authority grants system during the 1980s and 1990s.

Twin Roots

In short, the present systems of grant allocation we have in the United Kingdom have two long intellectual lineages. They come together to produce a wide political consensus that may seem strange unless seen in this light. The idea of achieving a national minimum standard of life consistent with citizenship proved compatible with the idea of fixed grants to authorities in need which did not encourage profligate spending. One had radical roots, the other conservative. Such principles reflected the strong sense of nationhood, reinforced by the Second World War and the unitary form of government which the United Kingdom has enjoyed, or suffered. How far different interpretations of a 'national' minimum will evolve under the United Kingdom's new devolved government remains to be seen. The hidden subsidies to Scotland and Wales implied by their allocation formulae (the 'Barnett formula') are already being called into question. So far, however, the concept of a United Kingdom citizenship and its attendant social rights has remained powerful in the popular imagination.

Who Does What at What Level of Government?

So far we have been mainly concerned with issues of equity. There is a second strand of thinking that owes little to what has gone before but turns out to produce a very similar outcome. It begins with this question: at what level of government can services most efficiently be provided and what efficiency incentives should those levels of government be subject to?

Much of the economics literature which seeks to answer these questions derives from the United States. Naturally, therefore, it begins with the presumption of a federal structure to government. The whole literature, indeed, is categorized with the label 'fiscal federalism' (Oates 1972). What should the US federal government do, what should the states do, what should local communities do?

The UK, in contrast, has a unitary state and the starting presumptions are very different (Foster *et al.* 1980). In the end the Westminster government has supreme authority over taxation and delegation of power. This is well illustrated in the debate about the Scottish Parliament. It has been created by and could be abolished by the Westminster Parliament and its taxing powers are severely limited. In the United Kingdom only 5 per cent of total tax revenue is raised through local taxation. This is a very low share compared to most other advanced democracies. Only Italy, Ireland, and the Netherlands are lower. In Australia and Austria the figure is 20 per cent. In the United States 30 per cent of all tax revenue is raised by local and state government. In West Germany the figure is similar, while in Switzerland the figure is 40 per cent and in Canada 45 per cent (Groenewegen 1990). Such a presumption of central power is something Americans, and those in many other nations, find incomprehensible. It certainly throws doubt on the proposition that general economic theories can set an ideal allocation based on technical considerations. Why have different nations come to such different conclusions about the split between local and national funding?

The Efficiency Case for a Mix of Central and Local Funding

The economic efficiency case for some fiscal powers being local and others national (or indeed international) is usually attributed to an American economist, Tiebout (1956). He may have formulated the theory elegantly but the origins of the argument can be found in the British economists Alfred Marshall and John Stuart Mill (Foster *et al.* 1980).

A generally accepted case for government involvement is the existence of public goods. Yet these goods are of different kinds. The public that benefits from them may be very local (street lighting in a residential area) or may be rather wider (county-wide roads and bridges not used by national traffic) or national public goods such as defence. Here the whole national community receives the benefit whether it likes it or not.

The essential thrust of the Mill, Marshall, and Tiebout theorems is that local public goods are best financed locally and national ones nationally. Preferences about the quality of local roads may differ. Enforcing one national standard will leave some areas over- or under-provided relative to those preferences. With local taxation and provision something analogous to a market will exist. Those who find the tax price of high-class roads too high will move to those areas with a different and more acceptable tax and benefit trade-off.

There are, of course, problems with this line of argument. Jurisdictions do not readily conform to the great variety of natural boundaries that public goods may have. Indeed no clearly defined boundaries can be set to public goods. There are spillovers from one area to another.

The smaller the country, the more important the spillover effect. Britain is a very small country.

Nevertheless, this kind of objection is not fatal to the overall thrust of the argument. The classic statement of 'fiscal federalism' is stated in Oates's (1972) book of that name. Central government should be assigned responsibility for activities with significant externalities that occur over a wider geographical area than existing or feasible local jurisdictions.

This line of reasoning has been reinforced by more modern theories of the firm and contracting which emphasize the transaction costs of central agencies trying to control local branches. Whatever it is the state chooses to do, it will be wise not to try to run it all from the centre. Local diversity will tend to bring experimentation and the capacity to copy the more successful local agencies.

One real difficulty with the theory as a general justification for local funding, however, is that relatively few of the activities of local government can be described as pure public goods, even less purely *local* public goods. That is especially true of social services like education or health or even housing, which are not strictly pure public goods at all and which have important externalities (spillover effects) that cannot be captured locally. Human capital may leave an area, indeed may have a greater capacity to do so, once its value is enhanced by local investment. Local finance alone would lead to under-investment in education from a national point of view. Just like firms, local areas might have an incentive to leave human capital investment to other areas and then to poach the skilled people. Moreover, a lot of political concern is aroused if it is felt that people in one part of the country are receiving much quicker access to education or hospital care than others. Rights to these services are, in the UK at least, nationally perceived. Moreover, given that Westminster has had ultimate power to act, it has been impossible for national politicians to resist claims of unfairness when access to services is seen to be significantly different in one part of the country compared to another.

In the USA voters seem to have a very different scale of values and the variety of the nation is so great that the same pressures do not arise. Distrust of the federal government is much greater than the distrust of Westminster—although that may be changing in the UK. Responsibility for the basic welfare safety net has recently been turned back to the states in the USA—a form of devolution that would simply be unacceptable in the UK. Constitutional differences are both caused by and reinforce the different value systems in the two countries. Thus economists begin from too narrow a conception of technical public goods. In their strict sense, education and health care are not pure national public goods. Yet, in the UK voters seem to treat them as if they were. They expect a national service or at least a high national minimum. The same is true of a national poverty line.

This leads on directly to a related problem. Many social services, and notably those we are concerned with in this study, have two distinct purposes. They are partly justified on efficiency grounds—they have a public good element. But they are also redistributive in function. One of the difficulties with the Tiebout theorem is that there is no stable equilibrium so long as any progressive taxation is assumed and costs of moving are low. As Epple *et al.* put it, 'Equilibrium will fail because the poor seek to enter wealthy communities in order to consume the high level of public goods provided there, the wealthy move elsewhere to avoid being taxed to provide a high level of public services shared by the poor, and a game of 'musical suburbs' results' (1984: 283). This result is even more pronounced if the very purpose of the service is redistribution.

It is precisely this problem that has concerned analysts in the UK over the past century. Indeed one of the major reasons why the UK has escaped some of the consequences of deep area-based social exclusion the USA has suffered is the kind of centralized redistribution of centrally raised taxation which is the subject of this book.

A third difficulty with local revenue independence is that there may be striking differences between different areas' capacity to tax. The tax base in some areas may be much lower for reasons of natural economic endowment. The delivery of national citizenship goods like education or health care may not be consistent with local funding. This leads to the case for tax-equalizing grants from national government to redress some localities' low economic bases (Le Grand 1975).

A fourth difficulty is that local authorities simply may not have access to the most lucrative sources of revenue. This has been a fact of life in the UK and for periods in the USA. If the centre wanted things done it had to be prepared to use its taxable capacity to make it happen.

As Foster *et al.* (1980) point out, many of these ideas were essentially grasped in the UK as long ago as the beginning of this century, through the work of Mill, Goschen, Cannan, and Marshall. The principles they advocated of shared fiscal and administrative responsibility found their way into the Royal Commission on Local Taxation Report in 1901 and into the Kemp Committee Report in 1914. The former minority report famously distinguishes 'onerous' from 'beneficial' spending. 'Onerous' is what we would call redistributive—the Poor Law, maintaining asylums—and public goods from which the whole local community benefited, such as the police. Here, the committee argued, such services should be financed on a capacity to pay basis. 'Beneficial' spending should be financed by those who gained from it. Local government had access to very little progressive taxation. Poor areas needed most support but had little revenue to fund such activities. The national government was the only jurisdiction that could effectively levy such taxes.

The Efficiency Case for Devolved Budgeting

In the light of all these arguments why not let central government do all the taxing *and* the *administering* of onerous services? The answer, which Foster *et al.* (1980) quote from the Royal Commission of 1901, sums up much of the central dilemma our present system is supposed to reconcile: 'the services in question are of such a nature as to make local management almost indispensable, because there must be investigation and minute supervision on the spot, and there ought to be personal knowledge of individuals and circumstances' (Royal Commission on Local Taxation 1901: 121). This line of argument led the committee to suggest shared tax responsibilities between local and central government. If local authorities were given a 100 per cent tax subsidy they would have no incentive to do an efficient job. Hence they should pay some of the cost. They would receive some of the benefit after all. The Commission suggested a maximum 50 per cent contribution from the centre.

In short, a Tiebout or Oates type theory makes a strong case for the decentralization of purely local public goods. It has much less salience for services like health and education or housing for the poor. They are not local public goods. Spillover effects are large; their purposes have a large element of redistribution, which leads to free rider problems with local taxation. National notions of equity between areas and the central state's greater capacity to levy progressive taxation have left the central state as the main tax authority for these services in the UK.

At the same time, an efficiency case can be made for local provision and administration. Indeed, more recent management theories and theories of the firm have emphasized the importance of delegating budgets down to small units over which a manager can have effective control. Here the lines of communication are shorter and the distortion of messages between centre and provider is less. The manager can identify with the unit for which he or she is responsible. The central office needs to keep its interference to the minimum and give local managers their head, so long as the incentive structure in which they operate is consistent with maximizing the profit or objectives of the organization (McGuire and Radner 1986; Peters and Waterman 1982).

It is from such theories that devolved budgeting and the quasi-market reforms of the 1990s in the UK originated. They are paralleled by notions of 'reinventing government' in the United States (Osborne and Gaebler 1992). Estate-based management of public housing estates (Power 1987), local management of schools (Glennerster 1991; Chubb and Moe 1990), and GP fundholding (Glennerster *et al.* 1994) are all consistent with this line of reasoning. Thus, while the funding of social provision in the UK has become more and more centralized, the administration of services has been increasingly devolved down to units that are small enough to be managed effectively but with considerable and growing central definition and oversight of policy outputs.

Economists have more recently incorporated theories of the firm into thinking about central–local government relations, especially the costs of information. As so often they were building on earlier insights (Burgess 1997; Coase 1937; Cremer *et al.* 1993; Grossman and Hart 1986). What they have to say is entirely compatible with the previous conclusions.

The critical importance of dropping the basic assumption of perfect knowledge required to make markets work perfectly was not really grasped until the 1970s. The asymmetry of information had implications for the way health insurance markets work, for example (Akerlof 1970). The same was true of notions of how organizations work (Groves 1973; Williamson 1975). Who holds information and how costly it is to get has profound implications for organizational design, for the way contracts work, and for the relative advantages of contracts versus markets as a way of doing business.

It is possible to see relations between central and local governments as similar in nature to contracts between a company and its suppliers. Central or federal government can pay local government to do things on its behalf or subsidize it. There is, essentially, a contract between the two. If all information were free and fully available to all parties, perfectly available to an altruistically motivated central government, then the central government might be an optimal provider. It would be possible to internalize all the inter-area externalities, co-ordinating inter-area issues. It would be the superior co-ordinator, to use Lindblom's (1965) phrase. But, in fact, the centre is poorly informed about what happens locally. It is possible in theory to invent a system of incentives to ensure that local actors give accurate information to the centre. However, given that local actors benefit from holding such valuable information, it will be costly to buy it or 'bribe' it from them. The complexity of human service decisions and the fact that so many crucial decisions are made by professionals interacting with clients means that it is all but inconceivable that perfect, or even good enough information, could be available to some central bureaucrat (Hirschman 1970).

There are even more fundamental problems which principal–agent theory has explored. Moral hazard and adverse selection problems in combination make it extremely difficult for one principal to cope with diverse agents. Because local actors have access to more information than the centre, the centre cannot judge what to pay the local agent to get a job done effectively. Local agents may be able to produce the outcomes the centre wants more cheaply if they really have to, but the centre does not know this. Local actors can change behaviour to maximize income without producing the real quality improvements the centre wants. One mechanism to check on such abuses is to rely on local voters who also have local knowledge. If it is true that local voters are better informed about the quality of their services than central politicians can ever be, they will be in a better position to police the use of central government money for their benefit. The more directly they experience the service the more information they have and the more incentive to use it to hold their politicians or receivers of funds to account (Cremer *et al.* 1993). Parents involved in their local school or tenants on housing estates have more interest in the quality of the service than local politicians. This, at least, has been the logic behind devolving budgets to that level. However, tenants or parents may not be in a good position to judge the quality of the service they are getting. They may be able to judge the *non-technical* features of education—the friendliness of the teachers, the atmosphere in the school and the facilities—but not necessarily the academic achievements of the school. It is costly for local people to get at this information unaided and it is not in the interests of the local school to give it, especially if it is doing badly (Cremer *et al.* 1993).

Central government may be in a better position to collect and disseminate such technical information. This is the case for a National Curriculum, national testing, and the enforced publication of test results which the Conservative government introduced in the UK. The Labour government has accepted these regular national tests of school children, although it is elaborating the nature of the statistical work done to compare results by school to take account of the capacity of children when they enter the school. The same logic lies behind the introduction of a National Institute for Clinical Effectiveness for the NHS and for national inspections of clinical effectiveness in hospitals that the new Labour government have proposed.

In short, it could be argued that modern economic theory provides some justification for the system which the UK has evolved—national funding of basic education and health care, combined with devolved budgets to small units of organization and national standard setting. Central government in the UK is essentially writing a contract with its local agents to perform certain functions. It is relying on local actors to help enforce that contract using their superior local knowledge on local factors, enhanced by national expert information on standards. These local actors may be parents of children who use the local school, or tenants who live in local public housing, or general practitioners who use the local hospitals.

What the economic theory presupposes, however, is that these local units are democratically accountable to users or that users can exercise exit power. Democratic representation and accountability is partly present in the case of schools, where parents elect representatives to the school-managing body that has a budget devolved to it based on the numbers of pupils who sign on at the school. It is not true of the new primary care groups, combinations of local family doctors, and only intermittently true for housing estates and housing associations.

The previous Conservative government in the UK thought in terms of market disciplines operating. Exit power would be the sanction laid on these organizations with devolved budgets to make them operate effectively. Schoolchildren signed on at a school and thus triggered a formula-based cash sum which the school collected. Parents had choice of school guaranteed by law. The consequence was a type of quasi-voucher scheme (Barrow 1998; Glennerster 1991). When a child signed on at a school, that essentially triggered a sum of money for that school. In practice there are severe limits to such freedom of choice, and many parents (especially working-class ones) have considerable loyalty to the local school, or inertia in choosing another. They do not act as classic market choosers (Gerwitz *et al.* 1995). A survey of school performance in 1993–7 undertaken by the Centre for Research in the Economics of Education at Lancaster University did suggest that the competition and the quasi-voucher scheme had been associated with improved performance. Performance improved most in those schools facing most competition and the worst performing schools improved most (Bradley *et al.* 1999). Over much the same period, however, evidence on individual performance of children suggests that it is the average and above average performing children who have improved, while the results of the bottom 20 per cent have not budged (West and Pennell forthcoming). School choice as, Americans call this policy, has had its critics in the UK precisely because it seems to conflict with the principles of equity with which we began the chapter.

Efficiency and Equity in Conflict?

In an early study of school choice in the UK, Gerwitz, Ball, and Bowe argue that since some parents are able to use their powers of choice more effectively than others, and some schools are able to manage themselves more effectively than others, school choice and devolved budgets result in unequal opportunities. 'This is not perhaps surprising given that the architects of the English market were not primarily committed to needs-based equity', they conclude (1995: 189). The debate neatly encapsulates the tension between the efficiency goals we have been analysing in this part of the chapter and the equity goals we traced at the start. Schools provide a good exemplar for all the other services we shall be discussing.

If all schools had similar pupils, all similarly endowed, it would be clear how to allocate funds between them. They could be allocated on the basis of equality—so much per pupil. Then, local parents would be able to judge the effectiveness of the service they were receiving compared to other schools from the performance of the pupils in their school compared to others. In practice, the mix of pupils in schools differs, as does the mix of problems that face a local GP or a local housing association.

If a local parent is to be able to make judgements about the effective use of national resources in her child's school, that school must be receiving resources that will enable it to gain the same results as schools with more, or less, able students. Or there must be a way of ensuring that the intake to the various schools is equivalent. A school with special needs children, who are slow learners, needs to gain sufficient resources to enable it to look after those children effectively without taking resources away from other children in the school. The same goes for those children with rather less severe problems.

The Conflict Resolved by Needs-Based Funding?

It turns out, then, that the goal of efficiency though local delegation requires needs-based allocation right down to the most local unit to which budgets are allocated. For local users to make efficient judgements in choosing a school, or in using their voice to change its practices, the school must have needs-based funding. Without such needs-based funding parents or local voters will be making incorrect judgements about the performance of their local schools. Given parental choice, an unstable equilibrium will follow if there is no needs-based funding. Parents will see their school as under-performing and will take their children away. This puts the school in a worse position and provokes more parents to leave. Individual parents are, of course, right to do so in the interests of their own child. However, all the remaining children do worse as a result. The human capital of the whole society is reduced.

What applies to schools, of course, applies to some extent to other services like health and housing. The consequences of 'cream-skimming' cannot be met by simply denying parental choice, as many of the critics of school choice and quasi-markets more generally claim. Denying choice will drive many of the most effective parents out of the state system altogether. The loss of any exit sanction will remove an incentive to maintain the efficiency of the schooling system as a whole and reduce the general quality of the state system of schooling.

A solution is advocated by a Belgian economist (Vandenberghe 1998), who has studied the operation of school choice in Belgium where a voucher-like scheme has been in operation since the end of the Second World War. Schools attempt to take the best children because they boost the performance of other children and parents know that. The aim of a formula, Vandenberghe argues, should be to compensate the schools that take a higher than average intake of low performing pupils sufficiently to make them indifferent whether they take a high or a low performing student. The level of the subsidy would be fixed at a point that achieved a full ability mix. A non-economist might want to argue that quotas might be used in combination. The detail is not important. The issue is. If the production of education is largely the result of the social and educational mix of the pupils in a school the nature of the formula funding of those devolved units becomes crucial.

We know enough from the health literature in the USA to realize that such attempts to counteract cream-skimming are very difficult to devise in such a way that they cannot be manipulated by the agencies receiving the funds (Grumbach 1998; Newhouse 1989). Extra money may be gained to educate low-ability children but be used to educate the more able. Quotas can be manipulated too. This leads to a game of ever-increasing complexity between the principal and the agent—the need groups get more and more closely defined to prevent the formula being gamed. We return to these issues in the final chapter.

Nevertheless, to recap, if we go down the route of separating funding from the centre from central administration, for the reasons advanced earlier, the same logic requires some kind of needs-based funding of those lower agencies, not just for equity reasons but for efficiency reasons too.

The Fiscal Wedge Argument

So far we have seen that a case can be made out for what Alan Day in his minority contribution to the Layfield Report (DoE 1976) characterized as a mixed model or (his words!) a 'middle way'. However, it does leave itself open to the fundamental criticism that those who are buying the service—the centre to a large degree or national voters—are not the same as the local consumers. They may have different preferences to the national median voter.

The case against separating payers from beneficiaries is, of course, as old as Adam Smith. If a good is free or subsidized there is no way for an individual consumer to judge the marginal benefit being gained from the marginal extra resources being spent. By analogy, the only way local voters can efficiently express their preferences about the scale of local public goods they want is to be faced with the full cost and vote for them or reject them, as happens with School Boards in the United States.

How does this relate to the substantial subsidy central government pays to local government to provide schools or other local services in the United Kingdom? What Alan Day argued in his minority report was that services like education *were* to a large extent national services which the national electorate voted for. The national electorate expected at least a national minimum standard of education to be provided to all UK children. The logic was for central government explicitly to fund that level of service in each area. Local electorates that wanted more could 'top up' this central voucher, in effect, out of local revenues. Echoes here of Balfour! Local electorates would judge the size of this top-up and decide whether the marginal extra results were worth it. Local education or other services like it were a joint product:

the base amount national, the marginal extras local. He rejected both matching grants and the regression-based formula system used in the 1970s precisely because they did not face local voters with the full marginal costs of the extra resources any expansion of services would result in. The only case for the centre to subsidize local services below marginal cost would be an 'infant industry' type argument. Education or public health were national merit goods where the centre knew best and had a duty to encourage local agencies to spend above the level they would of the own volition choose to spend. Once a mature system had evolved the central state met the costs of the national standard and the local area added and paid for extras. He went on:

> The Report also emphasises the difficulty of identifying the costs of providing a given standard of service in differing circumstances in different parts of the country. These difficulties are considerable, although it is easy to exaggerate them. They are, for example handled reasonably satisfactorily in the case of those services, such as the National Health Service, which are nationally provided but where there are significant differences in costs in different areas. Any reasonable approximation to a definition of the cost of providing a defined standard of service in differing circumstances would be a considerable improvement on the present (1976) regression equation basis for allocation of the needs element of the Rate Support Grant.

Giving extra discretion to local authorities would make things worse. They would be encouraged to spend more in order to increase central funding. '. . . there is an unavoidable requirement in logic for some measure of needs or the costs of minimum standards which is independent of past expenditure decisions' (DoE 1976: Minority Report, para. 17). It was, indeed, this logic that has carried the day in the 1980s and brought the methodology of National Health Service funding and local authority funding closer together. The centre has moved to define minimum national standards in education and to largely pay for them. It still requires some local contribution on grounds similar to that employed by the Kemp Committee and the Royal Commission at the turn of the century.

Summary

We have seen that the United Kingdom's funding of its basic in-kind social services like health and education and housing is unusual. Unlike federal countries, such as the United States, Canada or Germany, almost the whole of these services is funded from national sources of taxation.

There is a powerful political sense that standards of provision should be nationally set and maintained. They are 'citizenship goods'—a peculiarly British idea in origin. What constitutes citizenship is undergoing change in the wake of Scottish and Welsh devolution. Even before that there were Scottish and Welsh versions of the various formulae we are discussing here and a formula that cut the cake for Scotland and Wales overall, the Barnett formula.

That aside, the central fact is that, partly by accident and partly by design, the UK has ended up with a highly centralized form of funding its social services. That requires some kind of allocation method and the means that has evolved is formula funding. We have argued that the formula funding of local services in the UK serves two quite different purposes. The first line of reasoning dates back to the nineteenth century. The Webb intention was to provide each citizen with a minimum standard of civilized life that included access to basic schooling, housing, and health care wherever they lived. The second line of reasoning derives from a concern with efficiency. That comes from devolved budgetary responsibility to small units of service delivery which rely on local residents and users to act as efficiency promoters for services they know well and can influence. Unless the sums these local agencies receive match the difficulty of the tasks they face, local users will not be able to judge the efficiency of the services they are getting.

This dual-strand logic, which has never been spelt out all that clearly, lies behind some of the recent developments in formula funding. The formula funding of schools and of primary care groups take us well down that road. Yet the incremental and obscure way we have reached the present situation means that most people simply do not understand what is going on. The logic may be good but the understanding is weak. Moreover, in many respects how we fund social services in the UK does not fully conform to that—or indeed any—logic. In the next chapter we trace the incremental steps by which we reached the present situation.

3

Needs-Based Funding from the Nineteenth Century to the 1980s

This chapter examines the historical development of funding systems for our services (drawing on a more detailed discussion in Hendry 1998). In any historical study used as a precursor to the analysis of current systems it is important not to extrapolate contemporary values backwards into assessing schemes formed in very different conditions to those existing today. Nevertheless, a central question is whether there is any common thread to the evolution of these allocation mechanisms. In recent years a series of quite complicated mathematically based funding formulae has developed, underpinning allocations to health services, housing, education, and local government more generally. They are all based on some concept of need. This is a fundamentally non-market, not to say socialistic concept (Doyal and Gough 1991). How did it even gain prominence during the 1980s period of Conservative, profoundly pro-market, rule? Why should mathematical formulation, beyond most electors' understanding, gain such sway? We begin by setting out a theory that might answer some of these questions and explain the evolution of formula funding mechanisms.

A Crude Stage Theory for the Development of Funding Formulae

In all three services the state only came to be a major *provider* during this century and a prime actor only after the Second World War. However, the early history of service funding tells us a great deal about the forms we have today (Glennerster 1996).

Why the state and, in the UK, the central state, became such a major source of funding has been discussed elsewhere (for example, Foster *et al.* 1980). Given that development, major questions arise about how central government should perform its rationing role. Should it provide matching grants to reward local initiative, base its allocations on some equity rule, or reward the government's political friends? All would be, a priori, rational strategies. The Foster *et al.* (1980) explanation relies primarily on agency theory. The UK is a unitary state. Central government might be expected to act like the headquarters of a firm, using subordinate levels of administration to carry out its will, minimizing transaction costs and maximizing control. Funding mechanisms would be designed to achieve this and to maximize incentives for its agents to act efficiently. Yet this perspective does not convincingly explain the dramatic changes that funding systems have gone through in the past hundred years, and especially in the last twenty. We therefore consider an approach that owes more to a modified form of public choice theory (Dunleavy 1991; Mueller 1989). This alternative stage theory is outlined in Figure 3.1 below, taking as our starting-point that services and their funding mechanisms respond to the varied self-interests of voters, politicians, and public bureaucrats.

Given the extended franchise in the late nineteenth century, a range of voters with a new set of interests became part of the electoral game. They and public bureaucrats had an interest in extending the boundaries of the services we are concerned with (see, for example, West 1975). This is not the whole story but, in so far as politicians and central bureaucrats see it as in their interests to expand local services, we would expect the grant mechanisms they devise to be largely devoted to extending their scope and access to them. Civil servants may be less opportunistic and self-interested than this model suggests, and many work within a moral framework in which they view well-managed public services as integral to a better society. However, in either case the aim will be to expand service activity into previously virgin territory. This is consistent with national politicians and the electorate having some notion of a basic national minimum standard of provision. This view was articulated by writers like Sidney Webb, discussed in Chapter 2. This context may be called stage one.

State funding does not entail state provision. Service provision may begin with state support of existing private agencies, then go on to fund state and private providers equally, and then as public provision expands it may be given preferential support. Once state services have been firmly established in a comprehensive, if not uniform, fashion, political concern will change to maximizing shares of the incremental budget for local interests. This may be called stage two.

In a political system with a strong legislature, and locally based politicians, this process will come to be dominated by 'log-rolling' (or

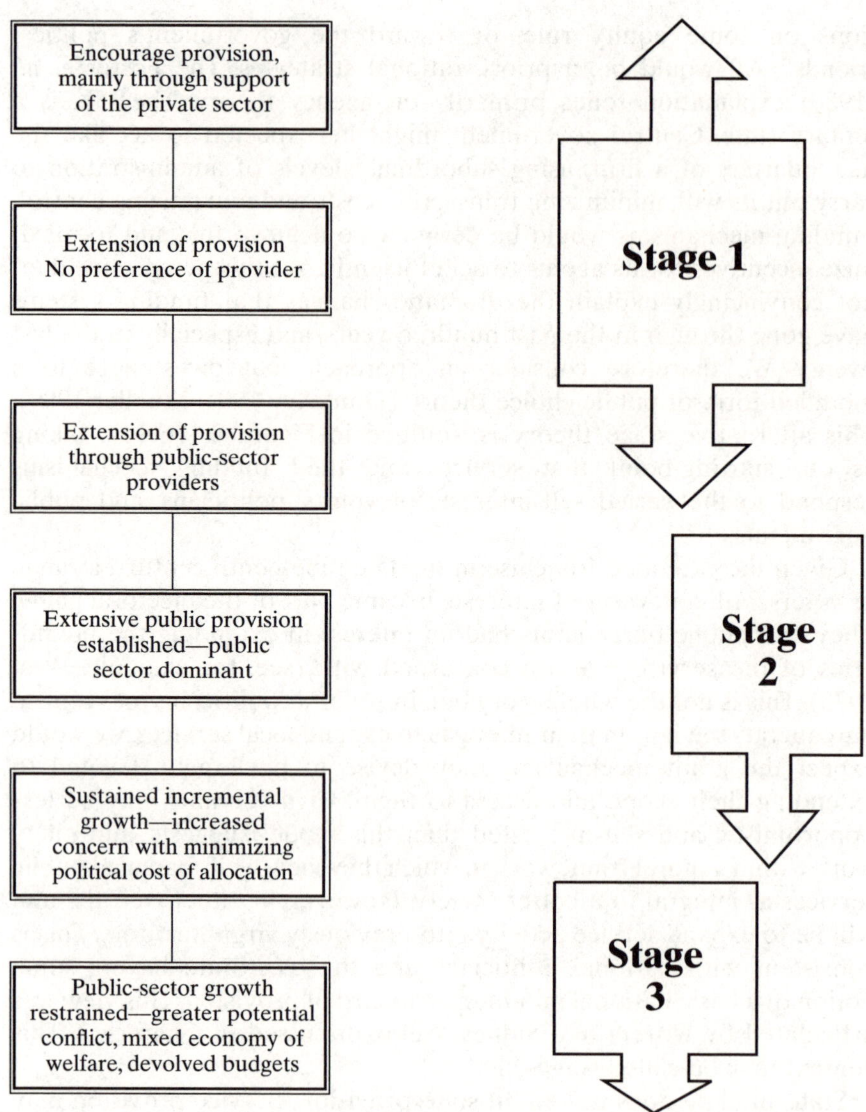

FIGURE 3.1. Stage Theory Structure of Development of Education, Health, and Housing Funding Formulae

back-scratching), lobbying, and temporary coalitions (Wildavsky 1975). However, in one like the UK with a strong national party system, a powerful executive, and a unitary state the outcome will be different. National parties will want to minimize public conflict about territorial budgets. Such open divisions bring the national party into disrepute and weaken party discipline. Party politicians will be expected to search for rules that internalize and formalize disputes about area allocations. They will not wish to rule out local political influence but to minimize its capacity to produce external dispute. External validation and agreement on the rules will help.

For bureaucrats the problems are different but the solution may be the same. If budget allocations are determined politically, by log-rolling or local deals with central politicians, bureaucrats are deprived of power and influence. Conversely, the more technical the solution, the more power they wield and the more work they have to do.

During stage one, when service provision is only partial, debate on priorities tends to centre on which new groups or areas should be brought in. This will reflect area-based interests, while judgements about the existing service base will tend to be largely subjective or political. This stage can be characterized by incremental legislation extending the scope of the service. Basic legislation in stage two is more stable and increments become the focus of interest.

Once budgets become tight as voter resistance to high taxes grows, regular budget increments cease, and the scale and costs of disputes will tend to rise. Instead of basking in the glory of additional funds, central politicians will be responsible for allocating cuts or resisting significant additions. Two strategies may minimize these political costs: first, more technical solutions to the allocation process; and second, devolved responsibility for budgets to smaller non-political units—schools, GPs, housing associations. In Figure 3.1, this is stage three.

All of this will be much more acceptable if it is done within a normative framework that is widely accepted—geographical 'equity', 'fairness', or 'need'. These are all widely accepted in the abstract but have ambiguous meanings (Doyal and Gough 1991). Tight budgets increase pressure on politicians to get more services from any given pound of tax. Thus formulae may come to be used more to encourage efficiency and prevent manipulation and perverse outcomes. The tasks these formulae will be asked to perform thus become more complex. They must minimize the conflict that derives from a tight budget and rising expectations. They must be capable of devolution to much smaller units where ordinary people or front-line professionals will come in direct contact with them. They must encourage efficiency. They may be being asked to do too much. In what follows we examine the history of formula funding through each of these stylized stages to see how far this framework can be sustained.

Stage 1: Allocating Limited Resources to Enable Provision, Education and Health

Our first stage covers the extension of service provision up to where public resources are mainly spent on state provision. Broadly, the pace and means of this development can be controlled in one of three ways (Glennerster 1996): legislation, hierarchical/management control, or financial arrangements. *Legislation* covers the statutory powers granted to ensure provision. Statutes define what providers from ministers to street level are allowed to do. Legal action can be taken if anyone in the chain exceeds their authority, or does not fulfil obligations. *Hierarchical powers* cover the bureaucratic means by which central government can influence provision, including inspection, audit, and ministerial guidance. *Finance* may be unit grants, linked to performance, percentage or matching grants, general revenue enhancement, or needs-based.

Education funding from 1800 to the 1930s

The development of a system of school education in England, Wales, and Scotland was seen during the nineteenth century as a way of enhancing the country's economic development. As the industrial revolution created an urban, factory-based workforce, entrepreneurs and enlightened liberals conspired to generate a demand for at least some form of basic education (Birchenough 1938: 28). Robert Owen proposed a universal system of elementary education from infancy, embracing explicit demands for equality of opportunity (Birchenough 1938: 31). In 1804, the Society for Bettering the Condition of the Poor sought (unsuccessfully) a parliamentary return to assess the education needs of different localities. In the early years of the nineteenth century, the extension of education was seen as a way of reducing Poor Law costs: if the poor were educated, they would need less parochial support (Birchenough 1938: 35–6).

Early government intervention was both small and governed by a belief that provision should be private. The first state grant to education was made in 1833, when £20,000 was given to two national voluntary church bodies to cover half the cost of building new schools. Allocation of such grants favoured projects intended to provide at least 400 places (Gosden 1966). Those receiving state finance were required to open up their schools to Her Majesty's Inspectors (HMIs), first appointed in 1835.

Expenditure by, and the influence of, central government grew steadily through the 1830s, 1840s, and 1850s, covering a variety of specific costs.

From 1846, further grants were paid to encourage schools to improve their teaching standards. Any school subsidized by grants had to prove it had local subscriptions (Goldstrom 1972: 103). Capitation payments were used for the first time in 1853. Officials believed that flat-rate per-pupil funding promoted efficiency and economy. Qualification for payments continued to depend on recommendations of government inspectors, and central government 'acquired a degree of control over the internal workings of the schools, which was never to be equalled again, despite the fact that they were private institutions' (Glennerster 1996).

Most resources were allocated through a proliferation of specific percentage grants and complexity became a major issue. The *Revised Code of Regulations* in 1862 therefore established a capitation grant based on both payment-by-results and attendance. In time it was thought that this would replace the need for HMIs. This system survived more or less unchanged until 1895. Although the operation of the payment-by-results method of funding schools is still viewed with distaste by much of the education establishment in Britain, it is clear that the original intentions of the Royal Commission were, in reality, partly concerned with equity and efficiency. The objectives of the 1862 system could easily be applied to the English schools system of the late 1990s.

The 1870 Education Act was more immediately significant in the development of provision than funding, but its long-term implications were profound. Financially it repealed government support for school building, and exclusive support of private education institutions. Instead, where the voluntary and private sector had failed to provide enough places for elementary education, 'Board schools', built out of the local rate fund, were allowed to fill the gap. Current costs of both Board and voluntary schools would remain funded by the government, but annual capitation grants would now be supplemented in areas with large school populations relative to their rateable value. This showed understanding that there was a negative relationship in deprived areas between need and the ability to pay for provision. The schools were not free, but boards were given the powers to pay the fees of poorer children (Birchenough 1938: 106). In 1891, parents were given the right to demand free education for their children. Schools received a fixed government grant per 'free' child. Thus was universal provision, underpinned by public funding, created. Controversy surrounds the state's move into provision of schooling. West (1975) argues that central bureaucrats eager to extend their role exaggerated the need for the state to step in. Sutherland (1971) shows that politicians were prime movers in extending the role of the Boards of Education and accepting the logic that compulsory education entailed state funding. External pressure from highly organized Nonconformist groups within the Liberal Party played a crucial part.

In 1895 exam-based funding for primary education was abolished. Instead, separate grants covering a percentage of expenditure were seen as a more flexible way of tailoring funding for individual schools. However, by 1918 the funding system had returned to an array of specific grants 'which stimulated and promoted expenditure in the particular ways thought desirable, rather than in other ways' (Webb 1920).

The 1902 Education Act established local education authorities (LEAs) to run parallel to the new local government authorities, and obliged them either to supply or to aid provision of non-elementary education. Those voluntary sector secondary schools that could attract sufficient pupils from the elementary sector received a per capita grant, forming the basis of the 'direct grant list', which survived until 1976. A new 'unified' grant would now be paid to the LEA who assumed responsibility for local distribution. This was based on an area's poverty (using rateable values as a proxy), its population, and school attendance.

The 1918 Education Act ended the common capitation grant for private and public sectors and the bias towards public provision became firmly established. There was yet another attempt in 1926 to simplify the structure of the grants, whose number and complexity had again multiplied. The new formula was a 50 per cent grant for secondary education, and a block grant for elementary schooling based on spending, pupil numbers, and the area's rateable value.

Increased provision and standards were the goal of the 1918 Act, but worsening economic conditions soon dampened the desire to increase public spending. A Committee on National Expenditure appointed in 1921 strongly criticized the percentage grant system for encouraging spending at the expense of economy and efficiency, and the open-ended commitment central government had made. In response the Board of Education proposed a switch from a percentage grant to a block grant fixed three years in advance. This faced hostility from every sector of the education lobby, and was not implemented. Again, when spending was cut in 1931, the percentage system remained intact (Vaizey and Sheehan 1968). Education was still in the development phase.

Health: evolution of a two-sector system up to 1948

Hospitals and health care had existed in England since medieval times, and great strides had been made in establishing medicine as a reputable and regulated profession during the course of the nineteenth century. During the same period state-financed health care was strictly limited to the provision for destitute paupers through the Poor Law. The rapid growth of voluntary hospitals and private practices occurred without state financial or legislative support. Within this system, the state workhouses became providers of last resort for the very poor or terminally ill, and the voluntary societies had little need for state assistance in their finances before the 1920s (Abel-Smith 1964).

The resulting health sector had little to do with equity of access. Indeed, need and provision were inversely related. Doctors and hospitals were located in prosperous areas that could pay for them, whereas areas of social deprivation where ill health was prevalent simply could not afford to pay. These problems led to the 1911 National Insurance Act, and an insurance scheme with contributions from individuals, employers, and the government. At its inception in 1913 the scheme was compulsory for all manual and other workers who earned less than £160 per year, and ensured cash benefits during periods of sickness, full and free general practitioner (GP) care, and limited pharmaceutical benefits. Lloyd George played on the fears of voluntary hospitals that government grants would lead to government control, but argued that for GPs, National Insurance was a means of preserving not eroding independence (Abel-Smith 1964). The 1911 Act thus brought most GPs into dependence on state finance, whilst leaving the hospital system much as it was before. Although the provision of secondary care was to change radically within forty years, the 1911 Act defined the form of finance for GPs that essentially lasted the remainder of the century. These independent agents were set a basic per capita sum to look after individuals accepted onto their 'list' (although the 1997 Primary Care Act did, for the first time, introduce a category of salaried GPs).

By 1938 43 per cent of the population was covered by the scheme and 90 per cent of all GPs had accepted a panel (list) of National Insurance patients (Webster 1988). More than a third of their income came from the Insurance Fund, although it was said that two-thirds of their time was spent dealing with insured patients (Stevens 1966). National Insurance still did not cover many of those groups excluded from the 'clubs' which were its forerunners, or treatment by specialists in voluntary hospitals. This gap was closed with the foundation of the National Health Service in 1948. Despite the universal coverage now guaranteed by legislation, and the use of general taxation to fund part of the service, GPs remained independent contractors, not state employees. Their basic relationship with the state did not change with the foundation of the

NHS, even though they may have become more dependent on public finances. By contrast, the secondary sector is directly accountable to, and controlled by, the Secretary of State.

Statutory responsibility for determining the number of GP practices in an area was handed to the Medical Practices Committee (MPC) by the 1946 National Health Act, with the Committee required to secure that the number of medical practitioners undertaking to provide general medical services in the area of different Executive Councils or in different parts of those areas are adequate. Chapter 4 discusses how this system operates.

Before the NHS, secondary health care consisted of independent voluntary hospitals and municipal institutions run by local authorities. With most active authorities, the latter's role steadily expanded throughout the inter-war period. Although voluntary hospitals were more prestigious, they were also more likely to be expensive, more selective in whom they treated, and in more affluent locations.

By 1938 this had led to the paradoxical situation whereby the most prestigious institutions—the voluntary hospitals—supplied the fewest beds and faced the greatest financial difficulties in the medical sector. Their dependence upon public resources intensified under the wartime Emergency Medical Service. Between 1938 and 1947 donations fell from 33 to 16 per cent of hospitals' revenue, while fees paid by public authorities rose from 8 per cent to 45 per cent. Yet even the best endowed group of voluntary hospitals at the top of the pyramid—London teaching hospitals—had a revenue deficit of £2 million by the time they were nationalized (Forsyth 1966). Municipal hospitals by contrast were mainly financed through local rates supplemented by the Exchequer block grants. Within this framework responsible authorities were assumed to charge patients according to their means, the method adopted by voluntary hospitals—although inability to pay coupled with long-term or particularly costly illnesses often meant patients were turned away from voluntary institutions under the assumption that they could then turn to municipal provision.

Stage 1 so far

Education most closely fits the first stage of the theory outlined above. Private provision was increasingly subsidized and public provision introduced first in cases where the voluntary sector failed to provide. Once established, the public sector gradually expanded at the expense of the private and not-for-profit sectors, notably after free provision was introduced. While payments to private secondary schools remained an important avenue of provision up to and after the 1944 Education Act, public provision steadily extended its scope, responding to carefully devised funding mechanisms.

Health care followed a rather less steady incremental progress, but the end result was similar. GPs remained private agents but were to be largely publicly funded as the scope of National Insurance brought in successive extensions of groups covered during the 1920s and 1930s. Voluntary hospitals' private funding declined steadily over the same period, but the war brought a sudden infusion of public money. Local medical officers working in combination with active politicians in London, the North of England, and Wales extended the scope of public hospitals.

The Cyclical Nature of Resource Allocation in Social Housing

For social housing the story is rather different. For example, central government did attempt to encourage provision through subsidies to the private sector, but only *after* a similar offer to local authorities. Looking at subsidy structures, they seem to follow a cyclical pattern, rather than the linear pattern of our model, and that seen in education and health (Malpass and Murie 1987). Also, social housing never became a universal service in the same way as education and health, so there is no period that adequately corresponds to stage two.

Shelter was only funded for destitute paupers within workhouses under the provisions of the 1834 Poor Law. Legislation was enabling, and committed no resources from central government for the construction of low rent housing. Bills in 1912, 1913, and 1914 proposing financial assistance for local authorities to build working-class homes failed to gain any significant support. Government intervention before 1919 remained limited to granting local authorities the power to build new homes and to control rents. The first government housing subsidy in 1919 was therefore significant for its positive financial incentives to build. Subsidies were deemed necessary to build the 500,000 new 'homes fit for heroes' for returning troops. The government believed this number could be built within three years given the generous subsidies offered to local authorities under the 1919 (Addison) Housing Act. But to get local authorities even to consider undertaking the construction needed, the government had to guarantee that their liability would be limited to a penny rate. The Exchequer would fund the difference between the income from a rent level set by a government officer and the cost of the project. While the construction cost of the average working-class house in 1914 was £250, inflation, scarce resources, and higher standards meant completion costs for subsidized housing in 1921 of £1,200 (Malpass and Murie 1987). It was left to the government to meet this increase, with no incentive for local authorities to economize. In the longer term the subsidy set an important precedent. The Exchequer would forever be shy of any system with an open-ended liability. Nevertheless, the Addison Act proved that government subsidies encouraged the construction of social housing.

One can identify three periods of local authority construction for general housing needs, all beginning with a generous central government subsidy: 1919 to 1930; 1946 to 1956; and 1961 to 1972. The beginning of each was marked by a desire to build high-quality homes, exemplified through the recommendations of the Tudor Walters Committee (1918), the 1944 Dudley Committee, and Parker Morris (CHAC 1961). But high standards meant slower, more costly construction, and within several years of their publication the standards initially advocated were diluted under the pressure to build more units quicker and cheaper (Malpass and Murie 1987; Merrett 1979). Each period concluded with general subsidies being cut back, and resources targeted more narrowly into slum clearances and renovations (Figure 3.2).

The 1919 Act had seen local government as the only viable sector able to build the amount of homes needed in the timescale. Chamberlain's 1923 subsidy broadened access to subsidies to include public and private builders alike. The recurrent subsidy, set at £6 a year for twenty years, became the blueprint for the 'classic British housing subsidy' of £x per year for y years (Holmans 1987: 306). The 1923 Act was designed to stimulate the private sector, with no control on the rent of the new houses. Local authorities could only apply for the subsidy having proved local need. Although this was not difficult, given the chronic housing shortages, it weeded out all but the most enthusiastic authorities. During the six years the subsidy operated, 76,000 homes were built by local authorities, but 362,000 by private landlords (Malpass and Murie 1987).

In 1924 a more generous additional subsidy introduced by the minority Labour government was only available to local authorities and other 'public utility societies', and over half a million local authority homes were built with this assistance before 1933. By then stronger financial constraints, and a lessening perceived demand for general need housing, led to resources being redirected into slum clearance.

After the Second World War policy went through a similar cycle, with initial emphasis on quality, then on numbers, and then, from 1956, slum

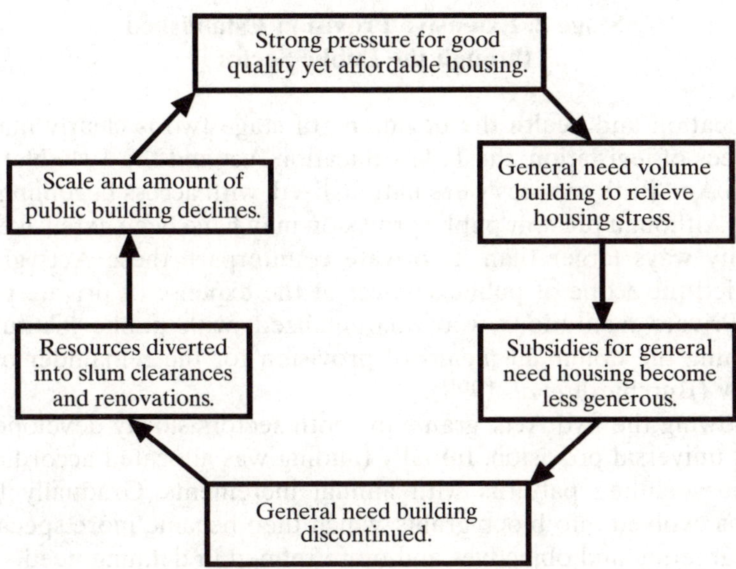

FIGURE 3.2. The Local Authority Housing Subsidy Cycle, 1919–1972

clearances. However, by 1961 general need subsidies had returned, and the third policy cycle began, culminating in the decline of large-scale council building after the mid-1970s.

A recent version of this cycle can be seen in the housing association sector over the last two decades. The generous capital grants to non-profit housing associations (housing association grant) established by the 1974 Housing Act were designed to encourage the growth of non-government providers of social housing. This system of capital grants was reformed in 1989 and far greater emphasis placed on value for money and increasing the numbers of units built (DoE 1987). After the mid-1990s the brakes went on this version of the house-building 'numbers game' as open competition for grants drove up rents and housing benefit. The 1998 Comprehensive Spending Review (HM Treasury 1998) suggested that the relative importance of renovation rather than new provision of social housing should be increased, echoing the final stage of the cycle shown in Figure 3.2.

Housing subsidies do not therefore fit the developmental pattern outlined earlier. Housing never moves from stage 1 to stage 2, mass universal provision. However, in many respects, it does, as we shall see, converge with other services in stage 3.

Stage 2: Extensive Provision Established through the Public Sector

In education and health the beginning of stage two is clearly marked by pieces of legislation: the 1944 Education Act and the 1946 National Health Act. Both services were nationalized, with access becoming universal. Although pre-war public provision may have been extensive, and in many ways larger than its private counterpart, these Acts greatly extended the scope of public services at the expense of private provision. Private institutions were marginalized, with public institutions remaining the dominant means of provision for the remainder of the century (Burchardt *et al.* 1999).

Following the two Acts, grants for both sectors slowly developed to reflect universal provision. Initially funding was allocated according to historic spending patterns with annual increments. Gradually these systems evolved into block grants, which then became more specific in their targeting and objectives and more refined in defining need.

The entitlement to *education* was radically altered by the 1944 Education Act. Provision, access, and quality were nevertheless restrained by the existing school buildings. Almost the entire debate surrounding the Act centred on the issue of religious instruction and church schools. Getting the churches on board was central to success. To ensure the support of churches, RAB Butler conceded a generous percentage grant for new building schemes. A similar agreement was made with local authorities. Comparable percentage grants were used to finance revenue expenditure, which remained independent of the local government block grant up until 1958. Thus from 1944 to 1958 primary and secondary education were funded to meet child population growth and to establish a full pattern of secondary education in England and Wales, with generous allocations provided out of general taxation.

When, in 1958, education funding was finally incorporated into the grant to local government the fear was that spending on schools would be squeezed by the demands of other services. The anxiety proved ill-founded. First, the Department of Education and Science 'had evolved a system of administrative control which enabled it to influence local authority programmes quite apart from any incentives which might be derived from the specific form of education grant' (Rhodes 1976). Second, a large amount of current expenditure in education is set by teachers' salaries, unaffected by the behaviour of individual authorities (Byrne 1974; Lawrence 1972). Between 1956 and 1972 a teachers' quota system was enforced. It sought to limit recruitment in popular areas, and to encourage teachers to seek jobs elsewhere, in much the same way as the MPC's system for GPs. Finally, it has been argued that when the child population is increasing the system of allocating revenue resources is of less importance than capital allocations (Griffiths 1966). The control exerted by the ministry over the form and location of capital spending has remained tight since the war. The result was that education funding increased rapidly even after incorporation into the local government grant.

In needs-equalization terms, the 'general' grant introduced in 1958 was in itself a major step forward from its predecessor. Since 1948 government support for general local services had been through a series of specific percentage grants, supplemented in poor areas with an 'Exchequer equalisation grant', whose aim was to raise the local rate base up to the average level (Hale and Travers 1993). Its 1958 replacement incorporated most of the individual specific grants into one block grant. This is described in more detail in Chapter 5, together with an analysis of the subsequent evolution of modern need-equalizing grants.

Funding for the *health* service between 1948 and 1962 was based on incremental increases set by the hospital management committees. If a formula did exist it was based on 'what you got last year, plus an allowance for growth, plus an allowance for scandals' (Maynard and Ludbrook 1988). Negligible amounts were spent on capital projects, and allocation was to the noisiest rather than the neediest (Mays and Bevan 1987). By the late 1950s the system was accentuating regional inequalities, and was further criticized for not sustaining adequate levels of funding (Ministry of Health 1956).

In response, the government committed itself to major capital investments as a partial solution to regional inequalities. The investment was to be guided by the 1962 Hospital Plan for England and Wales, which envisaged equalization through capital planning. In time the more equitable distribution of hospitals would work itself through to current spending through the 'Revenue Consequence of Capital Schemes' (RCCS). Areas with new hospitals would therefore gain more revenue to staff and run them. Capital spending did rise, but from a very low base. Yet the result was not an equitable distribution of resources, as capital expenditure was used to renovate existing buildings (Klein 1995). A 1966 reform to the plan did little to alter this, and regional inequalities remained the prevalent feature of hospital resources up to the 1970s. Never the less, the very existence of a 'national plan' for hospital building did begin to attract academic and expert attention to the issue of geographical equity in capital allocations and building standards.

Stage 2 Reviewed

During the early post-war years it was believed that abolishing fee payments and creating universal institutions would be enough to meet the needs of the population. But as the welfare state matured the realization grew that geographical differences created different levels of need or potential demand for services. Differential availability of service itself posed a second kind of problem: were there enough doctors, beds, teachers, or desks? Once universal primary and secondary education had been achieved, and once access to free universal health care had been (virtually) achieved in the 1950s and 1960s, so political pressure and academic critical interest began to turn to the question of distribution—income distribution in cash benefits and area distribution in services in-kind (Cooper and Culyer 1970; Davies 1968; Townsend and Bosanquet 1972). These issues emerged before the era of austerity began in the mid-1970s but serious attention devoted to geographical allocations rises sharply after the economic crises of that time. Stage 3 begins.

Stage 3: Universal Coverage Strains Resources—Funding Formulae Used to Make the Hard Choices

Up to the 1970s the primary concern of the *education* sector was the acquisition of enough resources to meet the needs of a rising school population and to ensure that all parts of the country made provision to meet the targets set out in the 1944 Education Act (secondary education for all and a framework of further education colleges). The comparison with health shows how more resources made this task far easier than it might have been. When demographic pressure began to ease during the late 1960s central government became increasingly preoccupied with standards and restraining spending increases. To achieve the latter the government promoted efficiency and encouraged local authorities to make the best use of their buildings and teachers. Safeguarding standards during resource-standstill required the government to develop an interest in how money was spent. This had distinct results.

First, capital spending was cut. Loan sanctions for building schemes had become one of the main ways in which the government could control local authority resource allocation after 1957 (Griffiths 1966).

Once the final loan sanction had been made, the LEA was free to choose which projects it wished to go ahead with. However, restricted budgets effectively restrained freedom of choice (Morris 1983; Regan 1977).

Second, the share of specific grants increased again during the 1970s. Although they remained a small proportion of overall spending, this did show an intention to direct spending very precisely. Such grants were often used by departments other than the DES, to promote policy objectives which crossed over into other areas such as employment or industry (Morris 1983). Despite the rise of specific grants, the majority of education funding remained an integral part of the local government block grant throughout this period, and allowed a great deal of local authority autonomy over subregional allocation. But between 1970 and the mid-1980s the distribution formula for local government changed three times, often resulting in greater central control over how and where resources were used (see Chapter 5).

Through the 1960s it became increasingly obvious that the distribution of *health* resources within the NHS bore little resemblance to the principles which Bevan had proclaimed two decades earlier. Equity of access was not nationally consistent, and the allocation of resources still depended on the historic distribution of hospitals. The 'inverse care law' that the NHS was meant to dispel still existed. The limited amounts of capital investment associated with the two Hospital Plans during the 1960s had done little to solve this.

Work done by academic economists at Exeter and later York University directed attention to the continuing if not growing inequalities in resource allocation between different regions (Cooper and Culyer 1970; Hurst, 1997). Interviews with civil servants who remember this period suggest they were strongly influenced by these findings and convinced by the logic. They had internalized the idea that the NHS was about equal access, but this goal was not being achieved. Work began within the Department of Health and Social Security (DHSS) to consider what to do about it. When Labour was returned to government in 1974, Brian Abel-Smith, Barbara Castle's adviser, urged the issue to be taken up again. This new health minister David Owen, himself a doctor, was committed to doing something about the allocation problem.

There was also growing political concern that strong Labour regions were losing out to more affluent areas. Before Labour's election defeat in 1970 Richard Crossman, prompted by Brian Abel-Smith and officials, had set in train work on a formula (used for the first time in 1971) that attempted to redirect resources. However, it had drawbacks. Although half the formula included some crude but objective measure of need (population), the other half remained wedded to historic spending. The basis of the formula was population, weighted by bed occupancy for different age groups, the cost of beds in each speciality, and the number of cases actually treated. This was a cross between demand and a rough measure of need, based on guesswork rather than evidence.

Finding a solution to the inverse care problem was finally given to a new 'Resource Allocation Working Party' (RAWP). Its conclusion was to create a new formula that assessed health needs according to measurements of population and mortality ratios. The full report, published in 1976, based funding on weighted populations and envisaged an equitable allocation of revenue and capital resources between and within regions. Resources were to be based primarily on the calculation of a Standardized Mortality Ratio (SMR), used as a measurement of morbidity and as a proxy for need. A region's need, and therefore allocation, would be calculated on the difference between national and regional SMRs for various forms of health care. The system was not without its critics (see Carr-Hill *et al.* 1994; Mays and Bevan 1987), but RAWP was the most significant step undertaken by the health sector towards an equitable distribution of resources based on some measure of need. As we discuss in more detail in Chapter 4, over the following decade RAWP did lessen regional differences, and achieved remarkable regional equality in the distribution of resources.

Local authority housing peaked as a proportion of the entire housing stock in 1978 (Hills 1998), but resources for new building were already in decline in the mid-1970s. By the mid-1980s the role of local authorities as the primary developers of social housing was being taken over by housing associations.

A series of controls on local authority housing capital spending were introduced between 1974 and 1976. These were largely introduced for macro-economic reasons, rather than to aid local authority planning and priority setting. For these the Labour government introduced the Housing Investment Programme (HIP) system in 1977. Local authorities were to develop four-year housing strategies to be approved by the Department of the Environment (DoE). Although the stated aims were needs-related and equity-driven, the implementation of the system gave the (not unjustified) impression that HIPs were more a means of controlling and cutting expenditure than of sensitivity to needs.

HIP submissions bid for a fixed pot of resources determined by central government. Resources are allocated first to DoE Regional Offices, and then down to local authorities according to criteria including the 'Generalized Needs Index' (GNI), based on a weighted index of nine measures of housing need. The rolling four-year capital programme was never achieved. Allocations have been made annually, with available resources falling substantially between the mid-1970s and mid-1980s (Hills 1998: figure 5.4). In 1980 the Local Government Planning and Land Act extended controls to all local authority capital projects. Allocations made for one service could be used for another, and the total would be supplemented by the receipts from the sale of local authority capital stock, particularly housing, under the 'Right to Buy'.

On the revenue side, the housing subsidy system also underwent major reforms between the early 1970s and the 1980s as government grappled with the effects of inflation and widely varying debt burdens between authorities. First, the Housing Finance Act 1972 attempted to establish equalized 'fair rents' across rented housing. Council rents would be raised over a number of years until they matched regulated private-sector rents. The poorest council tenants were to be protected by a national rent rebate scheme, replacing *ad hoc* local schemes. The aim was to reduce central government spending, but in the short life of the Act's operation the Exchequer's contribution to housing actually grew: the specified rent increases did not match costs and council spending rose with what became rapid inflation.

The new Labour government abolished the Housing Finance Act in 1975 and restored local authority autonomy over rent levels and their ability to make contributions to housing from the general rate fund. Under a new subsidy system, central government paid 66 per cent of loan charges on approved expenditure—a return to a system which encouraged construction. However, this was soon counterbalanced by the capital controls, outlined above, making the 1975 subsidy system look particularly incongruous. This was effectively a stopgap pending the results of the government's Housing Policy Review in 1977, which advocated a new subsidy system in the end brought in by the Conservatives in 1980 (see Chapter 6).

While the growth of local authority housing was first controlled and then reversed, the *housing association* sector was embarking on a twenty-five-year period of growth. Before the First World War associations had been the main source of social housing, but the subsidies taken up by local authorities during the inter-war years meant that associations were soon eclipsed. Their growth stagnated until some limited revival with new subsidies in the 1960s (Holmans 1987). However, it was the system of capital grants, the housing association grant (HAG), introduced in 1974, which set associations onto their most rapid phase of growth.

The idea of HAG was substantially to reduce the amount of capital borrowed, and hence debt servicing costs, allowing associations to charge 'fair rents' as set by a rent officer (Hills 1991). Fair rents (surviving for the private sector from the Housing Finance Act) played the key role, determining the size of grant. In simple terms, HAG equalled capital costs minus a residual loan. The residual loan was calculated so that debt servicing in the first year would equal the amount left from fair rents after deducting allowances for management and maintenance (M&M). Attempts were made to control capital costs through the total indicative costs (TIC) system, a matrix of average regional land and building costs for particular types of development. These costs were, however, indicative, and if a project over-ran, the extra spending would be met by grant.

This system—enough grant to allow associations to balance their books in the first year—was very generous. In later years, rents rose but loan servicing costs did not, giving associations the chance to build up surpluses. To correct for this, a system of claw-backs—Grant Redemption Fund (GRF)—was introduced in 1980. At the same time some associations had been left with large debts as a result of developments before 1974, and could receive a recurrent subsidy, Revenue Deficit Grant (RDG), to allow them to balance their books overall.

Summary

Figure 3.3 draws together the most important changes to funding formulae in education, health, and housing described above and places them within the stage theory postulated at the beginning. Although some reforms fit this model better than others, it does describe the general pattern.

Themes and Trends: Control and 'Equity'

One consistent central government objective running through the developments described above has been to control the behaviour of the institutions that receive its resources. This can be realized by formal restrictions or incentives. Incentives that alter or encourage certain responses are intrinsic to any funding formula. As well as formal restrictions, formulae have often been used to encourage frugality or at least not reward additional spending. Examples of this would include the 'classic British housing subsidy' or capitation payments in education.

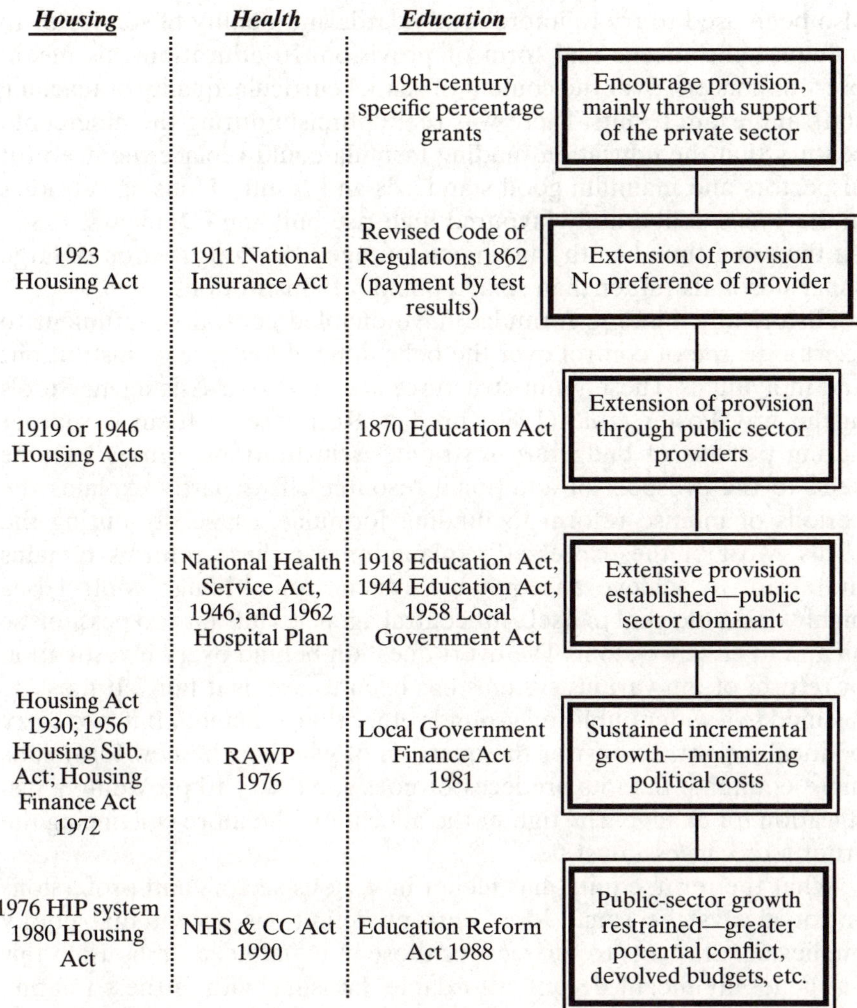

FIGURE 3.3. A Summary of Funding Formulae History (based on Hendry 1998)

Both involve a fixed amount per unit, which gives an incentive for the provider to perform the service as cheaply as possible. On the other hand, percentage grants, the 1919 Addison housing subsidy, or the local government finance system introduced in 1974 all encouraged providers to spend more to increase the size of their award.

Spending is not government's only concern. Funding formulae have also been used to try to improve standards and quality of service or to influence the means and form of provision. In education this meant pre-war concern over the content of school curricula, quality of teaching staff, and exam results. There was real optimism during the nineteenth century that the education funding formula could replace the need for inspectors and maintain good standards and results. Housing subsidies in the 1960s deliberately favoured high-rise building (Dunleavy, 1981). At the same time health funding encouraged the construction of large super hospitals rather than small community institutions.

Historically, funding formulae have enabled central government to exert a degree of control over the behaviour of lower level institutions and individuals. These grant structures are used as classic agency tools in the way Foster *et al.* (1980) predict. Response to them is sharper during periods of budgetary restraint, as institutions' senses become keen to the prospect of additional resources. This partly explains the periods of intense reform to funding formulae, especially during the 1970s. Most of the expressed explanation for these reforms remains the desire to achieve an equitable system, for although control is a highly desirable goal in itself, for central agencies it is far too pessimistic an aim to advance alone. The overt question behind every investigation or reform of the various systems has been to ask 'is it fair?' It must be justified to a wider public on grounds other than efficiency if it is to carry political weight. To answer the question of whether the new formula is more equitable than its predecessor goes some way to providing a justification for change. The tighter the allocation, the more convincing the criteria of fairness must be.

What the term 'equity' has meant in various sectors and professions is not always the same. Most current definitions accept that equity implies equal access to services for those in equal need. In housing this has generally meant decent 'affordable' housing, with fairness relating to the balances between incomes, rents paid, and the quality of housing occupied. In health it has been taken to mean that those with equal need of care (equally ill) should have equal opportunity and access to the same standard of care. Education has for the past forty years been part of the local government sector where equity is defined as a situation in which a person paying an average amount of council tax should expect a minimum standard of services. All these policy outcomes clearly echo Webb's thesis, discussed in Chapter 2.

In operational terms, equity has meant the degree to which funding is related to 'needs'. This can be broken down into two parts. The first is 'institutional needs'. One of the questions early formulae failed to answer was the extent to which allocations took account of geographical differences in costs. Most modern funding formulae acknowledge that costs may be greater in one area than another, and compensate for this. Another aspect of equity for local government, housing, and pre-war health funding is the differential ability of various communities to supplement central government resources. 'Resources elements' of local government finance have tried to adjust for this. The second criterion can be defined as 'individual needs'. It seems straightforward that there are some people and areas that have greater educational, health, or housing needs than others and consequently require additional resources. It has proved very difficult to find objective variables that can be accurately measured as an indicator or proxy for individual need. Even when suitable variables are found they may soon become outdated.

It is clear from the narrative above that during the 1970s far greater pressures were put on resources than ever before. A lid was placed on spending that was kept down through a combination of economic and ideological developments (Glennerster and Hills 1998; Timmins 1995). The effect was an unprecedented drive towards more explicit rationing through the funding formulae. If rationing was to be fiercer, it had to be based on some kind of preferably 'scientific' or at least agreed criteria. This was not a trend unique or new to the 1970s, but a continuation and acceleration of processes that had been at work for decades. Nevertheless it seems paradoxical that successive Conservative governments during the 1980s, dedicated to reining in spending on the social wage, implemented and administered formulae that were unprecedented in their equity-driven redistribution of resources. This question of why Conservative governments should make equity the guiding principle to resource allocation has not been fully answered in previous studies. Why should a government that advocated self-sufficiency, and whose power base remained in the South-East, implement formulaic changes that could see resources being directed towards groups and areas that had weak voices and little political advantage to offer? There were, however, several processes at work during these years that can in combination explain this paradox.

First, was the simple ability to devise, work, and administer formulae that were more sensitive to need. This was largely due to the advent of cheap and powerful computing, but also drew on the growing academic interest in funding mechanisms and equitable allocations that derived from research on poverty in the late 1960s.

The second is the timing of governmental financial crises, the high point of which occurred under a Labour government in 1976. Ideologically and politically Labour had far more invested in supporting socially deprived groups and areas than the post-1979 Conservative governments. According to measurements of need it was the North and the poor who were losing out through formulae based partly or wholly on historic spending. These also happened to be Labour's power bases. It was in the party's supporters' interest, therefore, to advocate more equitable systems of resource allocation. Such alterations then take time to be formulated and then implemented, so that although it was a Labour government which instituted the committees and reports that proposed the relevant changes, the consequences of reform were not fully worked out until the accession of the Conservatives to power. The second factor behind the paradox of New Right and equity, therefore, is procedural and legislative inertia.

A justifiable criticism to this viewpoint would argue that the areas that gained from formulae introduced during the 1970s were not necessarily poor or Labour. Population was the main driving force in the health formula, for example. This meant that many Labour inner-city areas lost out to the growing Conservative suburbs. Additions were made for high-cost areas in the South-East, and rural areas could also claim that their costs and needs were higher. Thus 'need' turned out to be a politically adaptable concept capable of appealing to both Conservative and Labour voters. The inherent political conflicts between members of the same party, between central and local government, or between government and the professions were very effectively sidetracked into technical debates about the weightings derived from various coefficient calculations. These were debates which could be left to committees of experts.

The third factor is a basic shared belief by politicians across the political spectrum that the most needy in society must always be protected. This claim was used to justify reduced but targeted social security benefits in the 1980s (Evans 1998). So, too, could it be used to support tight education, health, and housing budgets since the mid-1970s. Politicians were defending their policies by saying, 'Yes budgets are tight, but we are concentrating them on the most needy.' Nor does one have to be entirely cynical about this claim as it reflects a perfectly genuine belief in the virtues of equity. Despite the relative and absolute cuts in expenditure this simplistic sense that had permeated throughout British society stated that the poorest sections should not lose out equally to those better off. Rather cuts should be distributed so that the most needy suffer least. Another part of the story—as we discuss in Chapter

2 above—was the attempt to devolve budgets in the late 1980s and the 1990s and the need to achieve this via a route which did not involve negotiations with local politicians which the Conservative government wanted to avoid.

The final element which was at work during this period was the existence of a relatively small number of large and powerful local authorities. Their voice was too powerful and too loud to ignore, and their historic role in service provision, which extended back to the nineteenth century, had enabled them to build up historic spending levels which the government found hard to cut without facing a severe battle. The evidence for their success has been illustrated in studies which have shown inter-regional differences in the UK to be far smaller than those apparent in most, if not all, of her developed neighbours and industrial competitors. Similarly we could also note the power and influence of the medical profession as a powerful interest group, but representing it across the whole country.

Conclusion

The historical evidence reviewed above reveals a more complex picture than the simple model we ventured at the beginning, but it does hold in its essence. During the 1970s a greater academic awareness of the problems, more research and data, as well as an ability to process this data following the advent of cheap powerful computing, allowed formulae to become far more refined, sensitive, and complex. More complex needs-based formulae both appealed to some basic normative values that become attached to social service provision, and helped reduce political conflict in a period of resource constraint, and increased the power of the central bureaucracy. Yet we must also remember that reforms during the 1970s and 1980s drew upon an intellectual heritage that extends back over a century of political and ethical thought as described in Chapter 2. Some writers proposed changes that were only practical years later, following technical advances that introduced better data and calculating power.

In effect, there are short-, medium-, and long-term influences on funding systems (Table 3.1). Political thought and academic work on equity and needs have largely defined the principled framework within which change takes place. Formulae outside this framework would be very unlikely, given the lack of moral justification. The boundaries of this framework may have contracted over the period of our study as the

TABLE 3.1. *Factors that Influence the Development of Funding Formulae*

Timescale	Explanatory theory	Outcome
Long term	Principled/moral predisposition	A general societal belief in fairness; generally defined as those in equal need receiving equal resources
Medium term	Political expediency explained through public choice theory	Devolved formulae the objectives of which everybody agrees upon. Minimization of political conflict
Short term	Practical ability	The simple ability to collect enough data and process it in such a way as to make it useful as a tool for assessing measuring and allocating resources according to need

definition of equity has been refined and information regarding need has grown. Equity in health resource allocation, for example, was unambiguously defined in the 1976 RAWP report, and subsequent formulae are tested against its standards. Previously the lack of such a definition led to a lack of clarity regarding the meaning of equity and, more importantly for funding, how this could be achieved. Although definitions and ideals are less clear in the other two sectors, additional research and the greater public awareness that often follows place constraints on what various groups accept as a fair allocative formula. This implies that more restrictions are placed on new proposals. Funding formulae have to prove themselves more equitable and academically more rigorous than their predecessors.

Pressure in the other direction has come from increasing technical ability. Only through more information, more research, and better computing could the complex formulae of the 1970s and 1980s become practical to administer. As the ability to implement and administer more complex formulae becomes a reality, it has become more feasible to meet more ambitious objectives.

Exceptions to these gradual processes have been noted above. Reforms tended to accelerate after or during times of economic crises—most strikingly during the late 1920s and 1970s. The implementation of more complex formulae during these periods certainly had political influences as well, which can be explained through a revised form of public choice theory. This remains the core explanatory proposition, even though intellectual studies defined the principled disposition of policy-makers and public, and technical developments restricted complexity and scope. Devising, implementing, and justifying formulae is an intensely political process.

Electors, bureaucrats, and politicians are all self-interested groups. Agreement on equity as an agenda for resource allocation systems may have appealed to such individuals. Yet many of these players also have motivations or constraints outside their own self-interest, and to suggest that all is a political compromise may be an over-pessimistic world-view, just as an argument proposing equity as the sole objective of funding formulae is too optimistic. Yet the strength of a diluted public choice theory and the consistency of equity as a theme within the development of allocative systems are undeniable.

PART II

Formula Funding in the 1990s

4

Funding in the NHS: Life after RAWP

Parts Not Reached by RAWP

We saw in the previous chapter that the publication of the Resource Allocation Working Party (RAWP) Report in 1976, and the essential acceptance of its recommendations, was something of a milestone in establishing a quantifiable measure of relative need. However, it was only the beginning of an evolutionary process. Though the new RAWP formula allocated the greater part of the NHS recurrent budget, about three-quarters, the remaining quarter continued to be allocated to general practitioners and to dentists on quite different principles. They were not salaried employees of the service. They were individual contractors with it. The sums they received to run their essentially private businesses were designed to give them an average income negotiated with their trade unions each year. It was not until right at the end of the period we are studying that an attempt was made to bring these allocation systems together in a tentative way. We discuss that at the end of this chapter.

Capital expenditure remained in a separate box. RAWP had recommended that capital spending should be treated in the same way as current spending and its formula used to allocate capital funding. The Treasury was not happy to let the control of capital allocations pass from its control in this way, nor were politicians. All major schemes had to be submitted to the department and then to the Treasury and a judgement made about their relative cost effectiveness. Only highly rated schemes were approved. This distinct rationing system had its own notions of relative need and effectiveness. Finally, the RAWP allocations were made to the new regional health authorities created as part of the 1974 NHS reorganization. What regions did with the money they got was up to them. Allocations down to areas, and below them to districts, did not have to be on the basis of RAWP-type criteria. Old historical legacies would remain the prime basis of distribution for many years at this level.

The Resistance Movement

To begin with, the leading opponents of RAWP were, not unnaturally, the London teaching hospitals and London regional and area health authorities and the local authorities in those areas. They were the major losers. Moreover, much of the medical establishment was still London-based. Yet to attack the principle of allocation according to need was not felt to be an acceptable response. So the attacks took the form of technical criticisms of the formula itself. Those who made the criticisms were often well-equipped to do so and had valid points. Public health physicians trained in community medicine were now part of the new health service, having moved over from local authorities in 1974. They had both a medical and a demographic statistical training. Their consultant colleagues, when they got their heads round what the new formula was doing, also began to turn their not inconsiderable scientific talents to the problem. There emerged a considerable scientific debate in the medical and public health journals about the validity of the RAWP approach. This was not a debate about the principle of needs-based allocation but about the statistical means of achieving it. Economists also entered the methodological debate. It was they who had been instrumental in getting the issue of geographical inequity onto the public agenda in the 1970s, as we saw in the previous chapter.

A set of central questions began to emerge. Were standardized mortality ratios really such a good measure of need for health spending? Did the fact that people died earlier from certain conditions mean that more needed to be spent on those conditions? Perhaps less needed to be spent because people lived shorter lives or died before they could be treated. The RAWP committee had wanted to measure morbidity—how ill people are—but had no area-based data that could do that.

The formula did not take account of the extra needs for health resources that derived from poor social conditions such as poor housing or old people living alone. The fact that individuals with a given condition could not be discharged from hospital was often not because they were more ill but because the home conditions did not permit it. This was an argument deployed especially in places like inner London and Liverpool. RAWP did not take account of the higher costs of treating people in some areas, it was claimed. Again, this was mainly a London and big cities argument, but rural areas also argued the long travel distances and ambulance and other costs of rural isolation were not taken into account.

London authorities and hospitals lobbied hard to limit their potential losses. In response the Labour government did set up a review of RAWP before it left office but the Advisory Group on Resource Allocation, as it was called, reported after the Conservatives had returned to power in 1979. The result was that the government did introduce a 'market forces factor', accepting that services of a given standard are more expensive to provide in some areas because the competition for labour is greater and the wages needed to attract the same quality of staff are higher. This argument tended to benefit London.

Despite a growing debate, RAWP's basic approach was not modified more fundamentally for a number of years. The Department of Health and Social Security officials argued that there was no real disagreement with the general direction of change and it was important to get regions moving towards their target allocations and to get the system accepted and treated as normal. Crucial to its acceptance was the 'pace of change' principle. The target allocation was set according to the best scientific advice. *Politicians* decided how fast regions should 'move to target'. Moreover, the movement to target was achieved by allocating differentially the service's 'new money' each year. Regions kept their base budget, adjusted for prices, from last year but if they were above target they got no more. Extra real resources the Chancellor made available, 'growth money', went to the below-target regions. This gained the system acceptance.

Within regions the RAWP formula came increasingly to be applied to distribute funds to area health authorities and then to districts. This meant that some areas within the losing regions did suffer significant real declines in funding. They were being 'doubly RAWPed'. This was especially true of inner-city areas that were losing population. Since RAWP was a population-driven allocation measure, areas losing population were particularly vulnerable. This grew more problematic as the overall NHS budget was squeezed in Mrs Thatcher's second term. For gaining regions, less and less benefit accrued. So the political pressure to reconsider the way the targets were calculated grew, and, indeed, some wished to abandon the system altogether. As academics began to crystallize the arguments, criticism focused on three issues (Mays 1995):

- Standardized mortality rates (SMRs) were not good proxies for morbidity;
- they did not reflect the true resource costs associated with deprivation; and
- there was no empirical basis for the assumed 1:1 relationship between SMRs and variations in need for health-care resources.

There was also growing worry within the service. One regional statistician, Mike Butts, had started to do empirical research on the relationship between hospital admissions and standardized mortality. His results suggested that a one for one relationship between SMRs and hospital use was overstating the case. SMRs *were* correlated with hospital use but more weakly. The one for one relationship had merely been a guess by the RAWP committee. This finally prompted the department to advise a review.

The NHS Tries Again

Ten years after the RAWP committee had been set up, the NHS Management Board was asked to reappraise the operation of the RAWP formula in 1985. In making the request, however, the Secretary of State pointedly endorsed the basic principle of needs-based allocation: 'the underlying principle of RAWP, that of securing equal opportunity of access to health care for people in equal need, is not in question . . . The review will therefore look at the scope for improving the measurement of need' (DHSS 1986). This at the height of the Thatcher revolution!

The final report of this review was not ready until 1988 (DHSS 1988). It was not a purely internal job as the RAWP report had been. This was the age of consultants. The analytical work was done by Coopers & Lybrand, the management consultants. The consultants tried to answer the question as to whether the SMR of an area was a good indicator of demand for service by using the information that was now available on the areas from which patients were referred to hospital. The analysts could now test the factors that were associated with differential demand for hospital services by area. This was the single most important analytic breakthough the review made. It grounded the whole approach to measuring the relative needs of areas in the revealed demand (hospital utilization rates) deriving from areas with different population mixes and characteristics.

The review concluded that the basic RAWP approach did emerge reasonably well. SMRs were related to the demand for hospital beds, but so were other factors that could be associated with the character of the area. However, the internal worries had also been correct. The relationship was not as strong as the RAWP committee had suggested. The review recommended that SMRs should have a lower weight and be confined to the under-75s age group. Instead of using condition (or illness) specific SMRs, they suggested simplifying the process and only using an overall SMR for the region. The gain from the complexity of calculating SMRs for many conditions was not great enough to justify the effort. They also recommended introducing a measure of social deprivation, an Underprivileged Areas Measure. They suggested that the use of the Jarman deprivation score (see below) would be a useful measure to adopt. They also suggested adding a higher weighting for over-85s. In short, the review upheld the basic weighted-population approach but modified it in various ways.

Ministers have Their Say

The government accepted some of these recommendations but not all. The weight given to SMRs was reduced significantly, by half, in fact. But no social deprivation factor was included, very different from the education needs assessments at the same time. The overall effect was to reduce the variations in assumed need across the country as compared with the immediate post-RAWP calculation of need. The regions of the North were deemed to need less in relation to London than before. That further reduced the pressure to move resources out of London. At the same time teaching costs in medical schools were given more weight and higher costs were assumed for London health services. All told this significantly reduced the pressures on the London regions implied by the formula. The result looked very political since the results benefited the South. However, one of our respondents in the department at the time (NHSE1) doubted that it was a politically driven change, at least initially: 'RAWP is incredibly arcane and I would seriously doubt that a busy minister could foresee what would come out of the review.'

A deeper result was that the measures used were now more empirically based and the way opened up to use small-area based analysis as the basis for future developments. The fact remains that the review, and especially those bits of it the Conservative government chose to implement, did help the London regions, which extend far beyond the inner London Labour heartland down to the south coast and the Wash in the north: the Conservative south.

Debate Continues

None of this reduced the continuing debate about the formula, however. Indeed, it only encouraged more. The review itself and its report were associated with a significant further outburst of academic work on the formula (Butts 1986; Carstairs and Morris 1989; Mays 1989; Mays and

Bevan 1987; Milner and Nichol 1988; Morgan *et al.* 1987; Townsend *et al.* 1987). The department took these very seriously (NHSE1 and DoH).

The statistical methods used by the review team's consultants were criticized. The small-area basis was criticized. Summary measures for a ward based on averages for that ward may not be good proxies for the whole. There may be significant variations within it. There was a case for using even smaller units, Carr-Hill *et al.* (1990) argued, namely enumeration districts. That did not satisfy those who believed the whole approach was based on an ecological fallacy. The causal analysis should be done only at the level of individuals, this group argued. Yet, this was not practicable with the data available and it was areas, not individuals, who were receiving the funds.

A more fundamental criticism was that hospital usage (in-patient episodes) was too crude a measure. More than that, it could be misleading. Supply creates its own demand in health care. The more hospital beds an area has, the more people go to hospital for longer. There could be a systematic relationship between, say deprived inner-city areas and high hospital supply there. The greater use of hospital beds in these areas was not a measure of need but of over-supply.

In-patient hospital care was, anyway, not a good proxy for all NHS costs. It ignored out-patient, community services, and primary care. In-patient episodes are a crude measure not closely linked to costs. The socio-economic characteristics of patients from some areas may mean the episodes are more costly. Then again, use of services is not a good measure of need. Higher social groups use services more than their relative health needs would suggest because of superior education and class confidence.

Finally, there were more detailed statistical criticisms of the approach adopted by the consultants working for the review team (Mays 1989; Sheldon 1990; Sheldon and Carr-Hill 1992). The attempt to meet the technical criticisms of RAWP with a reasoned response had merely led to further debate among academics. As a respondent (NHSE1) said: 'The Department worries about this, rightly or wrongly, because they take the view that the system should be robust to serious external criticism and empirical challenges.'

More Adaptations

The report and the responses came out at a time when the design of the census for 1991 was being discussed. Some of those in what was now the

Department of Health thought that a number of criticisms could be met if there were much better census data, for example, on morbidity and self-reported long-standing illness. This could possibly be used to get a measure of the demand for community services as well as hospital services. After hard lobbying these questions were placed in the 1991 Census.

There were other factors at work too. The publication of this review of RAWP coincided with Mrs Thatcher's review of the whole of the NHS which led up to the White Paper *Working for Patients* (DoH 1989). Its results were incorporated into that White Paper. The new internal market was to have important implications for formula funding. District health authorities were to become the purchasers of health services. It was important that the sums they received should be based on the needs of their area and not on the budgets of existing hospitals and other providers. That would give them a claim on those resources and destroy the whole point of the internal market. If district health authorities were to be encouraged to buy services from the best providers for their populations, then their budgets had to be freed from history and the claims of particular institutions. That being so, there had to be an intellectually robust way of fixing those allocations down to a district level. RAWP, which had always only been, officially, an allocation to regions, would be 'abolished'. It would be replaced, the White Paper said, by a 'Weighted Capitation Formula' that could be used for subregional allocations. However, as a department informant (NHSE1) put it, 'If a hen says quack, you probably suspect that underneath it's a duck.'

The formula was not that different from what had preceded it. Moreover, regions did not move consistently to use the new formula to allocate money down to districts. Some used the age cost assumptions and the same SMR weightings. Others commissioned and implemented entirely new allocation methods (Balarajan, 1990; Carr-Hill *et al.* 1994). Others continued to use the old RAWP formula with the old needs-weightings.

There were other difficulties. For the first time part of the Hospital and Community Services budget was not to be allocated to health authorities but to general practitioners, GP fundholders. Those GPs who chose to do so would be given a part of that budget with which to buy hospital and community services for their own patients. They were to take their place alongside districts as purchasers. Hence, they would have to be funded in the same way, otherwise claims of unfairness would arise. That is what the White Paper proposed, though nobody knew how it could be done (Glennerster *et al.* 1994). In the interim, GP fundholding budgets were set on a historic cost basis. Regions and later districts calculated how many patients GPs had referred to which hospital in the past and what that would cost under the new regime.

Another Go

The need to move to a better and redesigned formula for districts was the first priority once the new 1991 census material was in. Some of the leading technical critics of the 1988 study won the competition to produce a new methodology. They were the leading exponents of some of the most advanced techniques available and they had available to them the much improved data. The study commissioned by the National Health Service Executive from the Centre for Health Economics at York University, took the whole methodology forward to a new generation of methods and a previously unmatched level of sophistication (Carr-Hill *et al.* 1994).

Essentially what the York team did was to look at the characteristics of small-area (5,000) populations that were associated with differences in demand for acute hospital care, non-acute care, mental illness, and geriatrics. They corrected for supply-induced demand since they were able to test how far high levels of bed supply generated higher demand and to correct for that. Using multi-level modelling they took into account differences in policies between health authorities.

As in previous studies they had to take as given the political priorities in spending between care groups. If we spend too little on the mentally ill, this approach cannot tell us we are doing so. All it can do is to say, given what we spend as a society on the mentally ill, this area, which has many likely to be affected by mental illness, should get more money relative to other areas. The study *did* take account of distance from hospital services as an indicator of access. In short, the study did take on board many of the criticisms levelled against the old formulae.

The models produced robust statistical results at a regional level. For acute specialties they identified five significant variables that affected demand for hospital care:

- All causes standardized mortality ratio (0–75)
- Proportion of those of pensionable age living alone
- Proportion of dependants living in households with only one carer
- The numbers with self-reported long-standing illness under 75
- The proportion of economically active persons unemployed (a good proxy indicator for other measures of deprivation in this case)

A larger range of variables were seen to be significant for the psychiatric and community services. The acute services index determined 70 per cent of the total allocation in 1997. The acute and community psychiatric indices had a weight of 16 per cent and the community services index the rest.

Ministers adopted the approach set out in the York report, though they dampened the impact somewhat (Peacock and Smith 1995). All the variables subsequently included in the formulae and the sources for each are all set out in an 'exposition handbook' produced each year by the NHS Executive (1997 and subsequent years). This York work still provided the basis for the resource allocation process used in the NHS at the time of writing in mid-1999.

York's work on the determinants of demand for hospital beds deriving from small-area characteristics was supplemented by work undertaken within the Department of Health by its Economic and Operational Research Division on the relative costs of providing services in different areas: the market forces factor. The resulting new formula was used in 1995–6 as part of the overall allocation process to the regional health authorities. Then, when they were abolished in 1996, the formula was used to allocate current account, or revenue, budgets to district health authorities. At the same time a new advisory group was set up to keep the formula under continuous review. Represented on it were not only academics but representative managers in the service who were on the receiving end and those in the medical profession. Thus, RAG, the Resource Allocation Group, became the national forum for policy debate about the funding formula and broader issues about resource allocation in the NHS. The more technical issues were discussed in the Technical Advisory Group (TAG). RAG continually assessed the effectiveness of the formula in achieving its objectives of a fair needs-based allocation of health resources and, in conjunction with TAG, formulated the future agenda of issues to be discussed.

RAG set the following criteria for evaluating the formula:

(1) Theoretical relevance: the formula should be plausible, logical, appropriate, and relevant.
(2) Practicality: the method should be readily calculable, statistically robust, and not require excessive judgement.
(3) Transparency: in general it should be simple to understand, although details may be complex.
(4) Outcome: it should not offer perverse incentives.

Early steps RAG took were to commission academic work to create an element in the formula to cover need for community health services and to have an independent review of the market forces factor. The Universities of Kent and Plymouth undertook the first study and Warwick the second. RAG also considered doing work on the costs imposed on areas with a high rural population. How should the goal of equal access be interpreted there? Homelessness was also considered a problem. The homeless were not properly accounted for in the enumerated population and they often generated a high demand for services. The allocation of budgets to GP fundholders also came up in early discussions. There was a great deal of feeling that they had been unfairly advantaged compared to health authorities and the original White Paper had said they would be treated in the same way. Could the formula be adapted for them?

In 1994 the government reaffirmed that a weighted capitation formula should be used to allocate 'benchmark' budgets to GP fundolders. These would be the starting-point for discussions with the practices. In 1996 the NHS Executive produced advice on the matter, *GP Fundholder Budget Setting*. That formula was also within the RAG remit, as was the question of setting cash limits for GP fundholders' drug spending and indicative budget ceilings for prescribing for non-fundholders. The broad issue of how to achieve more equal access to health care across the range of NHS services was also in their remit.

New Labour's Impact

Then, in 1997, the new Labour government came to power with an even higher priority to achieve not just equal access to health care but to reduce inequalities in health outcomes. It abolished RAG and replaced it with a new committee to reflect these wider concerns. It came to be called ACRA, the Advisory Committee on Resource Allocation in the NHS.

The rhetoric was new: 'The Government is determined to reduce the health inequalities that scar our nation. How we distribute NHS cash has a key role to play in that process.' (DoH press release, 11 Sept 1997). For a time work continued much as before. Refining the needs-based allocations continued within the same intellectual framework. The one significant addition was that its terms of reference emphasized that ACRA was to look across the board, not just at hospital and community services but at primary care too. The whole issue of how to allocate resources to the new, much smaller, primary care groups was to dominate the work of the new committee in its first year. The publication of the Labour government's White Paper: *The New NHS: Modern, Dependable* (DoH 1997), introduced three changes that affected resource allocation. The first was the introduction of primary care groups (PCGs). These replaced GP fundholding but in many ways extended its principles to the whole of the NHS. Groups of GPs and others in primary care serving populations of about 100,000 would have the main part of the NHS budget, devolved to them. This would include both the hospital and community services budget and the pharmaceutical budget, as well as the cash-limited part of the general practice budget (administration and non-GP staffing, mainly). These primary care groups would then make agreements with hospitals and other providers to provide services for their patients and pay them to do so. The full devolution of budgets would be reached in stages. Ultimately they would become free-standing primary care trusts with fully devolved budgets and autonomy to spend them.

This raised issues of extending the basis of formula funding and using the old formula to allocate money to much smaller units than a district. A formula that had been devised by RAWP to allocate mainly hospital revenue money to regions had now to be developed to allocate the whole NHS budget to populations of 100,000. More than that, the basis of the population was in dispute. Those brought up in the RAWP tradition and working for regions or districts saw the principle of allocation to a resident population as crucial. A local population was something public health researchers were used to studying. The information is census-based or relies on returns from the registration of births and deaths. This has its disadvantages, too. Census information is out of date and especially so for small areas where housing and population movement may be substantial. Most problematic for these purposes, GPs draw their populations beyond ward boundaries. Those who were GPs on the committee were only too aware of this. They argued it was crucial to begin with actual patients on GPs' books, not nearly ten-year-old guesses about the size and nature of populations unrelated to GPs lists. Ah, said their opponents, but GPs will cheat and inflate their lists by keeping dead patients on their lists and those who have moved long ago—they do that anyway to boost their capitation-based incomes. That is being stopped with new nationally cross-checked computer listing came the reply. Yet, in 1996 in England, the total of patients on GPs' lists still exceeded the Office of National Statistics census-based estimates of population by two and a half million! For the moment it was difficult to move to a GP patient list as the basis for setting budgets.

It was not just the population base that caused dispute but how robust the scientific basis of the results of the original York work would be for small populations. In the end ACRA decided that populations of 100,000 were big enough for confidence to continue in the York model. For the moment the population base would have to continue to be geographical and census-based. Adjustments would have to be made to health authority populations where GPs drew populations from beyond a particular health authority or PCG. Many believed that for budget control purposes it would be necessary to allocate a shadow budget down to practice level. That suggested that improved practice population data would have to be the eventual baseline.

ACRA recommended a method to set health authority budgets and a methodology for health authorities to set PCG budgets. Once PCGs have developed into full primary care trusts they will receive their own formal allocation direct. As under previous arrangements there are four elements to the procedure by which health authorities' and PCGs' budgets are set. First, there are the weighted capitation targets on which we have so far concentrated. These represent a world in which health resources are fully matched to the assessed relative needs of each area. Then there are the *actual* baseline budgets each health authority/PCG has in the current year. This is, of course, based on history and past attempts to move to target. The difference between the two is the 'distance from target'. Finally, there is the 'pace of change', the speed with which health authorities/PCGs are moved closer to target. Health authorities' pace of change is entirely in the hands of ministers. PCGs' pace of change is, for the moment, in the hands of health authorities.

In its first two years ACRA also undertook work refining the detailed approach to measuring need. It continued in the wake of its predecessor, elaborating separate components in the formula for acute hospital services, for community services, and, separately, for non-community and community-based psychiatric care. As a result of work by a team of consultants, rural low density of population was not found to be associated with higher costs, except for emergency ambulance cover. A measure was included to take this into account. Ethnicity was also investigated. For the most part its effects were already captured in the formulae, the committee thought.

RAWP Evolved into a Too Sophisticated Beast?

Thus, in a very different world from any that they could have foreseen, the basic approach adopted by RAWP committee survived for a quarter

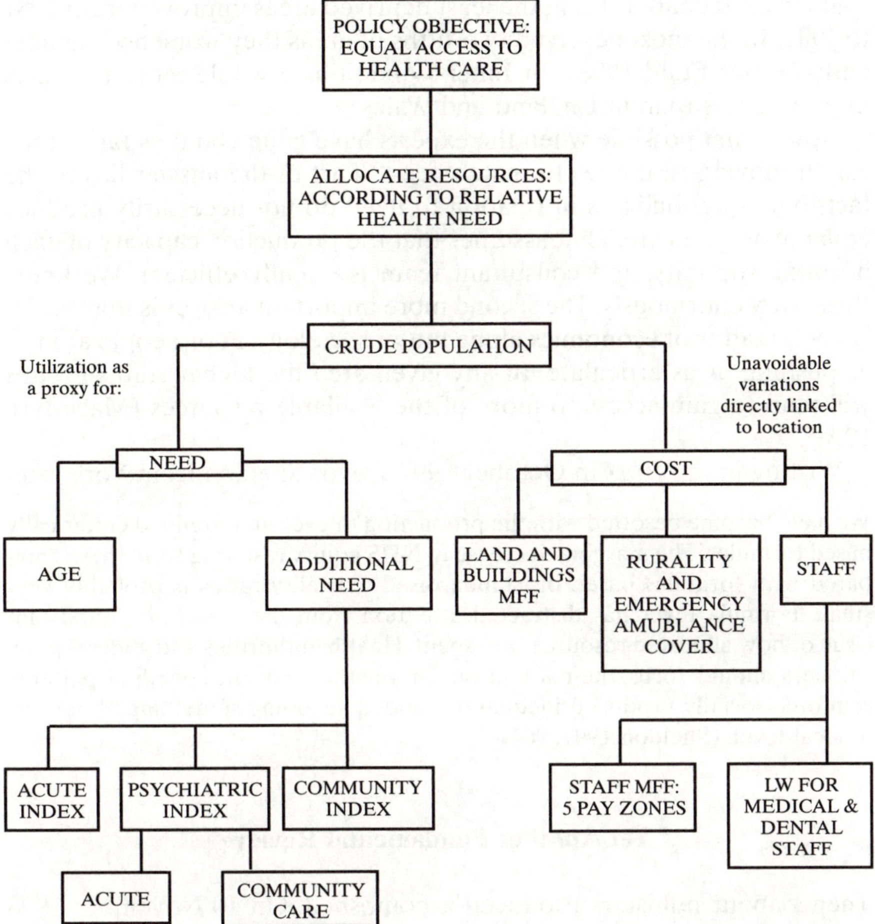

FIGURE 4.1. Schematic Outline of Main HCHS Weighted Capitation Formula, 1999 (*source*: NHS Executive, adapted by the authors; MFF = market forces factor, LW = London weighting)

of a century. A schematic outline of the methodology that had evolved by 1999, is set out in Figure 4.1. Yet all was not well. At the same time as ACRA was worrying about whether it could really go further in perfecting its measures of need, the Acheson Committee (DoH 1998) was delivering its verdict that, in many respects, inequalities in health status had not improved since the 1970s, when all the RAWPing began, and in some instances they had worsened. In London, for example, standardized death rates in the least deprived areas improved from 1981 to 1991. In the most deprived two-fifths of areas they worsened significantly (Kings Fund 1998). In Inner London as a whole mortality rates improved less than in England and Wales.

How is that possible when the experts have gone about as far as they can in moving resources to match need? Part of the answer lies in the fact that equal budgets in relation to need do not necessarily produce equal quality of care. That assumes that the production capacity of each hospital, specialty, and consultant team is equally efficient. We know these vary enormously. The second more important answer is that access is not a matter of economics alone but of sociology. Poor people are not as pushing or as articulate. In any given area the higher status groups will tend to gain access to more of the available resources (Macintyre 1998).

Writing in the *BMJ* in October 1997 Trevor Sheldon from York said:

> We have become besotted with the production of ever more refined empirically based formulas. The marginal increase in NHS equity resulting from these compared with formulas based on standardised mortality ratios is probably very small. Formula fever has distracted attention from the now more important issue of how allocated resources are spent. Health authorities and general practitioners should focus their attention on whether current spending patterns reinforce socially produced inequalities and, if so, doing something about this at local level. (Sheldon 1997: 964)

Yet Another Fundamental Review

Then Labour ministers produced a bombshell. On 10 November 1998 the Minister of State for Health Alan Milburn said ministers wished to undertake a 'wide ranging review' of the formula. The objective of the new formula should be ' to contribute to the reduction in avoidable health inequalities' (letter from John Denham, the new Minister of State to the Chair of ACRA, 23 March 1999). Ministers wanted NHS resource allocation to reflect and fully support the government's wider social agenda including combating social exclusion and reducing health inequalities.

As readers will appreciate, this is a very different set of objectives to those that had been followed since 1976, which sought to ensure that all citizens had an equal chance of accessing health care wherever they lived. Whether they did so and how effective the NHS was in each area was for a different part of the NHS machine to achieve. Most of the determinants of health inequality lay outside the NHS and officials' view was that that was for other social ministries to tackle. All the NHS formula funding could do was to ensure that resources available to each area reflected the differential demands that population was likely to put on the NHS. The reasons for that differential demand were for others to address. Now ministers were questioning that approach.

It posed major problems for ACRA. Should it throw overboard twenty-five years of work on a needs-based approach? Did it abandon the idea that people in different parts of the country in equal need of health care should be able to have an equal chance of access? How much attention should it pay to the NHS's task of being a sickness service in comparison to its newer concern with promoting health?

In the short run, at least, these two objectives were in conflict. If the NHS were to allocate only according to an index of health inequality, say high mortality rates, it would find itself giving resources to places where the population died young and had few old people, thus denying resources to areas with many old people to look after. Ministers would probably not want that. So the formula would have retain some of the old needs-based approach. But how much? We return to the wider issue in Chapter 13. ACRA also faced another uncompleted agenda—what to do about the allocation of resources to GPs and allocation of GPs themselves?

An Unfinished Agenda: General Practice and Equal Access

General practitioners have always jealously guarded their independence from the state. From the National Insurance Act of 1911 they have retained their separate contractual status, been paid for their services as private contractors. Their income from the state derived from a sum paid for each patient they took onto a list of patients they promised to treat. That originally applied to those who were in the 1911 scheme and the system was taken over for the whole population after 1948. In successive stages GPs have had to promise to deliver more and do more specific things for their capitation-based income. They have also gradually been given more lump-sum payments to enable them to set up and run their basic surgery. This combined system of complex payments remains quite separate from that we have so far been considering. GPs have resisted any idea that they be paid a salary. Only right at the end of the Conservative period in 1997 was legislation introduced enabling some GPs to opt for salaried status.

However, the fact that GPs have been paid separately did not prevent the issue of their geographical distribution being a key political concern right from the outset of the NHS. Indeed, more progress was made on this front in the early days of the NHS than with budget allocation. Responsibility for determining the number of practices in an area within the NHS was handed over, in the 1946 NHS Act, to the Medical Practices Committee. Section 34(2) required the committee to: 'secure that the number of medical practitioners undertaking to provide general medical services in the area of Executive Councils (forerunners of District Health Authorities) or in different parts of those areas are adequate'.

In 1949 the committee responded to calls for a more equal distribution of doctors by classifying each district in England and Wales as 'needy', 'open', 'doubtful', or 'closed'. The classification neatly met the professional restrictive practice interests of the BMA too, since it prevented too much competition in popular areas. This had been an aim of the BMA for a hundred years or more. Restriction on entry to popular areas was, however, balanced by encouragement to enter under-doctored areas. The definition of areas in each category list appears to have been based on crude average list sizes in each area. A needy area was defined as one where the average list size was over 3,000 per doctor. In 1952, after the BMA expressed concern with this, the limit was redefined to 2,500. An Initial Practice Allowance was introduced to encourage GPs to set up practices in these unattractive areas.

These measures did produce an improvement in the distribution of doctors, as did the minister's more direct power to spread consultant posts more evenly across the country. The NHS did employ consultants on a salaried basis and could decide which region and area they were employed in. The Labour government of 1964–70 was anxious to push things further. Yet recruitment was poor and morale low. So it was not an easy task.

An unsympathetic pay review body report lead to a not unprecedented row with the BMA. The BMA demanded a new contract and the Labour minister, Kenneth Robinson, saw the chance to link this to some other goals of government policy, namely distribution and the aim of introducing a salaried option for GPs to put them on a par with consultants. The resulting Charter for GPs did improve their conditions and pay. Capitation payments were supplemented by other payments. Better incentives were introduced both to encourage better services in primary care and to get GPs to go to less attractive areas. A basic practice allowance to cover the fixed costs of running a practice meant that it was less risky to set up practices in poor areas. There was an extra payment for practices in unattractive areas. There was a higher payment for patients over 65. There were loans to build and buy practice premises and money to set up health centres. Many of these were in poorer areas. The quality of general practice began to be evened out. Yet it remained remarkably varied, not least in inner-city areas and in London especially. This was the subject of a report by Donald Acheson (DHSS 1981).

One of those giving evidence to the committee was Brian Jarman, a GP in a working-class area of London, and Professor of General Practice at St Mary's Medical School. From day-to-day experience he was convinced that social deprivation was associated with increased attendance at GPs' surgeries and more difficult situations and pressure as well. He developed a measure that correlated census measures with medical conditions and levels of deprivation that were thought to be related to demands on the service. Compared to the complex modelling that RAWP and its successors engaged in this was unsophisticated. But Jarman (1984) convinced the BMA and then the Department of Health and Social Security that it was worth trying. The Jarman index came to be used to give extra payments to practices with high numbers of socially deprived patients. Patients' postcodes were used to identify them with the level of deprivation indicated by their census tract. The variables were:

- Pensioners living alone
- Children under 5
- One-parent families
- Unskilled heads of household
- Unemployed
- Overcrowding
- A mobile population
- Ethnic minorities

The next attempt to even up standards came with Kenneth Clarke's 'contract' imposed on an unwilling BMA in 1990. GPs would be paid to undertake preventive work and GPs in inner-city areas would be paid more, on Jarman criteria. At the same time the element of their income that GPs would receive from capitation payments would increase from about half to 60 per cent. Basing their income more on their capacity to attract and keep patients would increase the pressure to do a good job, it was thought. The BMA opposed the contract but to no avail.

Distributing Doctors

The Medical Practices Committee (MPC) claimed that out of 1,500 districts in England only fifteen were under-doctored in 1997. This fact must be treated with caution. The MPC cannot call for an area to be declared under-doctored unless the GPs in an area call for additional doctors. It may not be in their interests to do so. A large list brings a high income.

Certainly policy on access to general practice sits oddly with the integrated formula funding approach to the rest of the service. At some point these two parts of the service are going to have to begin to sing from the same hymn sheet, or at least from the same composer. A joint working group of ACRA and the MPC was set up to consider how far the needs-based formula approach used to allocate cash to hospitals and community services could be adapted to allocate primary care resources. Some progress was made in thinking how this could be done by 1999.

Inverse Care Law Reversed? Movements to Target

In 1971 the radical GP Tudor-Hart coined the phrase 'the inverse care law' (Tudor-Hart 1971). It said, 'The availability of good medical care tends to vary inversely with the need of the population served.' It was this law that RAWP and its various offspring were designed to repeal. Have they done so? Certainly both the RAWP measures to bring regions closer together and the post-1993 attempts to bring districts together have paid off significantly. The pause in the pressure to equalize had the opposite effect.

The Thames regions began mostly 10 per cent above target in 1976 and others nearly as far below. The average difference from target in 1979 was still 6.29 per cent (see Table 4.1), despite the fact that RAWP had been in operation for a few years. By 1987/8 the average percent-

TABLE 4.1. *Mean Distances of Regions from RAWP Target (% of regional allocation)*

1978/9	1982/3	1985/6	1987/8
6.29	5.71	4.14	2.64

Source: Le Grand *et al.* 1990.

age difference from target had fallen to 2.64 per cent. Then the 1988 review was published, changing the rules of the game and reducing London's distance from target.

It is difficult to get a consistent series that measures distance from a common need-based target. However, Le Grand and Vizard (1998) do show (see Table 4.2) that in terms of average spending per person in each region the variation in spending went on narrowing from 1985 to through to 1990 but then seems to have increased. It may that needs widened and allocations followed but that seems unlikely. What the figures suggest is that when the RAWP-type pressure was relaxed the inequalities grew.

In Table 4.3 we look at what happened when the new district-based formulae were introduced following the York work. In 1993–4 the most overtarget district was 21 per cent above target and the most under-target district was nearly 16 per cent below target. This was a range of nearly 37 per cent, much further than the original regions were apart in 1976. As smaller areas this was to be expected. By 1998–9 the range between top and bottom was only 14 per cent.

Thus both RAWP and its successors have gone a long way to pull health-service resources nearer to what experts, at least, think are those areas' relative needs. Those who look back to the record of the old

TABLE 4.2. *Variation in Real Recurrent Health Expenditure per capita 1985–1993*

	1985/6	1987/8	1990/1	1992/3	1993/4
Coefficient of variation between regions	0.103	0.097	0.093	0.091	0.140

Source: Le Grand and Vizard 1998.

TABLE 4.3. *Range of Distances from Target*

	Most over target HA (%)	Most under target HA (%)	Range
1993/4	21.13	−15.68	36.81
1994/5	15.50	−10.20	25.70
1995/6	14.60	−13.00	27.60
1996/7	13.08	−7.88	20.96
1997/8	8.16	−6.23	14.39
1998/9	8.64	−5.24	13.88

Source: NHS Executive, personal communication.

Ministry of Health in the 1950s and 1960s may find this surprising. The diagnosis Buxton and Klein (1978) were able to make in their paper for the Royal Commission on the NHS hardly stands now. The Ministry of Health compared very badly, they argued, with the Ministry of Education which had successfully pursued a centralized policy of equalizing access to education. That ministry had prevented over well-endowed areas from employing more teachers, had enforced equalizing measures of spending, and ruthlessly hounded the laggard education authorities. It was an active equalizing ministry.

The health service in contrast was locally invisible. It was local democracy combined with an active central department that had brought about an even spread of education they argued. The central health department had been weak and uninterested. The story, post-1976, hardly bears that out. The once weak central department has become more directive and continuously concerned with evening up resources. Ministries can change their spots. In Chapter 8 we report on interviews with civil servants concerned to throw some light on this change.

Has this pro-active stance made any difference to the larger goal of equalizing the health of the nation? We saw earlier in this chapter that ministers in the new Labour government have begun to ask just that question. ACRA met in June 1999 with a set of questions before it:

(*a*) What is meant by health and how should it be measured?
(*b*) What do we mean by health inequalities?
(*c*) What are the main determinants of health?
(*d*) How do we distinguish between 'avoidable' and 'unavoidable health inequalities?
(*e*) In what ways does the NHS impact on health inequalities?

The committee had a long and interesting road before it.

Summary

Over the last twenty years, health service funding has moved to an increasingly sophisticated needs-related basis. Improvements in data (via the census and utilization recording) and strong academic and professional interest have tested and refined the original 'RAWP' formula, based just on relative mortality ratios (SMRs). This system, now known as the Weighted Capitation Formula, is being applied to smaller and smaller sized areas. At present, moves are under way to apply the formula to funding for the new primary care groups of GPs, covering populations of around 100,000.

These moves started under a Labour government in the 1970s concerned with inequality between regions, but were reinforced in the 1980s under a Conservative government which was restraining overall health spending, and was introducing a 'purchaser–provider split' that required health authority budgets to be fixed in a way which did not simply reflect previous activity. By the end of this period, actual allocations to districts were converging quickly on needs-based targets, but the political agenda was moving onto new concerns with inequalities in health outcomes, rather than just in access to health services.

5

The Development of Education Needs Formulae from 1958 to 1990

The year 1958 saw the beginning of modern local government grant systems in England. The 1958 reform of central grants to local authorities had a single, efficiency-driven, objective. Whereas before there had been a number of percentage grants (that is, where the more a council spent on schools, the more grant it would receive), the post-1958 arrangements created a new, general, grant for education, health, fire, child care, planning, road safety, traffic controls, electoral registration, training, recreation, residential care, and school crossings. The proportion of all grants-in-aid which were not tied to specific services increased from one-sixth of all grants to almost two-thirds (Travers 1986: 9). There was also a (separate) grant to assist authorities which had low taxable resources.

The 1958 system was used until 1966, when it was somewhat modified by the introduction of a subsidy for domestic ratepayers. The post-1966 'Rate Support Grant' consisted of the 1958 'general grant' (now to be called the 'needs element'), a grant to assist authorities with low rateable resources (now to be called 'resources element'), and a new 'domestic element' to subsidize householder ratepayers.

One of the main reasons for introducing the new domestic element was to protect householders from the local tax implications of rapidly rising local expenditure. The 1960s and early 1970s were a time of rapid growth in local authority expenditure. In particular, spending on local welfare services such as education, personal social services, and council housing rose rapidly. In some years, real-terms spending rose by 6 or 7 per cent. In an attempt to shield ratepayers from the rising costs of local welfare, the percentage of local expenditure financed by government grant rose from 50 per cent in 1966–7 to 66.5 per cent in 1975–6.

Thus, despite the 'efficiency' arguments put forward in 1958 in support of the move from percentage to general grants, the massive expansion of public expenditure in Britain in the 1960s and early 1970s meant that education spending increased—with central government encouragement—throughout this period. Whether or not the move from percentage grants stimulated efficiency, local authorities were spending far more on schools (in real terms and as a proportion of GDP) by the mid-1970s than at any time in history.

The 1958 and 1966 grant systems sought to increase equity by successive moves to more sophisticated needs-related factors for education. Concern was largely for the maintenance and improvement of standards after the end of percentage grants. But there is little doubt that the factors used for allocation of local government grants implied a concern for the fair treatment of individuals in authorities with different economic and social circumstances.

Thus, in the General Grant Order 1958, there were factors for young children, schoolchildren, high density, low density, declining populations, and high London costs (Ministry of Housing and Local Government 1958: 9). The first Rate Support Grant Order, in 1966, allocated resources on the basis of young children, high density, low density, declining population, high London costs, and education units'. These education units introduced a more sophisticated subcalculation of need to spend, taking account of such indicators as the different costs of educating pupils of different ages. In addition, the 1966 Rate Support Grant Order allocated—for the first time—grant to take account of the higher costs of educating New Commonwealth immigrants (Ministry of Housing and Local Government 1966: 6, 9, and 10).

The reform of local government structure in England (outside London, which had been reformed in 1965) in 1974 coincided with a major period of turbulence for the British economy. Slow economic growth and rising inflation fed through to disenchantment with the system of local government finance. An official committee of inquiry into the funding of local authorities (the Layfield Committee) concluded that either the country should move to a more centrally financed system of council finance or, alternatively, one where there was far greater local autonomy (DoE 1976: 298). Layfield was also explicit about the pursuit of equity and the equalization of taxable capacity (DoE 1976: 213). However, no significant changes were made to the grant system (or local government finance more generally) as a result of Layfield's efforts.

Some things did change, nevertheless. By the mid-1970s, computing was becoming cheaper and more easily available. This coincidental change made it possible to introduce new and more complex techniques into needs element calculations for education and other services. Between 1974 and 1981 a system of weighted multiple regression analysis was used to determine the weightings of the factors in distributing the needs element of the Rate Support Grant. Regression analysis reflected actual spending patterns on the assumption that past spending was a plausible reflection of future need. Because of this link between past spending and future grant entitlements, a number of lower spending authorities argued that higher spenders could affect the size of their allocation by increasing their spending.

Notwithstanding such problems, the post-1974 system did highlight the fact that there was ministerial acceptance for needs-related assessments. Past spending might not have been a perfect needs indicator, but it did imply acceptance of some form of 'need' or equity requirement. The major problem with the government grant system during the late 1970s—apart from the allegation it encouraged high spending—was that the majority of individuals affected (or even ministers or senior civil servants) were unlikely to understand its complexity. Judgement over which indicators were used in the regressions was to a large extent handed over to technicians (civil servants). Problems of complexity and accusations of a lack of objectiveness led to another problem. Minor alterations to the RSG formula could result in unpredictable knock-on consequences elsewhere in the system. As ministers ultimately decided on which bundle of indicators were used, the system was open to accusations of political manipulation.

The priority of the new government in 1979 was to simplify the system of local government finance. However, there was no question of them not retaining a system of needs-based grants. The government was also keen not to become involved in telling local authorities how much to spend on each service. Local discretion was still deemed essential. The result was that in 1981, a new 'Block Grant' was introduced. This new system was based largely on a needs assessment known as the Grant Related Expenditure Assessment (GREs), with an allowance within the same grant for variations in rateable resources. The assumption underpinning this new system was that that needs assessment could be calculated according to a principal–client system in which regressions would assume a subordinate role. Precision in determining the grant was a problem, given the stated desire to achieve greater simplicity. This effort to trade off simplicity and fairness has dogged the local government grant system (and with it education) for the last twenty-five years of the twentieth century.

In the end, over sixty GRE factors were used in the post-1981 Block Grant. There were also subcomponents. At least thirty components or subcomponents were concerned with education. As far as possible, GREs were client-group-related, although some elements of regression analysis remained as the basis for the new needs calculation. While very different from the 1974 to 1981 arrangements, the 1981 system maintained (and increased the explicit sophistication of) needs assessments for education.

The Post-1990 Local Government Finance System

Although the Local Government Finance Act, 1988, is remembered more for the poll tax, its more lasting feature was the replacement of GRE by Standard Spending Assessments (SSAs). SSAs are the latest effort to measure need to spend, and form the basis of an authority-by-authority allocation of Revenue Support Grant (RSG). Variations in the local tax base are also taken into account within the RSG calculation. Expressed simply, an authority's RSG is the difference between its assessed spending need (SSA) and income—on the basis of a standard tax rate—from its local tax base. Councils with a higher SSA and/or lower tax yield will receive more grant per head than those with lower SSAs and/or higher tax yields.

Despite its aims of greater simplicity, transparency, and attempting to control local authority spending by making council expenditure more accountable to the taxpayer, one of the most notable features of the system is that it retained a strong redistributive element: 'The purpose of SSAs, then, is to provide a measure of relative need across all local authorities as a basis for distributing a given amount of RSG' (Sanderson 1995). The official definition states that an 'SSA is the Government's assessment of the appropriate amount of revenue expenditure which would allow the authority to provide a standard level of service, consistent with the Government's view of the appropriate amount of revenue expenditure for all local authorities' (DoE 1996). Current calculations of SSA are subdivided into seven main service blocks, each of which has a spending 'control total'. The seven service blocks are: education, personal social services, police, fire, highway maintenance, 'other services' (now known as 'environmental, protective and cultural services'), and capital finance. Each of these component blocks are, in turn, divided into subformulae which are mostly based on client group and unit cost data. The sum of all these component service-based SSAs produces an aggregate SSA for each authority.

The Education SSA Formula

It was noted earlier that education is the largest service undertaken by local government, and it accounted for over 40 per cent of the total SSA allocation in the late 1990s. Not surprisingly, this, the largest of the SSA component parts, is divided into five separate sub-blocks. The split between these sub-blocks is based on previous years' spending patterns. The full SSA method is set out in the *SSA Guide to Methodology* (DoE 1996; with similar documents for earlier and later years) on which the paragraphs below are based.

The sum of the five separate education sub-blocks thus adds up to the overall education SSA total. Each of the five sub-blocks is based upon a client group. For an individual authority, the numbers of pupils or students within a client group are multiplied by a unit cost figure, with additional add-ons for additional educational needs, sparsity, free school meals and regional cost variations. The SSA calculation for a particular factor or sub-factor, at its simplest, is as follows.

$$\begin{array}{c}\text{Number of individuals}\\\text{in a defined client group}\end{array} \times \begin{array}{c}\text{Unit cost of the}\\\text{service provided}\end{array} = \begin{array}{c}\text{SSA for a}\\\text{particular factor}\end{array}$$

The five client groups within the formula represent the needs of particular age group. These five subgroups are shown in Table 5.1. These definitions are relatively straightforward, and need little further explanation other than to acknowledge that the need to spend could be influenced by cross-boundary flows of population. In order to overcome this problem allowances are made in the education SSA itself and also within the 'other services' block of the overall SSA formula.

The SSA for a particular authority, for one of the sub-blocks of the education SSA, is shown in a simplified form, in Figure 5.1. A calcula-

TABLE 5.1. *Client Groups within the SSA Education Subgroup and SSA Total, 1996–7*

Education SSA sub-block	Client group	SSA 1996–7 (£m)
Under-5 education	Resident population aged 0–4	1,027
Primary education	Pupils and residents aged 5–10	7,303
Secondary education	Pupils and residents aged 11–15	7,514
Post-16 education	Pupils aged 16+, residents aged 11–15	1,067
Other education	Resident population aged 11+ and resident population aged 16–24	854
TOTAL		17,765

Number of **pupils aged 11–15**

×

unit cost for secondary pupils

+

unit cost for **additional educational needs**

+

sparsity measure (some authorities only)

+ **free school meals** allowance

Total of above calculation × **area cost adjustment**

=

Secondary schools Standard Spending Assessment

FIGURE 5.1. Secondary Schools SSA for a Particular Authority

tion of this kind is made for under-5s, primary, secondary, post-16, and 'other' education. Details, such as the basic unit cost per pupil and the area cost adjustment (for authorities in London and the South-East) are subject to annual negotiation between local and central government. This negotiation process is discussed below and a brief description of the key elements of the formula is included.

Unit costs

According to the DoE (now DETR) guide to SSAs, unit costs for a particular client group within education consist of two elements: a standard national amount and a 'supplementary amount' which is different for each authority. This supplementary amount is calculated taking account of additional educational needs, sparsity of population, and the demand for free school meals. For ease of understanding, it is simpler to think of a single, national, flat-rate amount per pupil plus different amounts for additional educational need, sparsity, and school meals. In 1996–7,

TABLE 5.2. *Shares of Education SSA Allocated by Elements of Formula, 1996–7 (%)*

	Client numbers	AEN	Sparsity	Free school meals
Under 5 s	65.60	34.4	n/a	n/a
Primary	81.05	15.7	1.65	1.6
Secondary	81.05	15.7	1.65	1.6
Post 16	81.85	16.5	1.65	n/a
Other	41.70	58.3	n/a	n/a

the proportion of the overall sub-block SSA allocated according to client numbers and other factors was as shown in Table 5.2. Thus, in 1996–7, the SSA for primary education was £7,303 million, of which 81.05 per cent (£5,919 million) was allocated on the basis of pupil numbers. There were 3.5 million primary school pupils, so the basic SSA unit cost for pupils aged 5 to 10 was £1,690. It is to this amount that additional sums for AEN, sparsity, and free meals were added.

Additional educational needs

The additional educational need (AEN) component of education SSA is by far the largest addition to the basic flat-rate unit cost per client amount. An AEN allowance is added to each of the five sub-blocks, though it has been much discussed and debated in the years since SSA was introduced (for example, West and Pennell, 1995). The additional pupil costs associated with AEN are generated by special schools, school support costs for services such as welfare officers, the additional costs incurred in ordinary schools on elements such as statemented or special needs pupils, and by particular needs associated with poverty or immigration.

In allocating grant the experience of the 1974 to 1981 RSG system highlighted the importance of finding needs factors which cannot be manipulated by local authorities. Regression analysis used in the grant system in the years after 1974 identified three such indicators which are still used in the grant system:

(*a*) lone parents: calculated from 1991 census data on the number of dependent children under 18 living with a lone parent;
(*b*) income support: the proportion of under-18 residents claiming income support as a proportion of the number of residents under 18;
(*c*) ethnicity: the proportion of under-16 residents who were them-

selves, or whose head of household was born outside the UK, Irish Republic and old Commonwealth.

Because of the high correlation between the 'lone parents' and 'income support' indicators, they are combined (as the result of statistical analysis) and given a weighting of 2.4 times the weighting given to ethnicity. Thus the composite measure of AEN is the sum of the ethnicity measure plus 2.4 times the combined 'lone parent' and 'income support' measures. The AEN weighting for allocation to each subgroup is then calculated using regression analysis and added to the basic unit cost. Calculations of AEN weightings are based on the position of authorities in 1990–1. DoE/DETR officials have argued that this (now distant) year is the most appropriate basis for calculations because it is the last one that was not affected by the move to (in effect) universal capping. Many critics of the AEN calculation point to the long period that has now elapsed since 1990.

Other criticisms of the AEN calculation include the close interrelationship between all three of the factors used within it, their urban bias, and the apparent absurdity of using the number of New Commonwealth immigrants as a proxy for English-language difficulties. Many local authorities, in particular those from rural and northern metropolitan areas have commissioned research from consultants and academics in an attempt to find more appropriate AEN indicators. Thus far, successive governments have not proved willing to make fundamental changes to the AEN calculation, although the proportion of the primary and secondary education SSA allocated in this way has been cut from 21 per cent to just over 15 per cent.

Sparsity

Sparsity is included as one of the additional weightings given to primary, secondary and post-16 education to take account of the additional costs incurred in areas of low population density. Those costs recognized by the government are (1) smaller schools, and (2) travel expenses. There are two categories of sparsity. 'Super-sparsity' is given twice the weighting of 'ordinary sparsity', on the assumption that costs are likely to be significantly higher in the very rural areas. Sparsity is defined as population density of between 0.5 and four people per hectare, whereas the value for super-sparsity is 0.5 or below. The sparsity factor, in common with other parts of education SSA, is based on regression analyses of past spending, whose method, calculation, and results are set out in official documentation (e.g. DoE 1996, 1997*a*).

Free school meals

The final supplement to unit cost calculations is free school meals. This measurement is only applied to the primary and secondary education sectors and is designed to compensate authorities that must, by law, provide free meals to children with poorer parents. This factor can certainly be seen as an additional measurement of social deprivation, as it is based on recording the proportion of children receiving income support.

Area cost adjustment (ACA)

This factor is intended to allow for the different costs of providing the same services in different parts of the country, though in reality it applies only to authorities in London and the South-East. There have been bitter debates between authorities on either side of the South-East boundary about the size of the ACA allowance (although not about the principle). Similar allowances exist in health and housing. Local authority housing, although ring-fenced into separate local authority accounts, also has an ACA for the calculation of management and maintenance costs, whilst the health sector includes a market forces factor in the determination of its formula. Each of the three calculations attempts to compensate for the same factor, that is, higher costs particularly within and surrounding London. The ACA component, which is applied to all SSA subformulae, is based upon higher labour and business rates costs.

SSAs and Spending in 1996–7

Table 5.3 shows the average education SSA, by class of authority, in 1996–7, and the maximum and minimum education SSAs within each class. It shows the wide range that exists between the highest and lowest SSAs in England. Inner London has education SSAs 24 per cent above the average per capita SSAs for the country as a whole. Tower Hamlets has an education SSA per head that is more than double the national average figure. Oddly, the lowest SSA per head is also in Inner London (Kensington and Chelsea). Kensington's SSA per head is low because of the relatively large proportion of its children educated in the private sector. The range between the highest and lowest SSA per head is far smaller in the metropolitan districts and shires.

Overall, local authorities spent 3.9 per cent above their SSAs in 1996–7. As might be expected, there was a significant range in perform-

TABLE 5.3. *Education SSAs per Head of Population, 1996–7*

	Average	Highest	Lowest
Shire counties	346	405 (Bedfordshire)	296 (Surrey)
Metropolitan districts	385	475 (Knowsley)	308 (Stockport)
London boroughs			
Inner	428	720 (Tower Hamlets)	226 (Kensington & C)
Outer	402	575 (Newham)	267 (Richmond)
Unitary authorities	354	419 (Middlesborough)	300 (Bristol)
England	365	720 (Tower Hamlets)	226 (Kensington & C)

TABLE 5.4. *Overspending and Underspending Education SSAs in 1996–7*

	SSA	Budget	Difference(%)
Overspenders			
Norfolk	243.4	263.3	+8.2
Leeds	252.5	277.5	+9.9
Kensington & Chelsea	34.2	48.2	+40.9
Barnet	117.0	126.6	+8.2
North Lincolnshire	56.4	65.6	+16.3
Underspenders			
Hereford & Worcester	229.0	228.9	
Bradford	209.9	206.0	−1.9
Newham	130.4	121.0	−7.2
Hartlepool	37.0	36.9	−0.3

ance, with some councils spending below SSA and others well above. Table 5.4 below gives examples of authorities spending above and below SSA in 1996–7 (DfEE 1999: annexe K). Few councils chose to spend below their education SSA. In the years since explicit needs assessments were first introduced (1981–2) spending has converged towards SSA. *De facto* capping of all authorities' budgets since 1991–2 forced many authorities to spend closer to SSA than they might otherwise have liked (spending caps were closely linked to SSAs).

Consultation about SSAs

The system of grant allocation has been open to scrutiny since the creation of the Consultative Council on Local Government Finance in 1975. But ministers had no inhibitions about carrying on the process of refining the formula after discussions with local authorities had finished:

the final formula each year used for grant distribution was influenced, but not constrained, by each year's negotiations between central and local government. One of the advances made with the introduction of the 1981–2 formula was that all the calculations involved were opened up for scrutiny. Ministers were still not confined to alter only those elements and changes to the formula discussed and agreed upon with local authorities, but the post-1981 system at least made the process of negotiation more transparent. All methodological calculations and data sources were published and thus open to scrutiny for the first time.

However, the size of task involved in calculating the formula and the number of possible options available did, perversely, limit the minister's choice. The impacts of particular grant changes on individual councils or groups of authorities became a key issue. Lobbying by authorities (individually and collectively) became an industry. By the late 1980s the formula was, like most of its predecessors, deemed too complicated to continue unchanged. The system introduced as part of the local government reforms of 1989–90 (with the poll tax) attempted to simplify the system by reducing the number of services assessed and the number of indicators used.

The process of consultation and determination about government grants is today conducted through the Department of the Environment, Transport, and the Regions (DETR, formerly Department of the Environment) in annual negotiations with local government. During the spring and summer each year an 'SSA subgroup'—specifically designed to deal with education issues—considers the education SSA. This subgroup has an intensive workload and timetable which involves the local authority associations, the Department for Education and Employment (DfEE), and DETR. The main task of this subgroup is to compile and study the many papers that reflect on new elements that might be adopted, and the new pattern of revenue distribution this would incur. There is much lobbying by authorities, often involving detained technical cases for or against particular changes to the formula.

The DETR has considerable influence over the SSA subgroup. Any local authority proposal is addressed to the DETR who then forward the work onto the subgroup. The forum in which these issues are ultimately discussed in the context of SSAs is one which considers all services. This means that on the government side education officials have to be present during discussions on issues affecting other local authority services. Inevitably, local government representatives tend to include few officers with detailed expertise of education (finance is a more likely background for most negotiators). There are few serious challenges to the education SSA formula during the course of each year's negotiating round. Some proposals may not be recorded, or in some cases may not be progressed if one or more groups of local authorities learn that the 'improvements' that have been suggested might work out against their financial interests. Nevertheless, as a result of the consultation process during 1997 approximately 150 different spreadsheet alternatives were considered. Despite this onslaught of proposals, none fundamentally challenged the system. The education SSA methodology has remained broadly unreformed since 1990.

A modernized process of central–local consultation was introduced after the 1997 general election, though grant negotiations have remained broadly similar to those outlined above during the 1980s and 1990s.

Outcomes and Objectives

The level of SSA calculated for each authority is not only significant in influencing the overall amount of resources an authority receives but can also send strong incentive signals about local costs and levels of efficiency. There is a strong implication that authorities with higher assessed needs should spend more than those with lower needs. By the late 1990s, both Conservative and Labour governments were demanding that local authorities pass on any year-on-year education SSA increases to schools.

However, it is important to remember that the education SSA is only part of a larger process of local authority resource allocation. An analysis from the view of the education service may produce different conclusions to those reached by other services within local authorities. Indeed, from the mid-1990s onwards, there is evidence that provision such as personal social services, fire, and highways have suffered resource pressures as a result of SSA being skewed towards education. At a time when governments have sought to restrain the overall spending of local authorities, maintaining real levels of education spending (via SSAs) has led to pressure on most other services.

There has certainly been no pressure from either central or local government to change or attack the equalization principle of distribution. The concept of expenditure needs equalization (a highly sophisticated version of such equalization) is now very well established. Many of the moves to ensure a fairer and more sophisticated grant system took place during the Conservative governments of 1979 to 1997 (Hale and Travers 1993: 9–12) .

Sub-Authority Allocation: The Development of School-by-School Allocation Formulae

The Education Reform Act, 1988

The 1988 Education Reform Act (ERA) was not concerned solely with financial reform. The Act was the largest piece of post-war education legislation and was designed to open up the schools sector to market forces. The success of schools, and their subsequent funding levels, would, in future, be based on their ability to attract more pupils/clients; funding would be based on the number of pupils attracted. Other changes included: the implementation of a National Curriculum; tests at 7, 11, 14, and 16; and, of key concern to this book, formula-based budget delegation from local authorities to schools. Although local management of schools (LMS) represented a major step towards public-sector financial devolution (Wallace 1992), it has received rather less publicity than another, separate, reform—grant-maintained (GM) schools. GM institutions, which never accounted for many more than 1,000 schools out of 24,000, have continued to attract far more attention than the majority which decided to stay within the LEA system, receiving their funding via the LMS formula.

The reason why GM institutions proved so interesting to critics and commentators was that a school which opted for GM status was subject to oversight by a new Whitehall-appointed body (the Funding Agency for Schools) and also received its funding directly from central government. The creation of a new centrally funded schools sector led to a debate about the possibility of creating a national funding formula for all schools (HoC 1994*c*: xiv–xvi).

In summary, therefore, a central feature of the Education Reform Act, 1988 (ERA) was a desire to introduce market forces into the schools sector, though with some increase in central regulation. This combination of local financial devolution and increased central oversight was not uncommon during the 1990s (Hood *et al.* 1999: 6). Devolved budgets were central to all these objectives, and were to be achieved by allocating resources below the level of the local authority, using a formula which had to be approved by the DfEE. There was never a government proposal to impose a national formula. Instead, it was envisaged that individual LEAs would design formulae that could reflect their own local circumstances. The formula would, nevertheless, have to be approved by DfEE, according to the following criteria:

(1) It should be mathematically rigorous.
(2) The majority of resources were to be allocated according to pupil numbers.
(3) There should be additional factors to achieve equity.

The decision to require local authorities to allocate resources to schools using a formula of this kind was indeed radical. Up to this point, virtually all LEAs had allocated resources to institutions on the basis of a series of one-off decisions made by town hall bureaucrats. LMS had the enormous advantage of making the allocation of resources a more explicit process. Although there was some initial resistance to LMS (particularly from within local government), there is no doubt that once introduced it contributed to the transparency of resource allocation. No political party is now lobbying for a return to the previous system.

LMS in action

In much the same way as the 1944 Education Act had been a general statement of intent, the wording of the ERA was not particularly specific or detailed. In the implementation of LEA formulae, departmental circulars played a key role in explaining how LMS should work. The two most important for this study are *Education Reform Act: Local Management of Schools* (DES 1988), which outlined the initial phase of LMS, and the later *Local Management of Schools: Further Guidance* (DES 1991).

The first of these circulars proposed that LEAs outside Inner London should produce an approved formula by 30 September 1989, so that it could be used for the allocation in April of the following year (for Inner London authorities equivalent dates were September 1991 and April 1992). Once approved these formulae could run indefinitely, although there was an obligation to review the system after three years. Any changes to the formula did, however, need to be approved and seek local consultation. The precise details of this approval process were first issued in 1990. In addition, the initial system did not compel LEAs to devolve budgets to all forms of school, only to all secondary and primary schools with over 200 pupils. Because of a combination of school support for LMS and lack of widespread opposition to financial delegation, LMS was extended so as to include all schools by 1995.

In conjunction with the extension of LMS to different types of school, the last few years have seen a gradual increase in the proportion of the overall education budget devolved to individual schools. Prior to LMS local authorities were free to decide what proportion of their overall budget (and thus the spending figure implied by SSA) they wished to spend on central services. Since 1990 this regime has changed dramatically, with formal delegation requirements being placed on LEAs. This feature of LMS restricted local authorities' autonomy (Lee 1997). One of the key purposes of LMS was thus to encourage greater delegation from town halls. The government laid down a requirement that the only items to be deducted from the total of the education budget devoted to schools were capital expenditure, specific grants, home to school transport, school meals, and certain transitional funding.

By 1996–7 the average share of LEA total budgets delegated to schools in England and Wales was slightly over 90 per cent. The range for individual councils lay between 85 and 96 per cent. The proportion of resources devolved has, nevertheless, not reached levels the government desired (Timmins 1995). Soon after Labour took office in 1997, they announced a move towards increased delegation, to be known as 'Fairer Funding'. Under this new system, authorities would be required to devolve a larger share of their central budget.

LMS formulae

There is no national formula for LEAs to apply in the delegation of their budgets: each authority has designed its own. It terms of national policy LMS has two objectives. First, it should devolve as large a proportion of resources as possible to schools. Second, it should require LEAs to distribute the amount that is to be delegated to schools according to a formula that has characteristics that apply to all schools, and which is open, transparent, and objective. In order to achieve this ERA specified that all formulae had to conform to guidance issued by the Secretary of State. Guidance issued by the government had a number of features: (*a*) general rules, (*b*) specific requirements, and (*c*) ministerial indications of an approaches that might be taken (Lee 1997).

General rules

These are set out in DES (1988) and state that a formula should be objectively seeking equity, based mainly on age-weighted pupil numbers, and simplicity. Central to these objectives is the implementation of age-weighted pupil number funding. Allocating resources according to age-weighted pupil numbers would lead to objective (formula-driven) rather than incremental funding based on historic spending patterns, would be relatively simple to understand, and, given accurate weightings, would be closely related to need.

Specific requirements

Given the importance of per-pupil funding in the guidelines stated above, the specific rules over LMS have generally dealt with the relative importance of this factor within an LEA formula. Up until 1993, 75 per cent of the money allocated through the formula had to be distributed on the basis of age-weighted pupil numbers. The remaining 25 per cent should allow for the additional costs incurred by special educational needs, and for the costs of small schools. In 1993 this system was altered so that now the LMS formula had to allocate at least 80 per cent of its budget according to 'pupil-led' factors. The definition of pupil-led was broader than that of age-weighted pupil numbers, as it included allowances for special educational needs or attendance in designated nursery classes.

Ministerial indication

The main issue that has concerned the government, beyond those that fell into the first two categories, is that of additional educational need. Ministers have expressed an expectation that a proportion of the available resources should be distributed on the basis of educational disadvantage. Most authorities have used the number of pupils in a school receiving free school meals as a proxy for social or educational disadvantage. This use of 'free school meals' as a proxy for spending need shows some consistency with the SSA formula. Efforts have also been made to ensure resource shifts from year to year are not too swift or too great.

The LMS formula and grant-maintained schools

During the period considered by this study, over 1,000 schools opted out of local authority control. The oversight of these institutions passed to the government-appointed Funding Agency for Schools, while their funding was provided by a 'common funding formula' (CFF). The CFF was, in reality, little more than a slight variant of each authority's local LMS formula. In the case of a particular school, the CFF was based on the SSA for the authority in which the school stood, though a national set of weightings was applied to the SSA-based schools budget. Thus, a GM school in an authority with a relatively high SSA would have the

CFF applied to a higher spending total than an institution in an authority with a lower SSA. (For a fuller discussion of the funding of GM schools as compared with LEA schools see HoC 1993*a*: paras. 16–25.)

The key issue raised by the creation of GM schools was whether or not they received more generous funding than the remaining LEA ones (HoC 1993*b*: paras. 12–17). Evidence published during the mid-1990s suggested that, while revenue funding for the two sectors was broadly consistent, the funding of capital was more generous for GM schools, particularly in the years immediately after they opted out. There was also some concern about the risk that LEA schools were being penalized by having to pay twice for the same central services provided by councils (HoC 1994*b*: para. 18).

The question of the relative fair treatment of LEA and GM schools had parallels with the debate about fundholding and non-fundholding GPs within the health service. The issue of the fair treatment of local authority and housing association tenants is also very similar. The question of equity in the treatment of two different kinds of devolved state-funded services was raised in the interviews with education, health service, and housing professionals which are considered in Chapters 8–11.

An overview of the LMS reform

At the outset of LMS most local authorities constructed formulae which were designed to be relatively stable from year to year and also to ensure that the distribution replicated previous spending patterns. Most authorities have maintained this priority of minimizing turbulence, while others have sought to simplify their formula. Whether this has led them to use the formula to redistribute resources between institutions remains unclear, though there has been pressure on councils to shift resources from secondary to primary schools (HoC 1994*a*: para. 106). It is not beyond the ability of LEAs to create a formula which would benefit certain schools disproportionately, but the number of complaints to DfEE and the number of rejected formulae are surprisingly few. There is no evidence that LEAs behave (or seek to behave) in a way that is unfair to particular schools or groups of institutions.

Another possible concern is the risk there could be major swings in school-to-school allocations from one year to the next. Given that such a large proportion of the LMS formula is now accounted for by components based on pupil numbers, changing the age-weighting could produce big shifts. There is no obligation on LEAs to refer such changes (in age-weightings) to the department, or seek approval. But again, there is no evidence of abuse.

There is little academic or other external pressure on the system of schools' funding, and there are no proposals to alter the system. Indeed, schools have in a number of cases been more critical of the SSA formula than of their own authority's funding distribution. Given the far greater per-pupil variations in education SSAs than in local authority funding formulae, schools are correct in judging that SSAs are a far greater source of differentiation in their funding than authorities' LMS formulae.

Conclusions

As local authority funding has gradually moved towards greater and greater precision in spending need equalization during the 1960s, 1970s, 1980s, and 1990s, it is unlikely that many education authorities or schools saw the change in precisely that way. Additional resources, rather than equity, have generally been the key interest for the education service. The move—in 1958—from specific to general grants was opposed by education interests, on the grounds that the education service might lose resources. It was not a debate about fairness. Reforms to the grant system in the subsequent decades have led to greater sophistication in education needs assessments, though debate has generally centred on whether or not the overall level of resources was sufficient.

This brief background to the modern debate about equity and efficiency within schools demonstrates that from the start of the nineteenth century the establishment of a publicly funded education system in England has been in the context of debates about the appropriateness (or otherwise) of having a universal system of education provision and also about the extent of equity to be achieved by the allocation of government funding.

At various times, Exchequer funding has been given directly to schools and to the local authorities who assumed responsibility for them. Grants have been made to fund buildings, as amounts per pupil, to take account of low rateable values, and to equalize for differences in spending needs. Some grants have been paid only on achievement of examination results, while others have been set at a fixed percentage of government-approved spending figures. Most recently, the bulk of central funding has been given as a general grant which is designed to equalize for differences in spending needs and taxable capacity.

It is the present arrangements for financing schools' education, based on local authority-set budgets funded by local taxation (25 per cent) and Exchequer support (75 per cent) which has been investigated by the research and interviews conducted for this project. The results of these interviews are considered in Chapter 9 below. The views of local government officers and headteachers should be seen in the context of the history outlined above and also of the longer term history of local government funding in Chapter 3.

Education in England has a strong 'establishment' of experts and professionals, and a complex set of central–local relations which have been formed over at least two hundred years. In this sense the service is similar both to health and housing. But what is certainly different to health is the extent of local political involvement in the debate about 'fair' treatment of particular areas. Councillors argue hard for the needs of their particular authority in a way that has no parallel in health. The territorial distribution of education funding is thus more 'political' than for health and probably, for rather different reasons, than for housing. Housing, after all, is not a universal service. Education funding, both the allocation of resources to local authorities and the second-tier distribution to schools, is now relatively open and subject to debate. Whether this transparency increases perceptions of equity is open to doubt.

6

Allocating Social Housing Subsidies

Housing differs from education and health services in that social landlords charge for their services through rents, so that their funding is only partly based on central government grants (although the majority of their rental income is, in fact, derived from central government indirectly via the housing benefit system). When they have been free to vary these rents, they have not therefore had to operate within fixed budgets in the same way as schools or health authorities (at times, however, their ability to set rents has been constrained, as explained below).

Second, capital spending plays a much greater part in the process. Funding systems for both capital and revenue are therefore important. The fact that so much of housing finance relates to borrowing and the cost of capital complicates housing finance by comparison with health and education. In particular, at times of inflation, real debt servicing costs are at their highest early on, but are then eroded (Hills 1991: ch. 5). Many of the developments in subsidies for social housing since the 1970s can be seen as responses to the problems this causes.

For local authorities, central government faced the problem that some had low costs as a result of old debts, while others had much higher spending as a result of recent, high-interest borrowing. These led to large cost variations between authorities which bore little relationship to the relative value of the properties owned. The development of local authority housing subsidies since 1980 has centred around attempts to equalize resources between such authorities. As Chapters 3 and 5 (for the case of the education Standard Spending Assessment) discussed, that this concern with equalization should dominate under the Conservative governments is not such a paradox as one might think at first sight. Especially within the housing sector, there was a strong priority to restrain, and even cut, public spending. If withdrawal of subsidies was not to lead to very high rents indeed for high-cost authorities, ways had to be found of putting more of the burden on low-debt ones, effectively moving towards greater equalization of costs.

The 1980s solution to the problems caused by inflation for housing association finance was to retain the very generous initial capital grants which had been introduced in the 1970s, but to try to claw back later surpluses as the burden of debt servicing fell. The 1990s solution was to give less generous initial grants, not claw back later surpluses, but leave associations with the responsibility for covering the major repair costs which would accrue later in the lives of their property.

What has emerged from this is a situation where two different kinds of provider—local authorities and non-profit housing associations (now technically known as registered social landlords, RSLs)—are doing essentially the same job. They both provide housing at below market rents to tenants who are granted tenancies mostly on the grounds of need. Indeed, in many cases, tenants are allocated to housing associations by local authorities from the same pool of potential tenants. However, the funding systems for the two subsectors are completely different. In this chapter we look first at the system which has evolved since the 1970s for the larger (though shrinking) sector, council housing, and then at the arrangements for the smaller (but growing) housing association sector. In each case there is a distinction to be made between the way the subsidies which allow submarket rents to be charged operate and the way in which their ability to undertake capital projects is controlled. We look at the situation in England; subsidy arrangements in Scotland in particular have differed from those described here.

Subsidies to Local Authority Housing Revenue Accounts

Since the introduction of the first housing subsidy in 1919 local authorities have played a significant role in the housing sector. At its peak in the late 1970s local government owned more than 30 per cent of the nation's housing stock, but even before 1979 spending controls were applying the brakes to the number of homes being built. By 1995 the proportion of the national housing stock owned by local authorities had fallen to below 19 per cent. This reduction resulted from the application of two principles by the Conservative administrations of the 1980s. The first was the general desire to promote owner-occupation, both through the new right for council tenants to buy the homes they lived in under the Right to Buy, and through general restraint in publicly funded house-building. At the same time, housing associations were to become the dominant providers of new social housing.

Changes to local authority subsidies began with the 1980 Housing Act, which brought in a new housing subsidy in England and Wales based on *notional* calculations of the change in income and spending on authorities' housing revenue accounts (HRAs) each year. Where the 1972 Housing Finance Act had provoked confrontation with local government through its use of compulsion to raise rents (Malpass 1989), the 1980 system simply *assumed* that rents would rise. If councils chose not to raise them, they would either have to find extra income from their own resources—higher rate fund contributions—or they would have to keep spending down.

The calculation of this new housing subsidy took as its starting-point a 'base amount' (effectively the total subsidy paid in the previous year). To this was added an allowance for increased spending over the year, while an assumed increase in income from rents was deducted. In general, the assumed increases in rents were higher than the allowances for higher spending, so subsidy would fall.

The allowance for increased spending included a percentage increase (set nationally each year) in management and maintenance costs per dwelling from the notional amount allowed for them the previous year (starting from average *actual* spending in the three years up to 1980–1 adjusted for inflation). It also included 75 per cent of the loan charges on new borrowing (or a notional equivalent if capital spending was financed in a different way). The system thus incorporated a high subsidy on new capital spending, but no additional subsidy on higher recurrent spending—except to the extent that using the base of actual spending in the late 1970s 'rewarded' high spenders at that point (with the ever-present possibility that any future change in subsidy might do the same, as indeed it did).

On the income side, the system was based on assumed flat-rate increases in weekly rent per dwelling across the whole of England and Wales. These increases totalled £12.50 between 1981–2 and 1989–90 (compared to an average weekly rent in 1980–1 of £7.71; DoE 1989, table 11.1). Whether it was intended or not, the system pushed authorities towards rent levels which varied little across the country (and in reality little between different kinds of property).

Councils could escape from these increases by increasing rate fund contributions (or, more rarely, by reducing the transfers made from the HRA to the general fund). However, changes in the Block Grant system made this an increasingly expensive option (by imposing 'penalties'—withdrawn grant—on those deemed to be 'overspenders'). To start with, at least, the system was very successful in reducing housing subsidy, which fell from £2.5 billion to £0.5 billion between 1979–80 and 1987–8 (at 1988–9 prices; Hills 1991, table 3.3). However, as the decade went by, more and more authorities dropped out of subsidy altogether—by

1987–8 three-quarters of them. This meant that central government could no longer use the system to lever rent increases or to extract further resources from them.

In July 1988 the government published a consultation document presenting what it saw as the problems with the existing system, the objectives of reform, and possible solutions (DoE 1988). This formed the basis of the system which is still in operation. The problems, as described by the government, included that subsidy, based on adjustments from an accretion of previous systems, was not being targeted on those who needed it most. Second, the ability to make rate fund contributions was said to be undermining the efficiency of housing management (as there was no 'hard budget constraint'). Third, the ability of councils which were out of subsidy to make surpluses on their HRAs could, it argued, be used to cushion inefficiency. The system was also seen as overcomplicated and giving inconsistent incentives. The new system, it was argued, should achieve rents which were set by reference to, 'what people can pay, and what the property is worth, rather than by reference to historic accounting figures'. The key elements of the new system, implemented under the 1989 Local Government and Housing Act from April 1990 were:

- 'Ring-fencing' the HRA, in effect outlawing rate fund contributions, and making an authority's landlord finances more self-contained.
- Unifying the different subsidies to the HRA. This meant not only ending RFCs (and the part of Block Grant which could actually support them), but also amalgamating what had been housing subsidy and the amounts paid by central government towards the costs of rent rebates (as housing benefits for council tenants are known) into a new housing revenue account subsidy.
- Basing subsidy on rent guidelines which reflected the capital value of an authority's stock (measured by Right to Buy values), and management and maintenance allowances, which would become more related to an external assessment of the cost of running different kinds of property, and less to historic spending patterns.

These changes served three objectives. First, the amalgamation of the old housing subsidy and rent rebate subsidy meant that virtually all authorities would be within the new system. Low-cost authorities could be given HRA subsidy which was *less* than the cost of their rent rebates, restoring central government's lever over them, and its ability to extract the surpluses which would otherwise accrue on their HRAs (up to the value of their rent rebates). This served the objective of allowing further cuts in net subsidy to HRAs (which became negative at a UK-wide level by 1995–6) and provided an implicit mechanism for transferring resources from 'surplus' to 'deficit' councils. On the other hand, the way it does so is not well understood, and the mixing of housing finance with social security payments has caused confusion in the housing world ever since.

Second, the reform made the current finances of the landlord part of councils much more self-contained. If spending was higher than the management and maintenance allowances, rents would have to be higher than the rent guidelines by the same amount. If spending was lower, rents would be lower (rather than potentially benefiting the council's general funds). This gave a much clearer link between spending and rents than had existed before. However, because so many tenants received housing benefit—which absorbed all of any rent increase for them—this still did not amount to a hard budget constraint on the HRA. Central government subsidy would still rise to reflect the full housing benefit cost of any rent increases or changes in the numbers receiving rent rebates.

Third, the idea was that subsidy should be 'calculated on a fundamental basis by comparing income and expenditure in each year', rather than the previous incremental approach under which the subsidy was calculated as an increase or decrease against the previous year's figure. The calculations involve almost complete adjustment for an authority's debt charges, not only equalizing between high- and low-debt authorities, but also meaning that any *new* capital spending is fully subsidized at the margin (but subject to the strong capital controls described below).

Rent Guidelines in the 1990s

These reforms—particularly the introduction of rent guidelines set in proportion to capital values—would potentially mean dramatic changes to individual councils' HRAs. To lessen the shock, a number of 'damping mechanisms' were applied to various parts of the formula. In particular, for many northern authorities, applying the rent guidelines implied by their Right to Buy values would have meant large cuts in rents; for others in London and the South-East, they would have meant dramatic rises. To prevent this, the Department of the Environment (now, with Transport and the Regions, known as DETR) sets minimum and maximum cash amounts by which the rent guideline actually used to calculate subsidy changes each year from the previous year's figure, starting from actual rents in 1989–90. For most of the 1990s, this 'damping' system was more important for many authorities than the underlying logic of basing guideline rents on capital values.

Indeed, it is not entirely clear that the DoE would actually have wanted rents to be in direct proportion to capital values, anyway. This would have meant rents in some northern authorities below their management and maintenance spending, for instance, and greater proportionate variation across the country than one would expect to see in market rents—a wild lurch from the flat-rate rent increases of the system in the 1980s. In confirmation of this, from 1996–7 the calculation of underlying rent guidelines was changed to have two elements: half depending as before on an authority's relative Right to Buy values, but the other half depending on relative regional earnings, which vary much less across the country.

Table 6.1 shows that rents did indeed come to vary more across the country by the late 1990s than they had at the start of the decade. 1989–90, London rents were one-third higher than those in the lowest rent region, Yorkshire and Humberside. By 1997–8, they were two-thirds higher. The spread of differentials became much more closely matched to regional house price differences. For instance, London house prices were 139 per cent of the UK average in 1997, and those in the rest of

TABLE 6.1. *Local Authority Rents and Rent Guidelines in England*

	1989–90	1997–8
Rent guideline for subsidy calculation (£/week)	20.97	35.36
Actual average rent (£/week)	20.70	40.98
Regional rents as percentage of English average		
London	118	132
Rest of South-East	107	114
West Midlands	100	93
Merseyside	99	102
South-West	96	99
North-East	95	83
North-West	95	91
Eastern	94	104
East Midlands	93	87
Yorkshire and Humberside	88	79

Source: Wilcox 1998: tables 68 and 69, and own calculations.

the South-East, 122 per cent. Meanwhile prices in Yorkshire and Humberside were 79 per cent and in the East Midlands 81 per cent of the UK average (Wilcox 1998: table 43a). The aim of rents varying with some kind of relationship to capital values was more closely achieved at regional level, at least.

However, the table also shows that actual rents rose faster than the increase in guideline for subsidy purposes. For the councils, this was because management and maintenance allowances were inadequate; central government feared that it was because councils knew that for most of their tenants, receiving housing benefit, central government would actually pay the bill (a similar concern about funding for the housing association sector is discussed below).

In reaction, the centre imposed limits on what it would contribute towards rent rebate costs. This restriction—also brought in from 1996–7—represents the most significant change to the subsidy system and its incentive structure since it started. Instead of fully reflecting the effect of higher rents on rent rebate costs through higher HRA subsidy, this would only apply for rent increases up to, but not beyond, a threshold. In effect, for an authority caught by the restriction, an increase in gross rents beyond the threshold only yields income from, say, the third of its tenants not receiving benefit, making rent increases much less attractive to the authority.

The threshold for the rent rebate restriction essentially takes as its starting-point the *higher* of an authority's 1995 rent guideline and its actual rents then. For most authorities, this means that the threshold is based on *increases* from whatever level actual rents had reached in March 1996, not on their underlying rent guidelines. Authorities which had high rents in relation to their guidelines (allowing higher spending) are thus less restricted by this than those who had low rents. This gives another in a long line of examples of new housing subsidy rules being based on past spending.

It also means that there are now effectively three different and not very well-related systems which affect the rental income side of the subsidy calculation: the 'underlying' rent guideline (based partly on capital values and partly on regional earnings); the actual guideline resulting from the cumulative impact of 'damping' via the maximum and minimum rent guideline increases as applied to actual rents back in 1989–90; and the rent rebate restriction threshold, generally based on increases from actual rents in 1995–6. As we shall see in Chapter 10, this is not conducive to a clear understanding on the ground (and possibly not anywhere else) of the principles underlying the system.

Management and Maintenance (M&M) Allowances in the 1990s

When the new regime was implemented for the first time in 1990–1 the newly required allowance levels for management and maintenance were based on an average of actual spending levels in the three years between 1986–7 and 1988–9, provided that this was higher than 'reckonable' spending under the previous system (derived from late 1970s spending) or a regional minimum. The objective, however, was to move towards a position where allowances were independent of previous spending—in effect, making them more 'formulaic'. This was achieved in 1991 for the maintenance element and in 1992 for the management component of the new 'target' system for allowances (DoE 1997*b*).

The *maintenance* target is now based on the varying requirements for recurrent repair of different kinds of building. There are up to sixty dwelling types in the calculation, all based on a classification by housing type (for example, high-rise flats), size (for example, number of bedrooms), and age (in bands). The weighting given for each category is related to the assumed need to repair, which has been based since 1996 on research and data from the 1991 English House Condition Survey. Moving to these weights meant smaller allowances for flats, which London authorities objected to. This loss was partly compensated for by taking into account the results of a study of the effect of social conditions, and of how factors such as vandalism affected repairs. This resulted in the introduction of a new 'social conditions element' (based on the DoE's 'Index of Local Conditions' for each local authority) whose weighting ranges from 1 to 1.2; in other words it can result in a 20 per cent increase in the target. The result of this calculation is then multiplied by an adjustment for regional cost variations.

The later introduction of *management* targets suggests that this was more difficult to formulate. DoE regression analysis found it hard to correlate management costs with explanatory variables, but in the end two factors proved significant and are used in the formula: the proportion of flats (in part a proxy for social conditions); and a measure of sparsity (with areas of extreme sparsity awarded double weighting). The result of this is then adjusted by a further 'geographical cost factor'.

The change from management and maintenance allowances based on actual spending to one based on these targets was—like the system of rent guidelines—accompanied by a system of 'damping'. The precise rules of this damping system vary from year to year. For authorities whose allowances are 'above target' the damping system constrains the fall in each year's allowance from the previous level. For those which are 'below target', the allowances converge upwards on the target (subject to a minimum allowance set as a percentage of the target, for instance 96.5 per cent in 1997–8).

Capital Controls on Local Authority Housing

Whereas, in the past, local authority housing capital programmes were mainly concerned with the building of new houses, today they are focused on renovation of existing housing (sometimes including regeneration schemes which involve demolition and rebuilding), together with support for the private sector, such as renovation grants or financing of housing association developments. These programmes are tightly controlled by central government.

As explained in Chapter 3, local authorities make bids to the DETR under the housing investment programme (HIP) system. Originally, controls applied to new borrowing. During the 1980s, authorities received substantial capital receipts from the sale of assets—particularly council houses under the Right to Buy. In the early 1980s, they were allowed to spend a percentage of their unspent accumulated receipts each year. This, however, led to two problems from the point of view of central government. First, it was hard to predict when councils would actually spend their receipts, leading to higher public borrowing in some years than the government had planned (as spending capital resources counts as 'negative borrowing'), affecting one of its central macroeconomic targets, the Public Sector Borrowing Requirement. Second, the authorities with the most capital receipts were not necessarily those with the greatest needs for capital spending. In addition, some authorities began to evade the controls, for instance through leasing deals under which they paid for new assets out of future revenues, rather than through capital spending.

To counter these problems, the control system was tightened under the 1989 Local Government and Housing Act. Controls now operate through a system of 'credit approvals', which apply to borrowing and leasing deals. Authorities are allowed much more restricted use of their capital receipts than before (although there have been certain years when authorities have been allowed to use a high proportion of receipts). Credit approvals adjust for an individual authority's capital receipts, so more resources can be steered to those with greater needs in relation to their resources. Again, the 1989 legislation can be seen as creating greater equalization of resources: under the pressure of tightly limited spending, it became of even greater importance to focus it where it was most needed.

The way in which credit approvals are distributed between authorities depends in part on DETR ministers' assessment of a local authority's relative performance carried out initially by government offices in the regions, but in part on the Generalized Needs Index (GNI), which attempts to measure local housing needs relative to other authorities. The GNI is weighted between elements reflecting local authority stock condition (60 per cent), need for new provision (30 per cent), and private-sector stock condition (10 per cent). The latter two elements are the same as those used in the equivalent index for housing association allocations, the HNI (see below), while local authority stock conditions reflect results from the English House Conditions Survey. The GNI is adjusted for local measures of deprivation (the Stress Area Enhancement), cost compensation (reflecting regional cost differences), and a damping element to prevent large changes in allocations from year to year. In the past, allocations between authorities were based mostly on DETR discretion, with the GNI acting only as a benchmark, but they are now based half on the GNI and half on the discretion of the DETR (Niner 1998). The elements of the GNI are currently (summer 1999) under review.

As explained in the previous section, once an authority has been allowed to borrow, any resulting loan charges are broadly reflected pound for pound within the revenue funding system. The efficiency pressures on councils' capital programmes thus come through the fact that they are allowed to spend only very limited amounts, and should be under tenant and political pressure not to squander them, rather than through any knock-on effects of high spending per dwelling on their net costs and hence future rents. This is very different from the environment now facing housing associations, as we now explain.

Housing Association Capital Grants

In the 1980s, the Conservative government decided that housing associations, not local authorities, should be the principal providers of new social housing. The role of associations was also to increase as an increasing number of authorities decided to transfer their entire stock to newly formed associations. For simplicity, we do not go into the details of how the financing of such transfers takes place here; in most respects the financial environment of transfer associations is similar to that of others, although they may face additional constraints as a result of guarantees on rent levels given to pre-transfer tenants before they were balloted on whether the transfer should go ahead.

As explained in Chapter 3, the expansion of housing associations after 1974 was based on a system of capital grants, made when a new project is completed, contrasting with the annual recurrent subsidies paid to local authorities described in the first part of this chapter. The housing association system gave a grant—originally known as housing association grant (HAG), but called social housing grant (SHG) since 1996—which was large enough to reduce costs to the level which could be serviced from 'fair rents' set by the local rent officer for an association's tenants. This was calculated by first deducting from the first year's fair rent a management and maintenance allowance (given by a matrix of property sizes and parts of the country, and varying between newly built and rehabilitated property). The amount left over was then available to service a 'residual loan', and the amount of grant was calculated as the difference between actual capital costs and this residual loan. The residual loan came from the Housing Corporation (responsible for giving out the grants and supervising associations) and counted as part of public spending.

This system had four features:

1. For their day-to-day operations, associations operated within a budget given by their management and maintenance allowances. Indeed, certain associations which were carrying high costs as a result of development during less generous systems before 1974, could receive an annual recurrent revenue deficit grant which covered their spending up to the level of the allowances, so there was little point in their spending any less.
2. For their capital spending, associations were effectively subsidized at a rate of 100 per cent at the margin. This did not in itself give any incentive to control capital costs, so the Housing Corporation used a system of 'total indicative costs' (TIC), a matrix of average land and building costs for particular types of development in each area. Costs in excess of the appropriate indicator would be subject to tighter scrutiny before grant would be approved.
3. Associations did not need to provide for future major repairs or depreciation on their stock. Instead, they would apply to the Housing Corporation for a major repairs grant to carry these out when needed.
4. After the first year of a development, inflation worked in an association's favour, as its rents rose, but not its debt servicing costs. To

remove this advantage, the 1980 Housing Act brought in a system of 'Grant Redemption Fund' (GRF) payments designed to remove the resulting surpluses (a version of this survived into the 1990s for stock developed before 1989 as 'Rent Surplus Fund').

In terms of cost control on the capital side, this system had some obvious weaknesses, although it gave associations a secure financial environment and a hard constraint on their current spending. In September 1987 the Department of the Environment proposed reforms which were eventually brought in by the 1988 Housing Act and applied from 1989. This had two aims (DoE 1987):

- To increase the volume of new development from any given amount of public spending. This was done by requiring associations to borrow privately for the capital costs not covered by grant and by cutting grant rates. Eventually grant rates were to fall to about 50 per cent, so that each pound of public spending was supporting twice the volume of capital spending.
- To give new incentives for cost-effectiveness in capital developments. This was done by moving away from grants that varied depending on out-turn costs, towards ones that were fixed in advance. Any cost-overruns would then be the association's responsibility. Initially this meant grant calculated as a percentage (varying by region) of fixed amounts giving expected costs for particular kinds of unit (total cost indicators, TCI). After a period of evolution in the first half of the 1990s, this ended up as a system under which associations would make bids to the housing corporation specifying how much (or rather little) grant they would like to undertake a development, with allocations heavily influenced by who was prepared to ask for least.

To allow all this to happen, with the risk associated with new developments transferred to associations, they were allowed to set their own rents for those who became tenants from 1989 onwards, known as 'assured tenants' (former tenants—now about a third of the total and known as 'secure tenants'—retain their right to a fair rent, set by the local rent officer). At the same time the expectation of grant for later major repairs for new developments was removed, and associations were expected to provide for these themselves.

The combination of major repairs provision and falling grant rates (and later, fierce competition for allocations though associations asking for even lower grant) meant that assured rents were much higher than fair rents, and rose quickly through the 1990s. In many ways the then government seemed quite relaxed about this, favouring a general move of social rents more in the direction of private rents, and appreciating the outcome of a larger number of new units built for each pound of public spending. However, as time went by it became increasingly apparent that much of the cost of these higher rents was in fact coming back to a different part of government through increased housing benefit bills (unlike the system for councils, this remains a separate part of government finance). The incentives to control capital costs which the 1989 system was supposed to introduce were weakened by this, while the previously hard limit on recurrent spending had been removed.

As well as leading to the rising housing benefit bill, higher rents represented a larger proportion of tenants' incomes (for those not receiving benefit) making them less 'affordable'. They also narrowed the difference between incomes in and out of work and extended the range of income over which the high marginal tax and benefit withdrawal rates of the 'poverty trap' applied. Eventually, the Housing Corporation announced that the rent levels of new units—and their impact on housing benefit costs—would be taken into account in making new allocations. Under 'rent-bidding', the competitiveness of bids would be assessed not only through looking at the grant requested, but also at the future value of the housing benefit implied by the proposed rent levels.

This change was a prelude to an even tighter restriction. After 1997–8 associations were told that they would not be eligible for grant at all if their *aggregate* rental income (for both assured and secure tenants) increased by more than RPI inflation plus 1 per cent. This restriction—which associations are by and large keeping to—parallels the rent cap for local authorities introduced by the rent rebate subsidy thresholds. In the same way, it starts from the level rents had actually reached before it came in, so the impact of the limit is tighter on those which had previously increased their rents least.

These changes raise a series of equity and efficiency issues which we explore in Chapter 11, where we examine the perceptions of associations themselves of whether the incentives introduced by the new capital finance system after 1989 did improve efficiency. We also look at the issues around the differences in rent paid by different categories of tenant, and the overall impact of the move of associations from the secure but limited financial environment of the 1970s and 1980s into the 'brave new world' of risk, private finance, and planning for major repairs in the 1990s.

Allocation of Housing Association Grants

The discussion above outlines the way in which capital grants to associations have evolved, and the impact of the changing system on their finances. The amount of money available to support new developments has, however, been limited, and these resources—its approved development programme (ADP)—have been rationed across the country by the Housing Corporation and its regional offices. This happens through a three-stage process:

(1) The Housing Corporation divides its available resources for the coming year between the regions of the country.
(2) Each regional office divides its own allocation into amounts available for new developments in each local authority area. The local authority draws up a list of priority developments.
(3) Associations bid against each other to the corporation's regional office for grant to carry out particular schemes.

To share out the available total allocation between English regions, the corporation has since 1985 used a measure of regional housing need, the Housing Needs Index (HNI). This is a development of the Generalized Needs Index used in allocating capital resources (in their case, credit approvals) between local authorities. The HNI takes account of information from the census, the five-yearly English House Condition Survey, and from local authorities. After reviews in 1989 and 1994 the current index is based on the following (DoE 1994; Niner 1998):

- The new provision indicator (75 per cent of the total), reflecting overcrowded households, numbers of households sharing, and privately owned unfit dwellings, as well as requirements for very sheltered provision for elderly and disabled people. It is reduced where there is evidence (like vacancies or under-occupation) of excess supply of social housing.
- A private stock condition index (25 per cent of the total), based on the cost to make all private-sector dwellings fit and carry out repairs needed over ten years (excluding owner-occupiers deemed able to afford such repairs).

A 'Stress Area Enhancement' increases allocations to local authority areas with a high score for deprivation on the DETR's Index of Local Conditions, and the cash available is adjusted for local cost variations.

Once regional allocations of the ADP have been made according to the HNI, regional offices make allocations at a subregional level. These are also based on the relative HNI scores of different local authority areas, but with regional office discretion to vary—by 20 per cent up or down—the amount going to each area, depending on its assessment of the quality of the authority's performance in its 'enabling role' (that is, in drawing up and delivering its priorities for housing in its area, and its support for corporation priorities, rather than its performance as a landlord). In order to give some consistency in planning, and to allow for the lumpiness of particular projects, the allocations are structured in three-year rolling programmes, rather than precisely hitting the desired relative allocations each year. It is these authority-by-authority allocations within which associations bid for new developments in the way described above. This system is currently under review, and the HNI may become less important at the subregional level in future (Housing Corporation 1999).

Summary

As a result of the developments described above, the two parts of social housing are financed in very different ways. This raises equity issues between individuals, as it means that the rents paid by different kinds of tenant can vary considerably, even if they are in identical buildings and have identical circumstances. There is also no clear relationship between the rents paid and the value of the property occupied or the amounts spent on managing and maintaining it. Figure 6.1 shows the scale of rent variations within the social housing sector, as well as the way rents rose in relation to earnings in the early 1980s and early 1990s, following the subsidy changes described above.

For local authority tenants, the key benchmark is the rent guideline in the recurrent subsidy system, and any difference between actual management and maintenance spending and the allowance for this spending set by the DETR. However, the rent guidelines themselves may still depend heavily on past actual rent levels, and the key threshold set for the rent rebate limitation rules depends largely on actual rents as they were in 1995–6. Despite the move towards the use of needs-based formulae for management and maintenance allowances, subsidy could still vary between two authorities, even if their stocks and debts were identical, as a result of this dependence on past rent and spending levels.

For housing association tenants, there is a difference in treatment of secure (pre-1989) tenants, with 'fair' rents set by local rent officers, and assured tenants, whose rents are set by the association. The level of assured tenancy rents has generally been much higher than either local

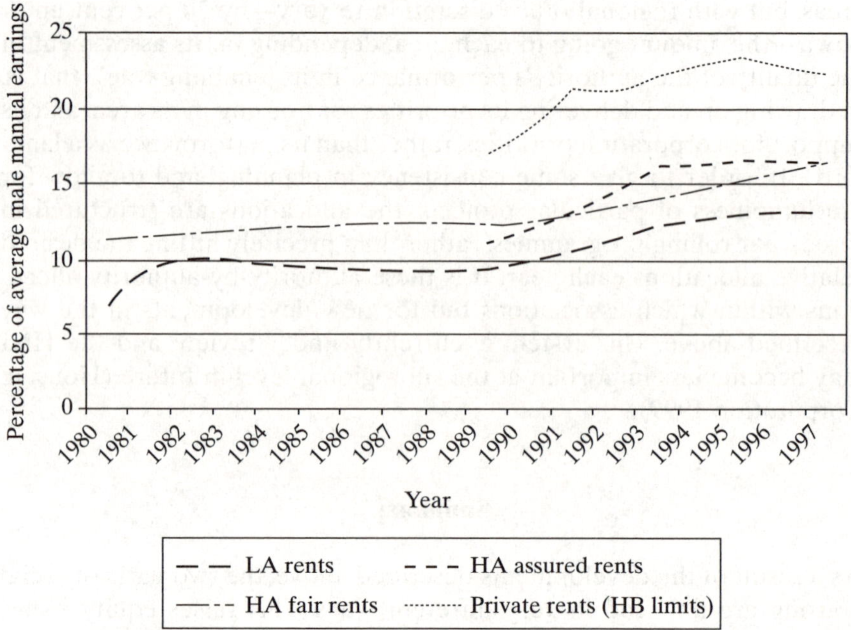

FIGURE 6.1. Rents in England as Percentage of Average Male Manual Earnings (*source*: Wilcox 1998: table 68)

authority or fair rents, but with variations between associations depending not just on relative efficiency, but also on how aggressively they pursued competition for grant for new developments in the mid-1990s. Some of these differences are now frozen into place by the 'RPI plus one' limit on increases in aggregate rent bills.

The incentives built into the funding systems have also changed for both subsectors over time. 'Ring-fencing' of local authority housing revenue accounts in 1990 and changes in the subsidy formula to become less related to past spending patterns have both meant a much more direct trade-off between spending and rent levels. For their recurrent spending, the pressures on local authorities now look more like those on housing associations in the 1970s and 1980s, when they had to operate within pre-set allowances. The subsidy system irons out most of the impact of variations in debt and capital spending between councils, while their capital spending is constrained by the rationing of the credit approval system. Housing associations, meanwhile, became *less* constrained after they gained the ability to set their own rents after 1989, as part of reforms which were designed to remove the potential for inefficiency in capital spending from the previous system which gave 100 per cent subsidy on spending variations at the margin.

Overarching these changes has been the operation of the housing benefit system. This removes any immediate effect of rent increases on tenants receiving it, and so reduces some of the potential downward pressure from them on rents and spending levels. In response, much tighter controls were brought in on both local authorities and housing associations in the late 1990s.

Both subsectors are subject to rationing in their capital funds. For local authorities their ability to make any capital spending (mostly on major repair and renovation work) is controlled by the credit approval systems. For housing associations, available capital grants (mainly for new developments) are rationed by the Housing Corporation. Both systems are based on an index of the relative housing needs of local authority areas, augmented by varying degrees of discretion in the hands of the regional offices of the DETR and Housing Coroporation. We examine social landlords' understanding and views of the impact of these systems in Chapters 10 and 11.

7

Three Services, Eight Formulae: Common Themes and Differences

Main Features of the Funding Systems

For those who have followed the story so far, not to mention those who have preferred to avoid the detail in the preceding three chapters, this is a useful moment to recap and summarize the funding systems for our three services as they had evolved by the late 1990s. In effect this means looking at eight different ways in which financial resources are allocated from Whitehall to service-providers at one level or another:

(1) District health authorities (and some primary care groups from April 1999) for hospitals, community health services, and pharmaceutical costs.
(2) General practitioners for GPs' income and practice costs.
(3) Local education authorities, largely for local schools.
(4) Individual schools, mostly as suballocations from LEAs, but with some direct allocations to grant-maintained schools.
(5) Subsidies to local authority housing revenue accounts for recurrent spending on council housing.
(6) Credit approvals for local authority capital spending.
(7) The level of capital grants for new housing association developments.
(8) The capital allocations available for such grants within each local authority area.

1. District health authorities

Following a review in the early 1990s, the system for distributing funding for Hospital and Community Health Services between district health authorities (DHAs) has been based on the 'York formula', derived from analysis of actual service use at small-area level (adjusted to remove the effects of better local supply leading to higher use). At the core of this is the Weighted Capitation Target. This depends on population and age structure adjusted for:

- Factors linked to greater needs, varying between allocations for acute hospital care, non-acute care, mental health services, and community services. For instance, for acute care the factors are standardized mortality ratios for those under 75; the proportion of those of pension age living alone; dependants living with only one carer; self-reported long-standing illness; and unemployment rates (as a deprivation measure).
- Additional costs on a geographical basis, reflected in a 'market forces factor', mainly relating to higher staff costs, and higher costs of delivering services in rural areas.

This formula is now to be applied to allocate funds to the new primary care groups covering populations of about 100,000 (although DHAs will have some discretion over this).

The amount a health authority actually receives each year is adjusted to prevent too rapid a change as it moves towards this target, with its actual allocation depending on its current baseline (previous spending), its 'distance from target', and the overall 'pace of change' (rate of convergence) decided by ministers. Convergence has been achieved by additional allocations to those below target, combined with a standstill in allocations to those above target in real terms.

2. Allocations to GPs

GPs receive payments based mainly on age-related capitation payments for each patient on their lists plus an amount for the costs of running their practice (more of a fixed-cost element). These payments are negotiated nationally and apply to all GPs across the country. Some practices receive extra amounts related to the number of patients living in postcode areas associated with deprivation (the 'Jarman index'). There are also small incentive payments for GPs to establish practices in 'under-doctored' areas (as well as a system of 'negative direction' which attempts to equalize GP list sizes by steering GPs away from over-served areas).

3. Local education authorities

Through the general system of local government finance, local authorities receive funding from central government (a fixed amount) and from council tax payers (which local authorities can vary in theory, although their ability to raise council tax rates is constrained). Since 1990 central government funding to LEAs has been a fixed amount, depending on each one's Standard Spending Assessment (replacing the previous calculation of Grant Related Expenditure) and its local tax capacity. SSAs are divided into seven blocks, one of which is education. Councils are free to vary the allocation of their total budgets between different services, so actual spending on education is not constrained to equal the education SSA (on average in 1996–7 actual spending was nearly 4 per cent above the education SSA). The education SSA in turn depends on five sub-blocks, relating to different tiers of the education system. The 'control total' for each of these is the product of:

- The size of the client group (for example, number of primary-aged children).
- A unit cost figure—a national standard amount for each group, adjusted for 'additional educational needs' (AEN), extra funding for rural areas (sparsity), and for the cost of free school meals. The AEN adjustment is based on three factors which are deemed to be outside local authority control (unlike elements in previous formulae before 1981): numbers of lone parents; income support receipt; and ethnicity (numbers with New Commonwealth origins). The first two of these elements have the greatest weight.
- An area costs adjustment, reflecting higher labour costs and business rates, mainly benefiting London and the South-East.

4. *Schools*

Under the 1988 Education Reform Act, a minimum proportion of the schools budget has to be passed from LEAs to the schools themselves (the current government wants at least 90 per cent to be delegated). LEAs can, subject to guidelines, choose their own subformulae to share money between their schools. Grant-maintained schools are funded separately, but the amounts of revenue funding they receive depend on the allocation system within that LEA. These subformulae have to be mostly dependent on fixed amounts per pupil of a given age, but up to 20 per cent of the budgets can be adjusted to reflect additional amounts for small schools or factors like deprivation (usually based on proportions receiving free school meals).

5. *Subsidies to local authority housing revenue accounts*

Housing differs from the other sectors in two important respects. First, social landlords charge for their services through rents, so that their funding is only partly based on central government grants. They are not therefore operating within fixed budgets in the same way as schools or health authorities. Second, capital spending plays a much greater part in the process. Funding systems for both capital and revenue are therefore important. On top of this there are two types of social landlord—local authorities and non-profit housing associations—whose funding systems are completely different.

Revenue funding for local authorities was reformed in 1990 to create a system under which central government pays an annual subsidy which would allow the council to charge rents averaging the 'rent guideline' set for it, if its management and maintenance spending equalled an allowance also set for it. The amount paid adjusts for the council's debt charges and the rent rebates it gives its tenants under the housing benefit system. If councils want to spend more, they have to charge higher rents. The critical elements in the formula are thus the rent guideline, now based in principle half on relative capital values and half on an element reflecting local earnings, and the management and maintenance allowances, based on formulae relating to stock composition. As with health authorities, the actual amount a council receives depends on various 'damping formulae' which slow convergence towards the underlying level of subsidy.

If an authority does charge higher rents, the cost of this will be met for most tenants through higher housing benefit, and the cost of this is added to the central government subsidy. However, since 1996–7, if a council increases its rents more rapidly than the rent guideline increases, central government does not reimburse the cost of increased rent rebates, so the net yield of higher rents is greatly reduced. This important constraint is generally based on actual rents in 1995–6, rather than on the rent guidelines underlying other parts of subsidy.

6. *Capital funding for council housing*

On the capital side, councils are not free to borrow, for instance to carry out major repairs or build new units, but can only do so if central government grants 'credit approvals' (these days almost entirely for major repairs). The allocation of these between authorities is made through the housing investment programme system. Allocations depend half on DETR regional office assessment of an authority's performance, and half on the Generalized Needs Index. The GNI attempts to measure local housing needs, weighted between elements reflecting local authority stock condition (60 per cent), need for new provision (30 per cent), and private-sector stock condition (10 per cent). The latter two elements are the same as those used in the equivalent index for housing association allocations, the HNI (see below), while local authority stock conditions reflect results from the English House Conditions Survey. The GNI is adjusted for local measures of deprivation (the Stress Area Enhancement), cost compensation (reflecting regional cost differences), and a damping element to prevent large changes in allocations from year to year.

Once an authority has been allowed to borrow, the resulting loan charges are generally reflected pound for pound within the revenue funding system, so that the system effectively equalizes between authorities carrying different levels of debt, regardless of whether these have been incurred recently or a long time ago.

7. *Housing association capital grants*

Housing associations (now technically 'registered social landlords') operate in a completely different way. Rather than annual revenue subsidies, they receive capital grants when they first build or renovate a dwelling. After that they have to raise enough money from rents to pay for management and maintenance, debt charges on the remaining money they have borrowed, and—unlike councils—to provide for periodic major repairs. The way grant is calculated has changed significantly. Up to the late 1980s, additional capital costs were (subject to Housing Corporation scrutiny) met at a rate of 100 per cent at the margin. Then, in the early part of the 1990s, capital grant rates were fixed, removing this feature. Later in the decade associations were encouraged to compete for new funding on the basis of the level of grant they required. The higher the rents they were prepared to charge, the lower the grant they needed. Much of the cost of this was passed on to central government through higher housing benefit. More recently, the cost to central government of projected rent levels via housing benefit has been taken into account in awarding new funding, and most recently associations increasing their rents faster than 'RPI plus one' have been ineligible for new funding.

8. *Housing association capital allocations*

Associations compete for capital funds available from the Housing Corporation (mainly for new building), which allocates amounts between local authority areas on the basis of the Housing Needs Index (HNI), 75 per cent of which is made up of an indicator of the need for new provision (which reflects demand factors like overcrowding, sharing households, and homelessness, but is reduced if there is evidence of excess local supply), and the rest reflecting local private-sector stock condition.

Adjustments are made for areas of deprivation and for geographical cost variations. The relative allocations between local authority areas also take into account the council's own plans and previous performance in its 'enabling' role, with the amount going to each are a varying up or down by 20 per cent from the HNI figure depending on the corporation's regional office assessment.

Common and Contrasting Themes

Changing systems in the 1990s

All of the funding systems we looked at changed in the 1990s as central government tried to bend them more to achieve its objectives (and to a lesser extent as those objectives themselves changed). Funding within the NHS became less based on historic patterns, and more on needs-based formulae, extending by the very end of the period to the move towards needs-based funding for primary care groups covering populations of 100,000. Education funding was also increasingly devolved, in this case to schools, but other changes reflected developments in the overall tussle over local government finance. Both local authority housing subsidies and housing association funding were changed significantly in the late 1980s/early 1990s and new constraints were introduced in the late 1990s to try to rein in some of the knock-on effects of the earlier changes.

Some of these changes—notably within the NHS—represent greater refinement of systems which were seen, at the centre at least, to be working well. Others look more like attempts to correct systems which were not working entirely as planned or had unintended side effects. In either case, lack of stability may have weakened understanding at lower levels of how the systems work, and may mean that there was not much time for them to have particular incentive effects, whether planned or unplanned.

The continuing stress on needs-related equity

Health and education funding systems are fundamentally about allocating resources between service providers in different areas. Notions of geographical equity are fundamental to them, and something of the same can be seen in the allocation of new capital resources to social housing. In the NHS the stress on geographical equity grew over the 1980s and 1990s, and this is now being measured at an increasingly low level. Within education the debate centres on relative allocations between local authorities, and justifications of the system at least became increasingly dominated by notions of geographical equity, even through the Thatcher years.

'Geographical equity' in the case of social housing might be taken as referring to the balance between the rents tenants pay, and the value of the services they receive. In one sense, funding systems, particularly for local authority housing, have moved more in this direction, with rent guidelines being related to local capital values and the subsidy system washing out the effects of variations between councils in historic debts. On the other hand, the lack of correspondence between the results for tenants of the respective systems for councils and for associations leads to patterns of rent variation which are hard to relate to any consistent notion of equity. More concretely, capital allocations seem to have been made on the basis both of formulae varying according to the 'needs' of different local authority areas (the GNI and HNI) and of principles which result in at least 'something for everyone', but with substantial discretion to DETR and Housing Corporation regional offices over allocations within their region.

One of the striking features of the account of the historical development of funding systems in Chapter 3, and of the more recent developments described in Chapters 4 to 6, is that needs-relation grew in most of the systems we describe under *both* Labour and Conservative governments. In the former case, developments like the 'RAWP' reallocation of health resources after the mid-1970s reflected explicit equity concerns. But during the Conservative period in the 1980s and 1990s many developments carried on in the same direction—for instance, the centrality of Standard Spending Assessments to education funding, or the way in which local authority housing subsidies have, since 1990, fully equalized for historic debt levels. The explanation of this is that this was also a period of strong constraints—in some cases cuts—in public spending in a period when demands for services were growing (Glennerster and Hills 1998). Minimizing the political cost of this restraint meant concentrating cuts on areas where the effects would be relatively least painful, in other words, where resources where greatest relative to 'needs'. The end result of what we describe as 'stage 3' of formula development in Chapter 3 was more stress on needs-relation.

Writing at the end of the 1990s, it appears as if we may be about to enter a fourth stage of funding formula development, with moves away from a stress on *inputs*—like pupil–teacher ratios or hospital beds per head of population—to much more stress on *outcomes*. For instance, within health care, equalizing *chances* of access is not the same as equal access, while equal access is not the same as equal treatment, which itself is only a small part of what determines good health. This has recently entered the NHS agenda. Equal treatment has, if at all, been seen as the responsibility of the management arm of the NHS. The Conservative administration relied more on competition to achieve this, while the new Labour administration relies more on central regulation and inspection. In 1999 ministers charged the Advisory Committee on Resource Allocation to consider how the funding formula could be used to achieve greater *health* equality (not just equality of access).

Damping

As the funding systems changed for all three services in the 1990s they incorporated elements which gave continuity in the amounts individual providers received from year to year. In funding for regional health authorities (and then districts) this was achieved through the system of measuring first 'distance from target' (the difference between current spending and the amount given by the formula) and then setting a 'pace of change', which gave the proportion of the gap to be closed that year, subject to the constraint that no one's allocation actually fell. For local authority housing, maximum and minimum flat-rate limits were set to the amount by which the rent guidelines on which subsidy depended could change each year, and there were similar constraints on management and maintenance allowances. For local education authority funding, there is explicit 'damping' in year-on-year changes in the total of SSAs, and, as we have seen in Chapter 6, the end result of the annual negotiation process over the SSA formula has in fact been remarkable stability in the overall shares of the total grant and SSA allocated to individual councils.

Looking at these systems both in terms of clarity and success in achieving convergence on the underlying target, the NHS system seems to have a much more to commend it than the local authority housing system. While the NHS system has prevented sudden year-to-year changes in funding, it has left the underlying target clear and explicit, and achieved faster moves where current spending was furthest from target.

By contrast, the damping of rent guideline changes for council housing meant that the underlying logic of the system has been left obscure. By choosing different maximum and minimum guideline increases from year to year, the DETR has had considerable control over the allocations to individual authorities. Indeed, in an earlier interview with one of the authors, a DoE official said that the damping system had the advantage that they could 'make music' with the allocations. This may have had short-term advantages, but did nothing to aid understanding of the basic system. Indeed, one of the reasons for heavy reliance on damping appears to have been that the centre did not actually *want* the degree of rent variation which the underlying targets, based solely on relative capital values, would have created up until 1996, when the system was changed. For clarity it would seem much better to set a robust underlying formula than to correct the results of an unsatisfactory one through mechanisms which are designed to do something else.

To make matters worse, when controls were brought in to slow the effects on housing benefit costs of both local authority and housing association rents rising in the late 1990s, these were done through setting limits to increases from *actual* rent levels, rather than by using the principles underlying the subsidy systems. Not only is this an example of systems which give a positive feedback to past spending (see below), but setting the limits like this added a further layer of obscurity to the aims of funding. We discuss the impact of this on providers in Chapters 10 and 11 below.

Changes in SSAs have been damped so as to limit their impact on council taxes and spending. There has been little discussion (or criticism) of such damping by LEAs, even those forgoing gains.

Regional price differences and deprivation

While the systems are heavily based on geographical equity, they also incorporate adjustments which recognize cost variations between areas. For the NHS, this lies in the market forces factor, increasing allocations to London and rural areas. The area cost adjustment in the education SSA does much the same (although sparsity is dealt with in a separate part of the formula). For local authority housing revenue subsidies, both rent guidelines and allowances for management and maintenance spending incorporate variations between regions, the former through the link to capital values and regional earnings, the latter through an explicit adjustment for regional costs.

The health and education formulae also allow extra amounts where providers are dealing with a more deprived population. For health authorities this takes the form of higher amounts depending on local unemployment rates, and for some GPs there are extra payments where they have numerous patients from deprived areas—a high Jarman index. For LEAs the elements of the area cost adjustment in the formula reflect deprivation directly—the number of lone parents, New Commonwealth immigrants, and local income support receipt. While the housing benefit system is the main way in which social housing subsidies adjust for particularly high levels of deprivation, the local authority management and maintenance allowances allow for up to 20 per cent extra maintenance spending in areas of 'poor social conditions'.

The kinds of cost faced by providers do differ between services, so it is not necessarily illogical for regional price differences or the impact of deprivation to be recognized in different ways by the funding systems, but there is a good case for those involved with this at the centre to discuss the relative merits of the approaches taken in case lessons can be learnt between them. For instance, the DETR makes a substantial investment in establishing and updating an 'Index of Local Deprivation' across local authority districts and wards within them. Information from this could assist other departments.

Positive, Perverse, and Passive Incentives

The systems we have described incorporate different kinds of incentive which might affect provider behaviour. Some of these are intended, 'positive' incentives, while others are unintended, and potentially 'perverse'. However, equally important are the 'passive' incentives affecting providers which face a hard budget constraint. If an organization cannot increase its budget (for instance, through a social landlord increasing its rents), and its managers have an aim of maximizing its activity in some respect, then the organization itself will look for ways of using its resources most efficiently to achieve its aim. By contrast, providers with a 'soft budget constraint' may be under much less pressure to improve efficiency, and there is a greater danger of perverse incentives.

Health services

For a long time funding within the health service reflected activity, with incremental changes in budgets for health authorities from year to year, and where those budgets were biting, accusations that the medical profession was prepared to 'shroud-wave' to increase them. The RAWP system has since the mid-1970s changed all this, and health authority budgets are far less dependent on past spending, although their ability to run increasing deficits means that this budget constraint is not entirely hard either. The centre's intention is now that efficiency pressures should operate through these passive incentives, together with inspection, supervision, and performance 'league tables', although there are special additional allocations for favoured activity, such as initiatives to reduce waiting lists since 1997.

One of the strengths of the UK system has always been seen as its use of largely salaried hospital doctors and GPs paid on the basis of capitation amounts, removing incentives from part of the medical profession at least to overtreat. The same was not true of referrals by GPs for hospital treatment or drug prescription, which were limited more by rationing through queues for hospitals or by exhortation for prescribing. The GP fundholding system was brought in to give GPs flexibility within a harder budget constraint (Glennerster *et al.* 1994), and a modification of this principle has been carried over to primary care groups. Again, apart from some incentive payments to locate in under-doctored areas or for particular initiatives (such as preventative clinics and screening of risk groups), the attempt is to move towards much more use of the passive incentives embodied in devolved but fixed budgets. This does not mean the system is entirely free of perverse incentives. With payments to GPs depending on their list size, there is no incentive for them to check that their lists correspond to those still resident. Regular 'trawls' are made to counter the potential problems this might mean, and a national list of patient records has now been set up to deal with double-counting. Also, any system which allocates flat-rate payments for each member of a list leaves an incentive for providers to 'cream-skim', by discouraging those who might be at the expensive end of any particular class of patients for funding purposes from registering. There was some danger of this with GP fundholding. The new much large primary care groups largely eliminate the danger at that level.

Education

Looking back at their historical development, the local authority finance systems involving 'matching' of actual spending up to 1958 were designed to encourage greater provision, by lowering the cost to local government. At the time this would have been seen as a positive incentive to councils to do more. However, by the mid-1980s, any incentives to higher spending built into the Block Grant system were seen as 'perverse' by a government which wanted to reduce local spending. The government first cash-limited the overall sum available to councils as a whole (which meant a complicated system under which one council's grant was readjusted depending on the actual spending of others). It also introduced penalties into the system, penalizing high spenders. Finally, as explained in Chapter 5, an enduring part of the 1988 Local Government Finance Act was to fix grant in advance from 1990 onwards, regardless of actual spending, removing any remaining elements of 'matching'.

Other features of the 1980s Grant Related Expenditure system were also seen as embodying perverse incentives, in that some of the elements of 'need' could—in theory—be affected by authorities themselves, or could feed back higher assessed need to high spenders through the regression formula based on actual past spending. The need elements now within the education SSA are intended to be outside LEA influence, and the role of regression analysis has been limited. This does not, however, put education spending under an entirely hard budget constraint—authorities can switch funding between other services and education, and can raise some additional funding by raising their Council Tax (although this was subject to capping until 1999, and is still restrained by limits on compensation for council tax benefit).

For schools, the budget constraint is much harder, especially with devolved budgets, apart from their important ability to attract more pupils. Back in the nineteenth century, there were positive incentives related to examination results. Today this kind of incentive operates indirectly, through school popularity—and hence pupil numbers and funding, as the clearest positive incentive is to maximize the school roll—which is strongly influenced by parental reaction to GCSE 'league tables'.

Housing

The incentive structures facing social landlords have lurched in different directions in the last two decades. For revenue spending on council housing, the budget constraint has been set by the combination of subsidy from central government, the amounts which can be raised by rents, and, until the 1990s, by flows from general local authority funds (rate fund contributions). While there was no 'matching' of revenue spending, this budget was soft in three ways: rents could be raised if councillors agreed; RFCs could be increased; and a succession of subsidy reforms from the 1970s onwards tended to use past spending as the base for new subsidies, in effect giving matching with a delay. The 'ring-fencing' reforms of 1990 hardened these constraints in two ways, cutting off RFCs and moving towards grant set more by formula than past spending (albeit limited in the pace of this by damping). However, with most tenants receiving housing benefit, the political cost of higher rents was restricted to the minority with higher incomes. The DoE eventually decided that this left too soft a budget constraint—in effect it was paying for more than 60 per cent of additional spending at the margin—and brought in the rent rebate subsidy limits described in Chapter 6 to harden the budget constraint again in 1996.

For capital spending, the 'classic British housing subsidy' gave fixed amounts to reduce loan charges up to the 1960s, but subsequent systems have—in an attempt to iron out the effects of historic borrowing patterns—been much more based on actual spending. The current subsidies to HRAs effectively pay for all of the cost of additional borrowing at the margin, but this borrowing is very tightly controlled through the credit approval system. The DETR relies on the passive incentives of these fixed allocations, the discretion of its regional offices to reduce credit approvals to poorly performing authorities, and political and tenant pressure on housing departments to make the best use of what they are allocated, now almost entirely for major repairs. However, authorities which concentrate spending on limited parts of their stock are still free to come back in later years to argue continuing need to spend on the rest. Under 'resource accounting' in the future they may face a sharper trade-off between different needs within a budget more under their own control, but with less ability to return to the DETR beadle for more (see Chapter 13).

Meanwhile, the funding system for housing associations somersaulted at the end of the 1980s. The previous system which matched extra capital spending pound for pound was reformed to give stronger incentives for capital cost control through what became fixed capital grants. However, at the same time the strong passive incentives on their revenue spending through controlled 'fair' rents were removed, leaving associations to set—and generally increase—their own rents. With housing benefit again taking the strain, the system embodied only relatively weak constraints on spending. Indeed this weakening also affected the capital side, as higher capital costs could also now be met by higher rents, undermining the incentives supposed to be built into the new system, until allocations of new grant also came to depend in the mid-1990s on promised rent levels ('rent bidding'). Eventually, a strong constraint was brought in through making associations which increased their rents by more than 'RPI plus one' ineligible for new funding, effectively restoring a hard budget constraint (at the level which spending had reached when the music stopped). We discuss perceptions of the effects of these changes in Chapter 11.

Summary

The discussion and design of housing subsidies is much more dominated by concerns about incentives than is the case for health and education. One reason for this is the way in which, without the freedom to raise revenue through charges, health and education providers generally operate within fixed budgets, unless government grants adjust to reflect higher spending. Under 'matching' systems in the past this was the case as positive incentives were used to encourage greater provision. Over time, our account in previous chapters of the way subsidies have developed shows a general move away from the positive incentives established during periods of expansion towards much greater reliance on passive ones achieved through fixed budgets, punctuated by periodic attempts to block breaches in the dyke when providers ran away with a perverse incentive. The growing use of needs-based funding is not just a matter of increasing concern with equity or avoiding cuts to the most politically sensitive, it also reflects a much stronger desire to control spending and hence to remove positive incentives to increase activity.

Constraints on the Design of Formulae

Some of the patterns we have described are the result of historical accident, the varying choices of central officials, or the outcomes of negotiations in which the strengths of actors at different levels varied. However, others reflect different constraints, either technical or inherent to the administrative structure of a service.

The clearest initial constraint is the technical ability to assess needs without relying on individual past spending. Here a crucial factor is the number of separate observations which can be made on which to assess the relative needs of individual beneficiaries of a service. The strength of the 'York formula' for funding district health authorities is that each year millions of independent decisions are taken about the treatment of people with different characteristics. While one health authority may have been better funded for historical reasons, or one doctor may be a heavy prescriber of drugs, this should not stop analysis from identifying the relative needs of the relevant populations: there are too many observations for individual behaviour to feed back into later 'needs' for funding. This allows the needs-based formula to be used with far more confidence.

By contrast, basing needs assessments on the past spending patterns of just a few hundred local authorities is much more difficult. First, the number of potential explanatory variables is itself large—approaching the number of authorities—so that, technically, there are not enough 'degrees of freedom' to identify the relationships involved. Second, particular characteristics may be correlated with political preferences. In the 1980s the Conservative government was concerned that high regression coefficients for factors related to inner cities were in fact reflecting the greater desire to spend by Labour-controlled authorities. Third, some of the factors which might explain need may be under potential local authority control. Avoiding this—as the current SSA formula does—severely restricts the range of needs factors which can be used, lowering its potential accuracy. There are, of course, many thousands of schools with pupils of varying characteristics, but the amount which has been spent on them historically does not necessarily reflect varying needs in the way that use of the NHS does for individual patients.

The same problem of 'feedback' from past spending to regression-based needs assessment caused problems for housing subsidy formulae in the 1970s. However, by the 1990s much more use was being made of observations by organizations like the Building Research Establishment of the relative costs to different organizations of maintaining different kinds of property—for instance, flats rather than houses—using data on individual dwellings, rather than basing it on regression analysis of just a few hundred landlords' aggregate spending. This has allowed management and maintenance allowances to be set without reference to past spending, although the formulae used only explain a small part of the variation in management spending. Of course, this may be because only a small part of the variation does reflect needs.

A second constraint is related to this, but is not inherent in the structure of the services. This reflects the technical resources put into establishing these kinds of relationship. We have noted above the greater academic involvement in both assessing and refining the health formula than the others, and this may have helped increase its acceptability. Certainly more people have been involved in this kind of assessment for health care than in the other services. Also, efforts have been made to improve data—for instance, by adding special questions to the census. By contrast, where 'research evidence' was used in, for instance, negotiations over the size of SSAs, it tended to be used as political ammunition where it would benefit a group of authorities, rather than as an external reference point.

The sophistication of techniques also seems much greater in the health case. Notably, the most recent developments have involved techniques for adjusting for past variations in local supply, for instance in available hospital beds, which might perhaps have been considered by those setting education and housing formulae, rather than just eliminating the use of information which might be tainted by 'supply-led demand' in this way. The health service—perhaps because of its centralized bureaucratic past—has also generated much more readily available data on individual treatment. In principle, similar data could be collected on the repair needs of different kinds of housing, or the management demands of different kinds of tenants, but there has up to now been little equivalent collection of data by social landlords (a factor which is already changing a little and may change more in future as funding changes give them a stronger interest in planned maintenance of their stock).

Third, the involvement of different political and administrative structures seems to have had important effects on the way formulae have evolved. While the London health authorities did raise objections to the consequences for them of introducing RAWP, those running them were part of an integrated national system. By contrast, local authorities—whether dealing with funding for their schools or allocations of capital funding for new social housing—are primarily charged with protecting the interests of their locality, not with making a judgement 'in the national interest'. This makes it much more likely that negotiations will revolve around battles to protect or maximize resources for individual authorities.

Finally, central political priorities have varied between services and over time, meaning that the fundamental objectives of the systems have differed. In the health service notions of equity have been fundamental since 1948, and were if anything reinforced rather than weakened during the Conservative years of the 1980s and 1990s. By contrast, education spending was caught up in the central–local government battles of the 1980s. Formula funding may have been strengthened as a by-product, but the key central aim was the restraint of local government 'overspenders', and education funding reflected this priority.

As far as housing is concerned, the primary political objective of recent years appears to have been to minimize the total of public spending. Current rent relativities between council housing and housing associations may look anarchic, but they have actually evolved to levels where central government could face higher net spending from the total of subsidies and housing benefit (and through knock-on effects on other index-linked spending if the RPI is affected) if rents were either lower or higher. The precise level they reached in the late 1990s reflected an arcane calculation of the balance between the number of tenants who would be moved on or off housing benefit if rents changed, and the different effects on the RPI of council and association rents. A greater concern with equity or with other factors like work incentives would have produced different rent structures, but would not have minimized public spending.

Summary

This chapter has summarized the main features of the funding systems described for each of the three services in the previous chapters. It draws out common themes like the increasing stress put on geographical equity within many of the systems, including under Conservative governments in the 1980s and 1990s. It also looks at differences, such as the systems used to slow—or 'damp'—changes from year-to-year (where the system for NHS funding has been most successful in achieving convergence while leaving the underlying principles clear).

Important comparisons relate to the extent to which the systems embody positive incentives intended to encourage particular behaviour, passive incentives through the effects of a fixed budget constraint, or perverse incentives which may encourage undesired behaviour.

Since the 1970s there have been moves in all three services away from positive incentives towards much more use of the passive incentives given by fixed budgets, particularly those devolved to provider units. This is another reason for the move towards more needs-based funding. Debate over housing subsidies has been much more dominated by worries about perverse incentives, and recent reforms have attempted—with mixed success—to correct for them.

The chapter also relates the structures of the formulae to technical constraints, such as the number of observations of spending behaviour available from which relative needs can be inferred. Here again, the health systems have been more successful in generating data and more sophisticated in using them. Another important difference comes from the involvement of local government in education and housing, strengthening political pressures for allocations to each area, rather than acceptance of 'national' equity objectives as in health.

What the chapter describes, however, is mostly the way in which different kinds of system appear to have been designed and the effects one might expect in principle. The next four chapters explore how these systems look from the perspectives of those running them, and particularly from those of the people involved in running the services which they fund.

PART III

The View from the Ground

8

Shared Values: Views from within the NHS

A Department Changes its Spots

We have seen in earlier chapters that equality of access to health care was an explicit founding principle of those who created the NHS in 1946. The abolition of fee-paying, an unequal financial barrier, was the major step, of course. Yet, the unequal geographical distribution of health-care resources was a natural consequence of the private market for health care that had existed pre-war. It came a close second in political concern.

In the very first memorandum Aneurin Bevan presented to the new Labour Cabinet after the Second World War, he stated: 'We have got to achieve as nearly as possible a uniform standard of service for all' (PRO/CAB 129/3 5, Oct 1945: quoted by Buxton and Klein 1978). We also saw that some initial steps were taken to achieve the stated goal in the 1940s' health service. Limits were put on GPs setting up practices in 'over-doctored areas', rather as there were limits put on local education authorities employing teachers in favoured areas like London. Senior hospital doctors were employed by regional hospital boards and a national Advisory Committee on Consultant Establishments was set up to approve applications to create new posts. However, it had no powers to consider which regions were in most need or to stimulate applications from them (Sir George Godber, the senior civil servant, quoted by Klein 1995). Consultant posts did come to be more evenly spread through the country than had been the case under the old free-market system but there was no active manpower planning attempted of the kind once envisaged in 1948. The ministry lost its driving role in the 1950s as the very existence of the NHS was called in question by the new Conservative government. It became largely responsive to demands from the profession, as Klein (1995) puts it. Then, in response to criticisms by the Guillebaud Committee (Ministry of Health 1956), and the BMA, the Ministry of Health developed a national hospital building plan to replace the legacy of old hospitals dating, in large measure, back to the Victorian era. It did so to an agreed national strategy based on population bed norms and the idea there should be a large, most-purpose, district hospital in every area. This was, in its way, a crude needs-based approach. In fact, London did rather well in the building boom as it had many prestigious, but old, teaching hospitals and lots of political leverage. Nationally, hospitals were able to argue that new buildings would cost more money to staff and maintain because they would be able to do more advanced medicine, so areas with new hospitals gained more funding—revenue consequence money, it was called. This, if anything, worsened old inequalities. Nothing was done to address the unequal distribution of revenue budgets that had been a feature of the pre-NHS world. One commentator (Griffiths 1966) described the ministry during this period as a 'laissez-faire' department.

Why this was so can only be speculated about, but one undoubted factor was the difficulty of putting together any obvious yardstick of unfairness. If class sizes were forty in Manchester and thirty in London there was an obvious political point to be made and local politicians to make it. Nothing of the same intuitive force seemed to be available in health and local politicians seemed not to think it part of their job to make the case beyond demanding a local hospital.

How then did the successors to the Ministry of Health become the equity leaders among Whitehall departments? Social science and a new political direction seem to be the answer. It was a very different story from that told by respondents in the other departments.

The Equity Vision at the Centre

We interviewed five senior civil servants about their views on the formula funding process and on its origins. When asked about the equity aims of the formula funding system there was some surprise that anyone should ask. It was obvious: 'equal access for equal need' (NHSE1). It had been set out in the RAWP report which everyone quoted like a biblical text.

One respondent had been at the Department of Health and its predecessor since the beginning of the 1970s and had been closely involved in resource allocation throughout the period since. He was asked how it came about that the department took on this much more pro-active stance? His response is worth quoting at some length. It sheds light on the account given in previous chapters.

This is a wonderful story of the interaction between social scientists and politicians. The story begins in the early 1970s. One of the first books I read (on the job) was *Health Service Financing* (BMA 1970) which had an appendix by Cooper and Culyer. This contained lots of evidence that created a puzzle over the question of health service expenditure. Expenditure did not seem to be well correlated with the regional distribution of death rates, waiting lists, and so on. The appendix was looking at efficiency, but a strong equity message came out.

Other economists published papers showing that, not only was regional inequality present, but it had remained remarkably similar in terms of the relative rankings for the previous fifteen years. This began to be discussed more and more between first academics and then politicians. John Rickard, an economist in the Oxford Regional Health Authority during the mid-1970s, the only one at that time to my knowledge, also did some work in this field. Martin Buxton and Rudolf Klein published something in the *New Statesman.* I am not sure what alerted David Owen, but by the time he came to office in 1975 he was sure that something (probably a lot) needed to be done, and a new formula was needed. [The alerting was almost certainly done by Professor Brian Abel-Smith from the LSE who was specialist adviser to the Secretary of State, Barbara Castle and David Owen, and had been Crossman's adviser.]

The story goes that Owen summoned officials into his office and told them that he was not happy with the Crossman formula [a previous attempt to get some regularity into the allocation process to regions] and that they were to go away and come back with something better. Officials went away for a week or two and returned stating that there did not seem to be a problem. Owen told them to go away and try again. Their second suggestion was to establish RAWP. This showed a clear political initiative at the outset, and whose ideas had been stimulated by the social sciences. It was not an internal civil service agenda.

There was no resistance from the civil service once RAWP was set up. . . . It is an interesting story about how a consensus was arrived at in the NHS in comparison to the conflict in local government, which seems to be very adversarial. This is not the case in health. Even the losers were intellectually persuaded of the need for reform. Another point is that a lot of the clinicians that could be harmed were not on the committees. The RAWP committees were surprisingly open to academic views, by Whitehall standards. Many academics were members. But it is striking to see how few medical professionals were on these committees. (NHSE1)

Politics is kept out of the formula setting approach as much as possible, he argued. But the 'pace of change' (movement to the targets) *is* a political decision and this has been done 'very very gradually . . . The politicians can be more objective about the formula because they are not arguing about next year's allocation but about a far off target. There is a continuity present in the DoH that other departments do not have' (NHSE1). This last remark is instructive. It is what civil servants in the old Ministry of Education used to say in the 1960s. It is what those in the Social Security Administration in Washington used to say in the 1960s and 1970s (Glennerster 1974). A sense of continuity is created not least by long-serving members who impart, and embody, an institutional memory and who have a driving commitment themselves.

Where does this come from, the respondent was asked:

> Surely the NHS was founded on the principle of equity. Statements made at its foundation stressed the removal of barriers to access. The NHS satisfied people's yearning for the idea of a publicly funded institution, that is, for the use of a better word, founded on socialist principles—payment according to ability to pay and treatment according to need. There seems to be continuity from the founding period of the NHS through to the present day. (NHSE1)

Others interviewed in the NHS Executive and the Department of Health shared the same view about the centrality of the equity objective and saw it lying behind not just the allocation of hospital and community service revenue allocations but family practitioner services too.

> [The] lead objective has to be the same . . . equity. But because the GMS (General Medical Services, mainly in general practice) is a negotiated settlement (we) have to reach some sort of agreement or at least acceptance within the profession. Until recently the equity objective has only applied to HCHS, but when RAG was established (it) began to form a single objective for the different services. (NHSE2)

The Equity Vision Down the Line

How far was this just an élite view not shared by those lower down the administrative chain who are directly affected? We interviewed people from the regional offices in the South of England, in the North of England, and in London. We also interviewed those working in district health authorities in those regions and GPs in those districts.

A remarkably consistent view emerged. The central value system was a shared one. Local actors might not understand the detailed methodology and they might be critical of the outcome in some respects but they shared the equity of access goal without exception.

> The objective is improving health care by getting resources to the right place—that's what equity is all about. (NHSER1: regional official)

> The objective is equity of access and resource allocation. In access this is probably achieved, even if we are still squawking over resource allocation because of how we interpret it locally. (ILHEA: district official)

We have a formula in order to get an objective measure of need. This is meant to achieve equity of allocation. That is a very important part of the definition of what the formula is about. (UNHEA: district official)

However, this northern Director of Finance was much less clear that it was achieving those ends.

You get the impression that the formula is not about getting an objective measurement. It is about justifying historical spending patterns. I know things have got better since RAWP and the 1970s but the South and London in particular get a great deal out of the system. Just look at who spends over target. Camden was miles over despite getting a very generous target in the first place. That would never happen in the North. (UNHEA)

A GP (ILFH) said: 'There is a near obsession in health with equity. It is a justifiable goal and does go back to the creation of the National Health Service.' Nor was this untypical of GPs. Here are others' views:

I do think that the allocation is generally fair, though of course I can point to areas where I think we get a rough deal. . . . We face particularly acute problems because we are in the capital near large railway stations. We have lots of refugees and psychiatric patients on our list. (ILGP)

Equity is defined at the top. It is a national statement of objectives that boils down to the general ethos of a National Health Service. (RSGP)

I have a friend who works in the regional office on these things full time. I am lucky because if it were not for conversations with him, then I probably would not have a clue about what was going on. . . . We will never be satisfied with the formula . . . that means we shall never reach a position where equity is achieved. But that does not mean we keep changing the formula either. There needs to be stability in the system. So a compromise has to be reached. We are probably as near that compromise as we will ever get. (OLGP)

The further down the system we interviewed, the less knowledge there was of the way the formula worked and the more it was taken on trust. The smaller the unit, the more there was a feeling that the allocations could not have fully taken this or that issue into account. Yet *none* of the general complaints about factors that ought to be taken into had not been discussed at some point on RAG or ACRA.

For example, from some GPs there were worries about psychiatric services and long-term illness. For others:

I know what I would like to see in the formula. I would like to see it measure poverty. There are probably some bits that pick it up somewhere but it is not obvious, is it? (USGP)

We are a deprived city, but this is not always on the indices that I have seen . . . . This area had a lot of heavy industry and mining was a big part. That means we have a lot of long-term illness. I have a lot of miners whose ill health has been caused by a life down the mines. But this is not official so there is no real recognition of the problem so no one addresses it with sufficient resources. (UNFH)

No ethnicity is measured in the formulae. (OLFH)

There is a concern that the formula does not take account of rurality. (RSFH)

All of these issues had been addressed and much work done on them, as we saw in Chapter 4. Long-term illness and deprivation and rurality and psychiatric illness are all in the formula. Some issues may be too local to be in a national formula. 'We deal with a very bad drug problem. We are lucky because we get extra resources to deal with this. We apply directly to the NHS Executive for it. So it is not included in the formula, and I am not sure it ever could' (UNFH).

The view at the centre that the various committees had tried to respond to issues raised in the field did seem to be borne out. What was more worrying was that those at the bottom seemed to have very little grasp of the process or its content. As the primary care groups get their own budgets this will be more of a problem. There is a considerable education job to be done. As one GP put it, of the proposed allocation to primary care groups: 'Most GPs need to be taught the system. It needs to be put in very simple terms and talked through at a very basic level. It's all new language to most of them' (OLFH). There was a residual anti-London feeling not far below the surface, despite its relative loss of funding: 'It did not take London long to dilute the effect of RAWP' (UNGP). Much the same views were expressed in the education interviews discussed in the next chapter.

It was entirely understandable that those on the extremes should feel their needs were not fully reflected. A measure of central tendency can never satisfy the outliers or get the allocation right for very small areas. Yet, as one of our respondents (ILGP) put it: 'At local level I do think the problem of equity is potentially worse. You can see the type of service your friends and neighbours are providing. I am not really interested in what goes on at the other end of the country.' The division between the funding of fundholders and other general practitioners had left deep scars. Most GPs supported the idea of primary care groups as a way forward, even though, when we interviewed in 1998, there was still a lot of uncertainty about what it would mean in practice. All agreed that they had to be formula-funded to achieve open fairness.

A doctor practising in the North of England summed up the general view of our GP sample: 'You can come up with lots of reasons to rubbish a target and why we shouldn't have a formula. But at the end of the day they also bring many benefits. Transparency must be the most important given the way things are done at the moment' (UNFH). Most thought that the formula should be suggested nationally but that there should be room for negotiation and variation on local factors. Some thought it would not work at practice level. Others thought the practice had to be the starting-point. Again, the national debate on ACRA was reflecting local views (see Chapter 4).

Is Equity in Inputs Enough?

Rightly or wrongly, there was no fundamental disagreement about the approach used to try and get an equitable distribution of resources. No one at local level raised the issues of using the formula to try to affect outcomes or whether the NHS should go beyond seeking to equalize inputs. Those at the centre were beginning to be exercised about the problem.

Was there much more they could do to improve the formula?

> There is a growing backlash against the growing complexity of the formula or diminishing returns. There comes a point when the system is as good as it needs to be. (NHSE2)

> The next debate will conclude that equal allocation of resources to similar needs is not enough. We may conclude that what has already been achieved is not enough. We have plenty of data showing where the money is going. We have very little knowledge about the effects of this money in achieving its ultimate goal of treating patients (DoH).

> We have come very far in achieving equity of resource allocation but have no information on what effect this has on health variations or on access. Evaluating outcomes is not the primary concern of the department. It is the health authorities' choice how to provide services locally. . . . Probably the main area to look at now is over outcomes. Should we be concerned? Should we be looking at unmet need? If there is any, to what extent can it be solved through a formula or subjective judgement? They are all questions that should be asked. (NHSE2)

Beyond Hospital and Community Services

All of these remarks concerned the allocation of hospital and community service budgets. Primary care and the variable quality of general practice had tended to be ignored until much more recently. One central department respondent said:

> It is odd that this had not been looked at before the hospital and community services budget. Logically attention over the distribution of primary care resources should have been achieved before the HCHS formula was reformed to such a level. In around 1990 primary care became very important. This was a late awareness of how resource allocation was significantly inequitable in this sector. Attention was not directed towards this area before then because there was no reliable and widespread figures, statistics or research done on the issue before the late 1980s. There was very little public attention on this issue and low public awareness of primary care. (DoH)

Analysis and Institutional Capacity

Asked about possible advances in analytical capacity one respondent made a revealing comparison:

> One area that could be looked at is the major work carried out in the US literature on risk assessment. They have outstanding data from insurance records and are streets ahead of us in doing sophisticated analysis on variations in risk or morbidity and the determinants in relation to populations and the consequence on health expenditure. This is a glimpse of what you can do given the resources and the data. In some ways it is a frustration not to have equivalent capabilities. In some ways we are insular and amateurish in what we are doing. But we do have the institutions that are far in advance of theirs. Both countries are looking with envy at each other—the US at our institutions and us at their research. We do have very sophisticated resource formulae which are used and affect every part of Britain. In this sense we are streets ahead of other countries. Finland has copied Britain; Spain has copied Britain and indeed so have many others. (NHSE1)

Efficiency Issues

Perverse?

It was part of the RAWP working party's original intention that the allocation formula should not be capable of being 'gamed'. Those at the receiving end should be incapable of affecting their allocations. It was an attempt to fund pure need and not existing supply. The brief given to both RAG and its successor ACRA make avoiding perverse incentives part of their remit. In our interviews we tried to ascertain whether there were any such incentives for good or bad. The firm conclusion was that none of those we interviewed could see perverse incentives in the current system. The allocations were determined in a way few really understood and certainly felt unable to manipulate by their own actions even as an authority. The misgivings about the possibility of using practice-level data to set primary care group budgets were driven by concern that this would open the way to manipulation. There was equal resistance to using the formula to encourage certain kinds of *efficient* action by GPs or others. The strong belief was that the funding process should be neutral.

The attempts to encourage GPs to hold clinics and undertake preventive work had led to some abuse. The 1990 GP contract had resulted in some unintended perverse consequences. It placed greater emphasis on capitation income. This was meant to give GPs greater incentives to attract patients and hence be better doctors. In fact, the only groups of GPs to have increased their list sizes consistently have been single-handed GPs. The public want to see the same doctor, often they like to see someone from their own ethnic group. The conventional expert wisdom is that single-handed practices offer less good services than group practices or health centres. These have more GPs who can specialize and community and nursing services on site. However, the public are going more for the single-handed GPs. GPs are also more reluctant to reduce their lists as this has a bigger impact on their incomes than it used to. There is now more resistance from existing GPs to new doctors entering under-doctored areas. The attempt to use a crude 'market' incentive may have backfired.

Passive/positive

On the other hand, the devolution of budgets first to fundholders and now to primary care groups had drawn GPs into the health service system of priority setting and forced them to think about efficiency and priority issues in a way that was never true pre-1990. One of the big attitudinal divides between fundholding GPs and those who resisted the scheme was the latter's reluctance to handle money or think about resources. Those who entered fundholding wanted to be involved in doing something to improve the service—to have an impact on local hospitals' efficiency, for example. They argued: 'if anyone is to do the rationing implicit in a National Health Service we want to be part of it' (Glennerster *et al.* 1994). Non-fundholders felt this was none of their business. Indeed they felt it wrong to be involved in a rationing process at all. They did not come into medicine to be bothered with money. (For a fuller reflection of both points of view see Glennerster *et al.* 1994; Glennerster *et al.* 1998.)

Contrasting these interviews in 1998 with those in the early 1990s a striking change does seem to have occurred. The remarks of fundholders sounded very familiar. 'It's a question of whether I wanted the responsibility of controlling my own destiny—my level and standard of care. The choice was ideological. Those who did not want anything to do with budgets didn't disagree about the benefits—they simply didn't think doctors should have to dirty their hands with money' (OLFH). All the fundholders, perhaps surprisingly, welcomed the move to primary care groups. One fairly typical attitude was the following:

> If you look at the proposals for PCGs then I think you will see how much they resemble all we fought for nearly ten years ago. They also make total sense for the government don't they. The government will now be able to turn around and complain about all the doctors who spend over budget. There will be a responsibility on us to show how often they are wrong . . . taking responsible decisions on behalf of (our) patients. It will be our role to point out the weaknesses in any allocation of resources and stand our ground. (ILFH)

So, for the ex-fundholders, the devolved PCG budgets, now covering most of the NHS, and including their old adversaries, was a logical extension of the efficiency gains they felt fundholding had brought.

Non-fundholders were more cautious. The new arrangements would end the divide and the unfairly generous treatment they felt fundholders had had. Even so the shift in attitude was clear.

> I can't say I think of these changes as beneficial. It is not our job to think about budgets but to care and to treat patients. But I do realize that this is a bit idyllic. We are not living in an ideal state and we have to make compromises. . . . The PCGs were as good as we could have expected under the last government but I would have hoped for something better under the new administration. But it was obvious that if fundholding were abolished, we would still be moving in that direction. (OLGP)

Others thought that PCGs were an admission that fundholding had not worked and were anxious to get involved.

I suppose we were both right in the decisions we made. Most of my colleagues that I have met have come to realize that things were never going to remain the same. I certainly would not go back to where we were and I think we have made a positive contribution to the way the health service is now run. (UNFH)

There are one or two figures at the helm but there's another five of us who are interested in the issues. We have a lot of catching up to do with others who have been coping with budgets for a while now. (USGP)

I generally do not really want to think about rationing and budgets but the reality is that I cannot run away from it. We have to face facts. It is probably only fair that if the health authority has a problem of sticking to a budget then we should be responsible enough to do so as well. I am looking forward to the changes. It is an exciting period to be a GP. The way ahead is more power to the grass roots. We do know what the best for this locality is. We do after all face the public day in day out. It is the sensible way to organize the service. If you were designing the system from scratch we would use all the same language of a primary care led service. I am not sure that we would have all thought of PCGs as the way to organize that principle, but we have to deal with history, don't we? In that case this is probably the least bad solution. It gets us all back into the same boat. (ILGP)

Apart from the relief at being in the same boat again, the revealing substance of these fairly typical reactions was a common recognition that GPs had to be involved in helping to run the service. The micro-efficiency gains that the evidence suggested did follow from this in both fundholding and commissioning groups (Le Grand *et al.* 1998) could spread more widely.

A Problem Unsolved

One boundary problem and perverse incentive that remains results not from the formula itself but the split between health and social care. This is particularly important in the case of the long-term care of the elderly but is also important for the mentally ill. Local authorities administer and fund, with central government assistance, the long-term social care of these groups. The NHS also cares for the same groups and the nature of the care overlaps. With a cash-limited budget, the NHS has every incentive to shift people across the boundary and have the local authority pay, and since these are means-tested services, the recipient pays too.

The formulae take no account of who is treated where. Since it is an age- and condition-weighted formula, an authority that has a large number of old people living alone and succeeds in getting the local authority and the families to do most of the care will do rather well. One Department of Health respondent suggested that much of the apparent gains in health service productivity claimed for the 1990 reforms had actually been achieved by shedding responsibility for the old to local authorities.

The issue had been studied by the Department of Health's economic advisers office. The personal social services element in the local authority grant had been looked at to see if there were major inconsistencies with the health formula. No significant ones were found but the incentive issue of cost shifting from the NHS could not be easily addressed. To do so would involve merging the NHS and local authority budgets for long-term care as the Royal Commission on Long-Term Care (1999) suggested, notably in the Minority Report.

However, the personal social services and the formula that applies to them have traditionally not been high on ministers' agenda. 'Ministers feel they can only fight for one cause and that is normally the NHS rather than PSS', as one civil servant put it (DoH). Since the PSS formula was in any case part of the Department of the Environment's responsibility, it tended not to be the focus of the resource allocation team's interest.

Conclusions

This chapter has reported on interviews with central NHS staff, health authorities, and both fundholding and non-fundholding GPs shortly before those categories were abolished and the new primary care groups came into being in April 1999. The equity aims of the resource allocation process were 'obvious'. It was striking the extent to which there was a shared view of what equity meant throughout the system from top to bottom: equal access to treatment for equal need. There was an acceptance away from the centre that this could imply others receiving more generous funding. Central officials were confident that the distribution formula they were using was very successful in achieving an equitable outcome and that it was based on sound scientific work. Lower down the system there were more sceptics. Respondents pointed to local factors which increased demands on them and which they thought should be taken into account. Yet virtually all of the factors mentioned had been discussed and worked on by the various advisory committees. The lower down the system we went, the less the understanding. As GPs and others on primary care groups get their own budgets, more information and explanation will be needed.

A measure of central tendency, however elaborate, can never capture the problems suffered by the extreme outliers or the very idiosyncratic problems some areas will face. This becomes especially true when the areas in question become very small, as PCGs will be. There was both a mature acceptance of this and a call for flexibility in the face of exceptional cases. Overall, there was an acceptance of the principles of the system—a population-weighted needs formula—and the general way in which it operated. Those at the centre felt there were decreasing returns to further elaboration of the complexity of the formula. They did feel there was a case for extending its principles to primary care where the distribution of GPs was not equitable.

Efficiency had not been seen by central administrators as an important issue in setting the formula. The intention had been to distribute resources fairly, not to affect behaviour. They had seen the avoidance of perverse incentives as being important. For the most part they seem to have succeeded. No one we talked to felt able to game the system. The GP capitation system was felt to be more open to abuse.

The devolving of budgets to localities and the involvement of GPs in micro-resource allocation and efficiency issues had come a long way since 1990. GPs, both fundholders and non-fundholders, now seemed willing to take on such involvement in a way that would have been unthinkable in 1990. The differences between fundholders and non-fundholders had created a deep sense of inequity, the 'two-tier system' it was called, which contrasted with the overall equity objective of equal access for equal need. However, the new primary care groups were surprisingly popular given this legacy. To the former fundholders they embodied devolved budgets and leverage; to the non-fundholders they were seen as restoring a uniform system. Now both in the same boat, they saw advantages in setting priorities and bringing efficiency pressures to bear on the hospitals as a joint enterprise.

The efficiency issues that were worrying the central civil servants had to do with the dilemma we highlighted in Chapter 4. A highly sophisticated system of resource allocation according to need was not delivering equal access or equal quality of care. This was the responsibility of other parts of the service. The new regulatory and advice-giving bodies set up following the new Labour White Paper—the National Institute for Clinical Effectiveness, for example, and clinical governance—may be ways of addressing some of these issues.

What we saw was a national service with very clear common values to which everyone we talked to signed up despite the deep divisions of the 1990s. It was in striking contrast to the responses we got from those in the education and housing services to which we now turn.

9

Central and Local Views of the Education Funding System

The development of public education services in England (and indeed the rest of Britain) has for much of the two hundred years since 1800 involved a balance of central intervention and degrees of local autonomy. As Chapter 5 showed, this local autonomy has, at different times, involved control by local authorities and at the level of schools themselves. The development of needs-based grants for education (considered in Chapters 3 and 5) has, by implication, meant a move towards a concern for ever-greater degrees of 'fairness'. The reduction of differences in resources in relation to the need to spend of individual authorities has become a key goal of policy.

But these grants have also had efficiency objectives. Chapter 5 described how a reform of the local government grant system in 1958 moved from percentage grants to 'block' grants. Cash limits have been applied to all the major local government grants since the early 1980s. Local authority expenditure capping operated—in varying degrees—from 1985–6 to 1998–9, heavily based on authorities' needs assessments.

Throughout this period of development of local government and education grant policy within central government, civil servants and other élite policy-advisers have been instrumental in shaping policy. As part of this study, we interviewed national and local policy-makers. Interviews were also undertaken with a cross-section of schools, within both the LEA and grant-maintained sectors. The results of these interviews are summarized in the sections below, looking first at central, then LEA, and then schools' views. In each case we consider equity issues and then efficiency ones.

Equity and Efficiency: Views from the Centre

One of the most interesting features of the existing system of central control over education resource distribution is the split between the Department of the Environment, Transport, and the Regions (who co-ordinate the overall SSA process) and spending departments—such as the Department for Education and Employment—which have responsibility for particular services. One DETR official stated: 'I don't know much about education in detail. SSA is a more general system and this is shown by the generalized criticisms raised' (DETR-LG). There was also a recognition that the government 'had done a very bad sales job on it [the SSA formula]' (DETR-LG).

DfEE officials consider proposed changes to the education SSA. They also have some input into the process of commissioning research about possible SSA reforms. Given the recent criticisms of key elements of the education SSA, in particular the calculation of the additional educational needs weightings, there has been surprisingly little new research about possible formulae changes. Unlike the health formula, there is no body of academic expertise working full-time on needs assessment and other qualitative issues. Academics and consultants do undertake such research, but generally only when commissioned by individual councils, groups of councils, or as a one-off commission from either DfEE or DETR.

Criticisms of the education SSA in comparison with authorities' own funding formulae are conceded by DETR: 'within education there is an acceptance of LMS as opposed to concerns with SSA' (DETR-LG). The education SSA formula is 'inherently complicated'. Having said that, DETR believe: 'There is a marked difference between the public arguments about SSA and what people will say behind closed doors . . . protagonists say they will put up with a particular situation' (DETR-LG).

Much of the debate about the education SSA (and, indeed, those for all other services) centres on the 'technical level' and takes place within a 'political/public affairs context' (DETR-LG). There is little detailed consideration of the importance of equity as such. Another DETR official commented, 'It's interesting nobody talks about equity' (DETR-H). This lack of discussion was even more surprising given that 'years ago the system was a black box. Now things are far more open and everyone can pick away at individual issues' (DETR-H).

Equity clearly plays a relatively small part in the Whitehall debate about education SSAs. Of far greater concern is the issue of the political pressures surrounding the distribution of resources between councils. Greater openness has led to more pressure to reform the system, but not to a significantly greater concern with 'fairness' as such. Authorities—led by elected councillors—lobby the government for larger SSAs, though the notion of equity is rarely referred to. What takes place is a debate between local and central government about particular geographical patterns of grant distribution. Fairness or equity is implied, but not often an explicit element in the negotiations. In the years since LMS was instituted, schools have in some cases joined in the lobbying for changes to the SSA formula.

Interviews with officials centred on issues of distribution. The use of the grant system to achieve particular efficiency objectives, rather like the concern with equity, is implied though not always explicit. It is clear from SSA policy documents that resources are distributed in the light of what the economy can afford. Officials work within a system which is simultaneously seeking to restrain expenditure while also being fair as between authorities. Local authorities and schools lobby for higher education expenditure over all and for larger shares for their particular area.

Equity: Local Authority Interviewees

Interviewees appeared to share a strong common view that the provision of school education should be provided in a fair and equitable way from one part of the country (and school) to another. But such a view was generally implicit and consideration of equity required prompting. More interviewees took it for granted that schools should be funded in such a way as to achieve a broad degree of fairness, though there was considerable scepticism about the complex formula-based system for allocating resources from central to local government. But none of the interviewees challenged the idea of the pursuit of equity through the allocation of central government resources.

The definition of equity

Most of the local authority interviewees were very aware of the system of Standard Spending Assessments as the basis of the revenue support grant (and thus of efforts to redistribute resources from one area to another). These views were expressed by two local authority chief executives:

> Equity means each according to their need—but we don't have it, and we'd never all agree on the same outcome anyway . . . the objective is equity of access and resource allocation, but you wouldn't recognize it if you saw it. We would still disagree if we had equal access because it is a matter of local interpretation. (UNCE)

Equity has never been discussed in any form in any meeting which I've been present in . . . I wouldn't recognise a fair system if I saw one, but I would recognize an acceptable one. (ILCE)

It is evident that senior local authority officers rarely, if ever, discuss equity or fairness in theoretical terms. But they continue to operate within a system which involves a distribution of resources which they know is supposed to achieve a fair or equitable result.

Local government officers see themselves as part of a significant and continuing political process. One chief executive put it thus: 'Nobody would claim the distribution was fair—not even the government. If it was fair, we wouldn't bother with the SSA round' (ILCE). Another senior council officer saw SSA as 'A mechanical attempt to allocate resources based on an assumption that people should have a set level of services and resources' (USCE). The overall sense of the interviews conducted was that the allocation of resources from central to local government—via education SSA—was a mechanistic and top–down effort to distribute a large sum of money between authorities. Most authorities appear to feel the current SSA serves them badly, though they do not think of this as 'inequitable', rather as yet another of the many problems which impede the proper delivery of services: 'There is an increased interest in standardisation. But because all providers face problems with the over-use of services, sustainability contrasts with local characteristics. SSA contradicts local objectives . . . SSA may bear no relationship to this city's objectives' (USCE).

The sense that SSA is allocated in such a way as to impede local service delivery is strong in a number of authorities (though this may be just another way of demanding more grant). Capping is seen as having undermined the objectives (equity included) of SSA. In short, there is little love for the current system of equalization and allocating resources to authorities. It is seen as a grim inevitability and a system that needs constantly to be put under pressure. But it is definitely not seen as tool for the achievement of equity.

Methodological issues

Local authority views about the method of distributing SSA are closely linked to those about equity discussed above. Officers see themselves as being involved in a dynamic process of annually negotiating and renegotiating the education SSA. All the authorities interviewed believed the SSA undercounted their particular needs. A view widely echoed was that the SSA formula 'doesn't recognize real spending needs' (ILCE).

Thus rural needs, the problems of coastal areas, the area cost adjustment (for the additional costs of providing services in the South-East of England), the additional costs of ports, authorities with 'bad council housing', and poverty were each cited as examples—by different authorities—of the methodological failures of SSA. London was seen as having particularly generous education SSAs by an interviewee in the North of England (UNCE). Interviewees in London believed social needs were not effectively measured.

The age of data was criticized, particularly in London where there can be rapid changes in the population make-up. Some authorities believe their own data cover a wider range of needs than those used in SSA (OLLEA). Authorities in all parts of the country stressed the importance of poverty as a driver of spending need. The existing measures of poverty are believed to be inadequate: 'Income support and lone parents [as a need indicator] don't tell us that much—it's pretty crude as we can show in this area' (UNCE).

The links between existing resource flows and educational outcomes were mentioned by two authorities. In the view of the chief executive and education officers of one authority, the government has come to accept that spending more money on a service does not necessarily improve it. SSAs based on the assumption that extra spending will improve quality are therefore wrong. Another chief executive praised OFSTED's database which is becoming a useful repository of information about the links (if any) between performance and spending need (ILCE).

Most authorities leave the detailed negotiation of education SSA to the Local Government Association and to special interest groups of councils. It is hard for local authority officers to distance themselves from proposals for changes in SSA which would specifically assist their own authorities. We met no interviewees who were prepared to argue for methodological changes in SSA that would explicitly take resources from their own council.

Thus it is clear that the debate about the SSA method is heavily influenced by the local needs of particular councils and their officers. Most authorities would be willing to tolerate an education SSA which was broadly acceptable, though not perfect. But as most authorities appear to want additional grant and spending power in the short term, it is difficult to see how it would ever be possible to move to a 'rough-justice' needs assessment.

Politicization

There is no widespread assumption that the grant system—and SSA as part of it—is politicized in any way. Chief executives are aware that the allocation of money is a political process, but they have not accused either the previous or present government of distributing grant for political advantage. A London officer put it thus: 'When there was a Conservative government there weren't many Conservative councils, but when Labour came in there were lots of Labour MPs who had Labour councils. This makes it more difficult to get a big influence' (UNCE).

Two of our interviewees used the language of sport in discussing the process of negotiating and allocating SSAs: 'It's all a game. We do take part because it's the only way we can make our feelings known. We wouldn't have much right to complain about SSA if we didn't take part in the annual consultations' (UNCE). And, 'When money flows out of London, we generally seem to win' (OLLEA). Evidently, senior local authority officers see the process of grant and SSA allocation as a winners-and-losers competition. In a sense they are correct: within any year's RSG, it is virtually impossible to change the distribution so that all authorities get additional grant or spending power (unless there were a very large increase in the amount of spending power and grant available).

Senior officers are aware that resource distribution is a political process, though none of them suggested it has been used for party-political advantage. Thus, we were told,

> It is a political priority of SSA to protect the government—it is designed to prevent challenge . . . (OLLEA)

> There is a pretence of objectivity, but after going through the whole process ministers can just turn round and pick an option we never discussed. The decision always seems to meet political objectives. (ILCE)

Yet none of our interviewees stated a belief the SSA is used for overtly party-political objectives, even if other political purposes might be supported.

A London chief executive believed that being in the capital 'does make a difference' (ILCE), while one outside London stated, 'We shout as loud as we like but London still can't hear us' (UNCE). A fruitful line of inquiry for future research might examine the thesis that closeness to government decision-making is an advantage.

There was no suggestion among interviewees that the system was becoming more political than in the past. Our interviewees were generally war-weary and cynical, but they did not state a belief that the system was becoming more overtly political. One change that was mentioned was the growing tendency for DfEE to bypass authorities and communicate directly with schools (ILCE).

Efficiency: Local Authority Interviewees

Spending benchmarks

All our interviewees accepted that both they and schools saw SSA as a (minimum) benchmark level of spending. Many authorities clearly spend above their SSA. One chief executive stated, 'Schools would be pretty unhappy if we only spent our SSA' (UNCE), while another said, 'We put much more money into education than SSA—schools would suffer a 25 per cent cut if we were at that level' (OLLEA). The clear implication is that SSA is a minimum level of acceptable spending.

One chief executive mentioned direct comparisons between his authority and others: 'We compare our SSA totals with other authorities, especially in relation to highway maintenance and education, and the Society of London Treasurers does an annual report comparing service spending in each authority with their SSA levels' (ILCE). It is also clear from some authorities that schools compare the authority's spending figures with SSA. Openness is not seen as wholly virtuous by senior officers as it encourages schools to ask questions.

Incentives were not generally mentioned by local authority officers. It does not appear that councils see SSA as giving them particular incentives to behave in a particular way. SSA is not hypothecated to par-ticular services, although there is pressure on authorities to passport additional RSG to education when ministers point this out in public statements. The need to passport money to schools in this way may lead to a suboptimal use of resources.

One chief executive did observe that, 'The current system provides an incentive for us to pack the schools as full as possible and increase class sizes' (ILCE). SSA is allocated in such a way that the more pupils in an authority's schools, the more needs assessment and grant it will receive. Thus there is an incentive to build up the size of school rolls so long as the authority does not reach the point where new schools have to be built (when, of course, there would be capital costs). But generally SSA is seen as a relatively neutral resource distributor, rather than as giving incentives to particular kinds of behaviour. It is also seen, increasingly, as a way as encouraging authorities to pass on year-to-year increases in education expenditure.

Complexity

SSA is seen as unpredictable and complex. 'Members are confused by the system' was a typical reaction (USLEA). Rather more dramatically, a chief executive in London described the system as 'bonkers: time-consuming and futile . . . nearly everyone says the same thing. Everybody battles against one another and nobody wins' (ILCE). Moreover, it is the control totals (of spending) which matter to authorities more than the actual allocation formula.

Resources versus equitable distribution

Most authorities are concerned with the total resources available to them rather more than the intricacies of debates about SSA. Some senior staff, notably chief executives and chief education officers, are heavily involved in the debate about SSA and its fairness (as they see it). But the main driving force for them is to get additional money for their authority, rather than an interest in equitable distribution as such. Indeed, when most authorities argue for greater 'fairness' or equity, they are, in reality, concerned with getting a larger total of grant for their own councils.

> We do not have an expert who understands the system and so we take it as given and spend our time looking elsewhere for money . . . We identify shortfalls and then identify how to bridge that gap. These are more issues of capital than revenue. We need money to keep the city developing and we are more likely to get that additional money through the SRB [Single Regeneration Budget], which is big here. This is more important than thinking about comparative SSA in other cities. (USCE: chief executive)

> I think we now see SSA as managing to do only so much. It's our basic income, which we have to supplement with other grants. European and other government specific grants allow us to provide the services we need and want. (UNCE)

The only major issue that raised a genuine concern about equity rather than simply a desire for more money was the treatment of grant-maintained schools. A number of authorities' officers felt that GM schools had been given an unfair advantage over LEA institutions, in particular in the allocation of capital resources. In some cases, a GM school within an authority had received more capital resources in a year than all the LEA schools put together.

But the debate about the equitable distribution of resources remains a second-order priority as compared with ensuring the education service within a particular authority is properly funded. Recent government increases in SSA, targeted at education, have put councils under pressure to increase education spending at the expense of other services. Thus there was now a debate within local government about how far education should be given priority simply because the DfEE required it. Again, this question overshadowed questions of equity.

The View from Individual Schools

Equity, in general

It is evident that the introduction of LMS has made most schools far more aware of the realities of education funding than ever before. In the words of one London LEA school, 'Things changed so much after LMS it's hard to believe we didn't think about money at all ten years ago' (ILSCH). Other schools stressed similar views: 'Most of us are treated fairly. LMS was a big leap forward. Before the 1990s the whole issue of how and why some schools got more than others was underhand. It was literally decided in smoke-filled rooms' (USSCH). 'LMS revolutionized the education sector. It dragged schools into the real world' (RSSCH). Thus, whether or not schools are convinced the system of funding is equitable, they are strongly in favour of the openness and transparency (and thus the increased probability of fair treatment) that LMS has led to.

In fact, the majority of schools interviewed believed that formula funding was leading to a result that is broadly fair. According to a grant-maintained school: 'Formula funding is the way things are. I don't doubt that it produces many benefits' (RSGMS). An outer London LEA schools took the highly realistic view that 'No system is perfect. If we are happy with our share then someone else will be moaning that they aren't getting enough' (OLSCH). Another LEA school was equally pragmatic: 'Given the restrictions—on us and the local authority—there isn't much room for big winners and losers' (USSCH). There appears to be no overriding belief that there is a fundamental inequity built into formula funding systems.

Even authority to authority differences (which are much debated within local government) are not much in evidence at the school level. As one London LEA school put it: 'We don't really look much at what's going on outside the area' (ILSCH). However, one urban southern LEA school did show a grasp of the wider issues raised by Standard Spending Assessments and other local government funding issues:

What looks like equity on paper often turns out very differently. For example, I agree with the principle of pupil-led funding, but also appreciate AEN. But that will differ across areas. The best example is over ethnic minorities. Local authorities get additional money for children from ethnic minorities through SSA. But in most places these groups are out-performing white kids. But where English is their second language or where there are small pockets then I do think a school needs more money to deal with them. So what would be the fair system? (USSCH)

Equity: grant-maintained versus LEA schools

As far as revenue funding was concerned, there was a high level of agreement between LEA and GM schools. There is no overriding feeling that GM schools are advantaged and some evidence of a desire to continue to maintain good relationships between the two competing sectors.

There has to be a degree of co-operation between the LEA and the schools—including those that are Grant-Maintained. GM schools have to work in the locality, and often use LEA services. (ILSCH)

Blaming shortfalls in LEA funding on the GM sector would be very convenient, but is something I am reluctant to do. (USSCH)

GM schools get an initial bribe then are on pretty much even keel with us. There are incentives to becoming GM but it certainly isn't more money in your annual budget. (ILSCH)

There's been a lot of emotion surrounding the different funding regimes between local GM schools and us. I don't think funding was the main reason why they decided to opt out. (OLSCH)

It is perhaps surprising that schools have readily accepted the different funding arrangements for GM and LEA schools with such equanimity. But the truth is that revenue finance, via the LMS formula and the common funding formula for GM schools, has had the same starting-points (a local authority's SSA or spending) and the split between the two sectors does appear to have been broadly fair.

Capital funding was seen in a very different light by our interviewees. A number of LEA schools made the same point:

Where we were clearly discriminated against is in the area of capital spending. (ILSCH)

It's clear that they have a pot of money that is far more generous than the one we draw upon. (OLSCH)

They were giving out grants like confetti to the early GM schools. (RSSCH)

Capital funding is the silver spoon that's never been taken out of their mouths . . . Who are they kidding when they try telling us they don't get additional money for buildings? It was the main carrot dangled in front of us all. (UNSCH)

Even some GM schools conceded they had enjoyed preferential treatment, though others disagreed:

We did get a good deal on capital funding . . . I think it was an opportunity for us to do work that had been blocked by the LEA for no good reason for many years. (RSGMS)

They [LEAs] always go on about our shiny new buildings. We are a growing school and we would have to put the children somewhere. (USGMS)

Capital funding is not as free and easy as the LEA would have people agree . . . We have to apply and prove our case before we get anything. That is the right way to do things . . . We have a fixed pot to bid from just like LEA schools. (ILGMS)

There was a broad consensus (apart from one or two GM schools) that capital funding for the grant-maintained sector had been more generous than for LEA schools, though it appears that this generosity was designed to tempt schools to opt out and that capital funding became more restricted after the initial year or two of GM status.

Relationships between LEAs, the Funding Agency for Schools, and other schools

LEA schools and GM schools have widely different views about their 'regulators', the local authorities and the Funding Agency for Schools (FAS). Typically, one GM school stated, 'We don't have much to do with the LEA. A lot of our relationship is conducted through the FAS' (ILGMS). An LEA school believed: 'We have the LEA and they have the FAS . . . It's funny how they go on and on about their independence, but they aren't really are they?' (USSCH). Separation of GM schools from the local government family is seen by many LEA and GM schools as partly ideological and partly practical. A GM school put it thus: 'There is a stand-off between us. We are politically too different. Our whole outlook on what schools could and should do is different' (USGMS). Rather more brutally, a northern urban LEA school stated, 'They [GM governors] are all Tory supporters and would love to see education being taken away from the local authority. GM schools were designed to undermine the role of the LEA' (UNSCH).

There is a perception that once a school has opted out, LEAs wash their hands of them. Nevertheless, there was general agreement that some kind of *realpolitik* was needed because the two sets of schools often coexisted within the same area and had many common interests. As one GM school put it, 'There's little point in them trying to sabotage our grants or make life difficult because we would just respond. We're not really that petty anyway' (UNGMS).

Incentives

LEA schools had stuck with their local authority in part because they had a relatively good relationship with them, rather than because they saw no particular financial incentive to encourage opting out. One outer London LEA school commented, almost with tenderness, 'There's no real reason to become GM. The LEA treats us very well. They're quite responsive. There's a lot to be said about having a comfort blanket. We get so much support from them that it cannot be counted in pounds and pence' (OLSCH). Another LEA school put it simply, though equally poetically: 'I dread the day when every school is an island' (UNSCH). In addition, schools saw no long-term financial benefits from opting out, 'There are no clear long-term financial reasons why we should become GM' (ILSCH).

But GM schools appear to be as content with their position as LEA schools are with theirs: it appears that particular kinds of school decided to opt out and now believe it was the correct decision. Equally, those which did not leave LEA control also believe they have behaved sensibly. As one GM school put it, 'Administrative independence was the key issue in our vote . . . The option was to control our own destiny or to hand it over to the LEA' (OLGMS). Another agreed:

> We chose GM status because it was the right thing for the school at the time . . . All the issues about freedom and diversity are very real considerations. Our ethos as a school did not tie in with many of our neighbours and councillors that were deciding our future . . . We had clear ideas about areas of the school and curriculum that needed to be strengthened. (USGMS)

The idea of a comfort blanket was referred to again, though this time as a criticism: 'LEAs foster a culture of dependency that LMS did not change. Schools are tied to the comfort blanket' (UNGMS).

The only revenue efficiency issue mentioned by schools was the per capita nature of their funding. GM and LEA schools agreed on this. A

GM school stated: 'Per capita funding is the most efficient way of financing schools. If that disadvantages inefficient schools—whatever their size—so be it' (ILGMS). A similar sentiment was expressed by an LEA school: 'The only incentive I can think of in the current funding system is to attract and many kids to the school as possible' (OLSCH).

There were capital funding incentives for schools to opt out, which both LEA and GM schools were aware of. But these capital grants were seen by both GM and LEA schools as one-off inducements that did not continue. After the initial allocation of capital funding, there was little expectation of continuing generosity. Indeed, with the change of government the two sectors were to be brought together again. There were no interviews that produced results suggesting LMS had led to more central control. This suggests that—at least in the early years of LMS and GM status—there was no sudden move to extend outright a control over schools. Tighter regulatory regimes may bring this in the future.

Conclusions

A number of general conclusions may be drawn from the interviews conducted with LEAs, schools, and other bodies. First, there is virtually no questioning of the policy of devolving budgets from LEAs to schools. We met no examples of interviewees who believed there should be a return to the previous regime of funding directly from town and county halls. Local management of schools and devolved budgets are now seen as the norm. Indeed, the way in which local management is now accepted is a considerable achievement, given the enormous criticism of it when it was being introduced in the late 1980s and early 1990s. This conclusion suggests a real gain in terms of marginal efficiency.

Funding—by the two-tier SSA and LMS arrangements—is heavily questioned by local government officers. They and their political masters fight hard for bigger shares of the overall SSA. The existing education SSA is seen as unacceptable because most authorities believe they should receive a larger share of the total. However, authorities do not believe the arrangements are politically skewed. In schools, there appears to be a far greater acceptance of the SSA and LMS arrangements. Individual institutions compare themselves with their neighbours, though rarely with schools in other areas. Schools accepted the idea of per capita funding.

Despite short-term capital funding advantages for GM schools, there is not seen to be any long-term revenue advantage attached to opting out. There seem to have been different characteristics attached to schools that affected their propensity to opt out. In the longer term, school-based budgets and management appear well bedded-in. When GM schools are transferred back to LEA control, their independence will be little affected. LEA schools will receive a greater share of the total schools' budget (and authorities correspondingly less) under the government's 'Fair Funding' proposals. The system researched in these interviews is unlikely to be radically reformed in the years ahead. There is certainly no evidence of pressure for such reform.

10

Struggling to Identify Objectives: Local Authority Housing

As Chapter 6 explains, subsidy for social housing involves different systems for two subsectors: those for local authorities and for housing associations (or registered social landlords, RSLs). Between the two, arrangements for transfers of housing from local authorities to associations involve what is, in effect, a third subsidy system through the financial terms on which transfers are made. Further, in contrast to the education and health sectors, where the bulk of spending is on current services, a large part of housing finance concerns capital assets—either the financing of new provision (or of repairs treated as capital spending) or the treatment of existing assets and liabilities. Adding to the complexity, a substantial part of the revenue of social landlords comes from the rents they charge (backed for the majority of their tenants by housing benefit). This means that issues like the 'affordability' of rents, or relativities between rents for different tenants, are major issues in a way which is not true for health or education finance, where charges are relatively insignificant. All this means that the sector offers a rich—and at times confusing—variety of subsidy and financial allocation systems through which the centre tries to influence and control the behaviour of social landlords.

In this chapter we look at the perceptions of these systems from those involved with local authority housing. We consider issues connected with housing associations separately in Chapter 11, as the funding systems are so distinct, but end that chapter with a comparison of the two subsectors. In each of these two chapters we look first at equity issues, and then at efficiency, dividing these responses in turn between current and capital finance. Table 10.1 shows the structure we have used to break down the issues raised in our interviews and discussions of social housing.

TABLE 10.1. *Equity and Efficiency Issues in Social Housing*

A. Local Authorities	
Equity: current finance	*Equity: capital finance*
Overall equity issues	Capital allocations and the GNI
Rent guidelines	
Local authority versus housing association rents	Lack of ring-fence for housing capital
The housing benefit rent cap	
Management and maintenance allowances	
Efficiency: current spending	*Efficiency: capital spending*
Effects of the ring-fence	Cost control
Trade-off between M&M and rents	Planning for future repairs
	Transfers
B. Housing Associations	
Equity: current finance	*Equity: capital allocations and the HNI*
Overall equity issues	
Local authority versus housing association rents	
Rent increase limitation	
Fair versus assured rents	
Affordability	
Efficiency: current spending	*Efficiency: capital spending*
Incentives before rent-bidding	Incentives before and after 1989
Incentives since rent-bidding	Planning for future repairs
	Becoming more business-like
	Grant levels and future development

Equity: Current Finance

Overall equity issues

What was most striking—in stark contrast to the health sector—was how unclear the notion of an 'equity' objective was within both central and local responses to our interviews. There appeared to be no guiding principle, equivalent to the idea of 'equal treatment for equal need', which people could point to as explaining why subsidies took the form they did. As we have explained in Chapter 6 above, the overall structure of Housing Revenue Account Subsidy is designed to allow local authorities to balance their books, provided that they charge rents at 'guideline' levels set down by the Department of Environment, Transport, and the Regions (DETR), while keeping annual spending on management and maintenance at 'allowance' levels set for each authority. Broadly speaking the system wipes out the effect of historic debt and of variations between authorities in the proportions of tenants entitled to housing benefit (although not the latter in recent years if rents are increased beyond a cap set by DETR). It could, therefore, be thought of as an attempt to achieve a form of 'equal treatment' for tenants in terms of the rents they pay for a standard level of service.

Central responses pointed to an underlying—but rather vague—idea of 'fair' rent relativities between regions, and a desire to set allowances for management and maintenance on as 'scientific' a basis as possible. However, the principles by which rent guidelines are set have been deeply obscured both by changes in their technical basis and by central concerns to minimize 'turbulence' in subsidy levels to individual authorities from year to year through *ad hoc* 'damping' adjustments. The change in the underlying basis of the rent guideline system in 1996 to incorporate an element depending on regional incomes appears to have reflected a general, but not very clearly defined, concern that underlying rent guidelines varied too much across the country: 'The income adjustment may not have been theoretically the strongest, but when exemplified it produced exactly what we were looking for' (DETR-H).

In other words, the centre has a view of the rough pattern of relative rents it wants to see between authorities, but the logic underlying this view is not very clearly articulated. It is hardly surprising, perhaps, that local authorities found it hard to explain what the system was trying to achieve in equity terms, as all of the local authority housing departments we interviewed showed:

> We did struggle—not only to identify what they were, but what the objectives should be. (ILLAH)

> I have never heard anyone describe equity or even fairness of distribution as an objective . . . we just get on with coping with what we get. (OLLAH)

> I suppose the objectives are for a fair distribution of resources between authorities, but it doesn't work out like that. (USLAH)

> No clear definition exists—no consultation documents in which fairness or equity appears. (OLCE)

> . . . the aim of the system must be to provide a fair level of subsidy on a consistent basis across the country . . . It is difficult to think of how to define the objective of the system. I can't think of any clear statement I have seen. (UNLAH)

Local respondents were more likely to put the aim of the system as being 'to spend as little as possible and restrict us as much as they can' (OLLAH), or similarly, 'to spend as little as possible and allow us to do as little as possible' (USLAH). There was little sense of what the system was supposed to achieve in terms of distribution between authorities, let alone between individual tenants.

Rent guidelines

Talking in 1997, an official explained the change in the underlying basis of rent guidelines from a straight proportion of capital values to involving a regional 'income' element as well:

> The Department was aware that the former capital values system produced great inequality. Northern local authorities could never expect to meet the very low level of rents calculated, which is why the damping formula played such a large role. . . . The system in the 1980s had produced a pattern that was far too flat, and gave hardly any regional variations, whereas the early 1990s system produced differences which were too large. (DETR-H)

Authorities have varied in the extent to which they have tried to follow the guidelines set down for their average rents (until the rent cap discussed below was brought in), and varied in their view of how equitable they were:

> We probably kept [rents] within guideline levels as long as possible, but the system does not accurately reflect our true costs. (USLAH)
>
> Setting some sort of guideline for rents is probably a good idea. . . . it was right that rents reflected how much we spent on M&M [management and maintenance]. (OLLAH)
>
> Politically it was not right to divorce tenants from an understanding of costs: enhanced levels of funding [should] be reflected in their burden. (ILLAH)

On the other hand, it was agreed that the system gives few signals about rent-setting between properties in the same authority:

> Rent guidelines do little for fairness within an authority. Like most authorities we charge the same rate for similar size properties, but the market value of some areas is far higher than others. (OLLAH)
>
> To the members [equity] means the same rents for the same type of property. We [the Housing Department] now think this is unfair. (USLAH)

Given the operation of the housing benefit system (which means that the level of gross rents is of little importance to many benefit recipients), the fairness of rent variations—or the lack of them—between properties does not seem to be a pressing concern: 'There tends to be a very low level of knowledge about rents at a tenant level, and those who are in the know tend to be non-HB tenants' (ILLAH).

Local authority versus housing association rents

An obvious potential equity issue is the difference between local authority and housing association rents, and one authority argued that 'equity between councils does not bother me as much as the gap between associations and local authorities' (OLCE). However, at the centre, the financial systems for the two subsectors have been driven by concerns (notably minimizing public spending) other than consistency in the treatment of their respective tenants. This may be beginning to change:

> One interesting aspect of rents is when you look over to the housing association sector, and the transfer of local authority stock to housing association control . . . One of the main issues tenants look at when voting is future rent levels. If a local authority has kept their rents down this has implications on how much a housing association would be able to raise them. . . . local authority rents have been constrained and therefore the gap is widening. (DETR-H)

For local authorities, with generally lower rents than associations, the issue was noted, but seen most often in terms of unfair constraints on authority revenue-raising rather than as an issue of equity between tenants:

> . . . it is not clear why there should be differences between associations and authorities . . . we believe that Housing Corporation resources could be better spent. (ILLAH)

> We do look at rents in the HA sector. It seems odd to us how they used to be held up as being models of efficiency, yet they still had to charge higher rents. [But] comparisons are of limited value because we have different roles and stocks. (OLLAH)

> We are treated very differently to housing associations. They have total freedom to raise money, and their rents are allowed to go far higher. (USLAH)

The northern authority did not see this as a major issue:

> I don't think the Government worry that much about the difference between LA and HA rents. I know tenants certainly don't. . . . For those not on Housing Benefit our rents offer far better value and are a lot cheaper. We both really rely on HB tenants to fill our stock now—them because their rents are high, us because they're old. (UNLAH)

The housing benefit rent cap

A different kind of equity issue at the time we interviewed authorities was the effect of the 'rent cap', designed to halt the growth in housing benefit costs. This meant that if rents were *increased* faster than the guidelines, subsidy would not be adjusted to meet the cost of this for tenants on housing benefit. To raise the same amount of revenue, gross rents therefore have to rise roughly three times as fast once rents are above the cap. However, the level of the cap depends on where rents were when the restriction was brought in, not on their *level* compared to rent guidelines. This was seen as unfair, particularly by those who had kept rents down close to the guideline levels:

In retrospect we would have been better off raising rents even higher during the early 1990s. (OLLAH)

It also does not allow us to vary our rents much. We have big variations in our stock so would think it was fair to raise some properties more than others. (USLAH)

One of the authorities had a high cap as a result of having had to raise rents in previous years to cover leasing payments: 'When rents were set and slowed down they were set at actual levels rather than guideline levels which was beneficial for us. We weren't aware then that the cap would be so stringent, but the system and events did benefit us' (ILLAH).

Management and maintenance allowances

At the end of the 1980s management and maintenance allowances were based on each authority's previous spending levels, again favouring those which had previously been relatively high spenders. The DETR wanted to make the system more 'formulaic', and commissioned research on the relative costs of different kinds of property, partly based on regression analysis of previous spending by authorities as a whole. However, such attempts to take the politics out of the system were not entirely successful: 'The reweighting [of maintenance allowances] transferred a lot of resources away from flats into houses, which London authorities resisted. The department then looked into the effect of social conditions . . . in order to compensate this loss. . . . in areas of high vandalism an authority could get 20 per cent extra' (DETR-H).

Establishing management allowances was even harder, and only the proportion of flats and measures of sparsity were found significant. Because of data problems, 'getting a significant regression is a matter of luck', and 'It is difficult to iron out the London effect' (DETR-H). This leads to deep suspicion outside London: 'They've tried to come up with a formula to calculate M&M, but it just shows how the system favours

London. Everybody knows that flats and tower blocks were included so that London would hold onto its share' (UNLAH).

More generally, there seemed little confidence in the way allowances are set, mainly because of their level:

There is no way we can stick to these. We do our best, but they are generally unrealistic. (USLAH)

You have to leave it to local discretion as to what level of M&M people want. A formula assumes that every area is going to have the same type of management. (OLCE)

Equity: Distribution of Capital Funds

Capital allocations and the GNI

With local authorities allowed to do very little by way of new building, the capital allocations system is mainly concerned with distributing limited resources for the renovation of existing stock. This depends on both the 'Generalized Needs Index' (GNI) and the housing investment programme (HIP) bids put in by each authority. But authorities are also involved in fighting for allocations to housing associations for new developments. Apart from complaints about their overall low level, capital allocations tend to be seen by authorities in terms of a fight between regions over available resources:

Within social housing we must question whether investment in the North East and West is sensible. (ILLAH)

It seems odd, but generally changes that benefit areas outside London bring most benefit to us. . . . it would probably be best for us to side with authorities outside the London area. (OLLAH)

The northern authority stressed the 'value for money' of building where costs are low, an argument which sounds rather weak if compared to those based on need:

The system tries to give a bit to everybody who says they need capital investment. But that's not the best way to spend the money. . . . I don't agree with the view that our need is less than in the South. Yes, it's different but no less severe. . . . We need to be careful not to assume that if somewhere has low overall demand it should be written off. If the government wants more units and output per pound than the sensible thing would be to build up where costs are far less. (UNLAH)

There was, however, a fair degree of cynicism about the whole process:

I do wonder whether the process is worth the effort either side puts into it. . . . We tend to fit our strategy to [look like] the department's strategy not vice versa. . . . It is true to say that we are stronger on presentation than content. (ILLAH).

Don't know much about national distribution—we have enough problems dealing with our own HRA. (USLAH)

Lack of a ring-fence for housing capital

Finally, both central and local respondents raised issues around the way in which capital allocations granted for housing can be used by authorities for other purposes:

The capital control system is quite flexible, as an approval for a housing project can be sneaked out of the ring fence and used for something completely different. (DETR-H)

There is the question of why the HRA is ring-fenced but capital allocations aren't. Nobody tries to justify that part of the system. (OLLAH)

The capital regime is one that can be breached, and a lot of authorities have not protected their allocations. (ILLAH)

But this issue did not worry everyone: 'The [HRA] ring fence was a good idea, but we're not really concerned that it does not extend to capital' (UNLAH).

Efficiency: Current Spending

Effects of the ring-fence

The big change at the end of the 1980s was the 'ring-fence' around local authority housing revenue accounts. This restricted authorities by stopping transfers into the HRA from general funds, but also had potential 'passive incentive' efficiency advantages (see Chapter 7), as savings within the housing department now stayed within the housing department. In general, despite the restrictions involved, it was seen as part of the process which led to local authority housing departments seeing themselves as more autonomous and business-like:

Ring-fencing did make people think about costs a lot more. (ILLAH)

Ring-fencing was probably a good thing. We were in favour of it because we could keep our own income. It made us more aware of our incomes and costs. The line used to be very blurred. (OLLAH)

The ring-fence on HRA was a good idea.... We saw it as way of controlling our own destiny... It probably did make us more aware of what we were doing and how much we were spending, though I can't remember cutting much costs as a result. (OLCE)

It was just another way of restricting our spending... But it's not all negative. Thinking about our own costs and having to stand on our own two feet has made us feel stronger. (UNLAH)

Trade-off between management and maintenance and rents

An important feature of the current subsidy regime as it was originally introduced was that authorities were free *not* to follow rent guidelines if they wanted to spend more (usually) or less than their management and maintenance allowances. At the margin, a pound of extra spending per unit would mean that rents would be higher by a pound, leaving a straightforward link between the authority's costs and the rents it would have to charge. When the authorities we spoke to had consulted tenants, they favoured higher spending:

Post ring-fencing we were able to go to tenants and say for rent increases we would improve services. (ILLAH)

They always used to choose higher rents with more improvements, [although] they didn't always go for the largest increase. (USLAH)

Tenants always chose more M&M spending instead of less. That encouraged us to know that we were on the right lines. (OLLAH)

From central government's point of view, however, the problem was that most of the cost of this kind of decision was carried by the housing benefit bill—only a minority of tenants were actually paying any price for this trade-off. The new 'rent cap' ends this, and has had clear effects on behaviour:

... now we have to stick to guideline increases. That is a severe restriction—there is no way to get around it because raising rents for only non-HB tenants is not really an option. (OLCE)

Theoretically we could [raise rents more than guideline increases], but when we explained to the members what it would mean it was ruled out very quickly. (USLAH)

We explained to members that it was like buying one pint of beer, but having to pay for three to do so.... Limiting increases in line with the guideline is most 'subsidy efficient'. (ILLAH)

Many people see the rent cap as vindictive. Government can talk about better planning, but restricting what we do on rents defeats the whole point. (UNLAH)

Efficiency: Capital Spending

Cost control

The local authority housing subsidy system offers no subsidy (except that coming through tenants' housing benefit receipt) on variations in current spending, but subsidy adjusts to absorb all the costs of additional borrowing. In other words, once an authority has won a capital allocation (credit approval), the borrowing this allows is effectively free, and there is no direct pressure on capital costs in the way there is on current spending (in contrast to the pressures now facing housing associations on their capital costs). 'On capital there is no incentive to save credit approvals—the incentive is to spend it all straight away.' (DETR-H). While conceding this, authorities point to the other pressures within a tightly constrained total:

There is political pressure to control capital costs . . . The big driver to spending decisions is tenant power and how their associations vote. . . . There is not much in the system for efficiency; the main checks are political. (ILLAH)

The pressure to control costs come from us having a limited budget and because we have to tell the tenants how we are spending the money. (OLLAH)

Planning for future repairs

Another major difference between the financial regimes for local authorities and housing associations is that the latter now have to plan for and take into account the costs of periodic major repairs to their stock (as well as having the freedom to borrow to pay for some of the cost of this if their finances allow). Local authorities are in the opposite position. They are not free to make their own decisions on major repairs, but instead have to persuade central government to grant a credit approval. Once this is given, however, the repairs are effectively free, because of the way loan charges affect HRA subsidy.

The system does not allow rational planning . . . We are reluctant to over-programme for the future because we are never sure about resources. (ILLAH)

We don't do that now because we can't. Guidelines are too strict, and we were penalised because our HRA and debt levels looked better. There is no incentive to improve your HRA. (OLCE)

All the moves want to move us closer to housing association behaviour . . . acting more business-like . . . [But] guidelines restrict what we can and are able to do . . . there is little incentive to do more or less. (UNLAH)

Transfers

As well as issues around the treatment of major repairs, authorities also reported problems with other aspects of managing their capital stock, such as disincentives to sell properties, resulting from controls on the use of receipts (ILLAH). On the other hand, several mentioned the financial incentives to transfer stock either through Large Scale Voluntary Transfer (LSVT) arrangements or through the (now discontinued) 'dowries' for partial stock transfer which had been available under the Estates Renewal Challenge Fund (ERCF). In some cases, such financial pressures were, however, secondary to strong preferences from councillors to retain ownership of the stock:

Members are worried that if they give up ownership, what policy influence would they have left? (ILLAH)

[There is] strong resistance to giving up stock. They feel that housing is an important council function. (USLAH)

There is a clear incentive for us to transfer . . . We are off-loading bits at a time . . . If we were to become a company could do so much more. We would have greater financial and administrative freedom. . . . The incentive to transfer is far greater since the [rent cap] came in. . . . If we were to transfer our stock we could raise rents to make improvements. We used to have this freedom . . . I can't see how much tighter government can pull the belt. (OLCE)

In Chapter 11 we look at the views of one of the associations formed from the transfer of its local authority's entire stock.

Conclusion

This summary of local authority views of their funding system shows few of the shared objectives found in the interviews with health service providers. On the other hand some of the concerns for 'local shares of the cake' echo views in local education authorities. The final part of the next chapter compares and contrasts views within the two parts of social housing in more detail.

11

A Runaway Train? Housing Associations

This chapter explores the views of those in the housing association (or registered social landlord, RSL) sector about their funding system, paralleling the discussion of local authority funding in Chapter 10, and broken down between topics as shown in Table 10.1.

Equity: Current Finance

Overall equity issues

Central Housing Corporation officials were clear that the equity aims of the system were not to be seen in terms of distribution between intermediaries, but between their tenants: 'The concern is not over an equitable distribution between RSLs, but over housing outcomes' (HC). By contrast, some regional offices—predominantly concerned with the capital allocations side of the business (discussed below)—saw things differently:

Fairness in a political sense is presumably happiness for the greatest number of providers. (HCRO1)

Not interested in equity between RSLs is the corporation's public line, but there is an undeclared eye kept on the process to ensure that competition between RSLs is kept high. (HCRO2)

As with local authority housing departments, some associations struggled to identify the equity aims of the system, and when they did so also tended to think in geographical terms and in terms of capital allocations rather than the rent and current finance implications of grant-setting:

The objectives of the social housing sector have never been clearly defined. For example, if we could decide on what an affordable rent level was, the appropriate grant or subsidy level could be provided. (RSBHA)

Does equity mean geographic equity, or are we talking about rents between private, council, and housing association rents within one area. How you define equity is going to have huge implications on policy—that's if we agree that equity, however, defined, *is* the overall aim—I'm not sure I'd agree with that. (UNBHA)

Local authority versus housing association rents

Rather than comparisons with local authority rents, the associations we spoke to were most concerned about relativities against private rents, particularly outside the South—understandably perhaps, given that if association rents are above market levels they will not be able to let their property. They were also at pains to explain the higher level of association rents as resulting from differences in grant regimes:

I don't think the difference between local authority and association rents is an issue. We all agree that we have different roles, different funding regimes, operate along very different principles, and have vastly different stock and historic debt levels. You've got to remember that we have to cover ourselves for major repairs. (OLBHA)

We do our best to compare ourselves with similar associations, but I don't really think that local authority stock [gives] valid comparisons. Generally speaking the local authority stock is far less desirable—it's old and not as well maintained. (OLSHA)

In the regions HA rents are not that low compared to the private sector . . . Associations pay a lot more attention to private sector rents in the North—this is not really an issue in the South-East. (NHF)

Some, however, saw more of a potential problem:

Rent differences between authorities and associations could be a future problem, but over the last few years the demand has been unending. (RSBHA)

Rents [are] a major issue for us as an association. We have to consider comparable rents in other sectors, which may be lower for historic reasons. There's not much we can do about it without higher grant. . . . Local authorities tend to be a bit smug in telling us how high our rents are. (UNBHA)

Rent increase limitation

As with councils, recent limits on overall housing association rent bills—now limited to the increase in the RPI plus 1 per cent, on pain of loss of new capital allocations from the Housing Corporation—were a major concern, particularly the way they had been introduced. We discuss the potential efficiency effects of this constraint below, but this was not the main central objective: 'The Department of Social Security were interested in fixing rent increases to RPI plus one because of its effects on the housing benefit bill, not on association behaviour' (HC).

Again, as with councils, the limits were introduced on the basis of where individual association rent levels had got to, rather than some formula which related to their absolute levels. This implies tighter constraints on associations which had previously kept their rents down.

We should be looking at absolute levels of rents rather than RPI plus one. (HCRO2)

RPI plus one is a crude attack. (USSHA)

RPI plus one is rough and ready. . . . Our rents did rise quickly after 1992, but so did everybody else's. Unlike local authorities we could do that. It would have been stupid not to. (ILSHA)

People's outlook is now very different to a couple of years ago, [when] nobody thought formal restrictions on rents would be introduced. (ILBHA)

We didn't bump up rents too much during the early 1990s as I suppose we could have done. (UNSHA)

In some respects, the subsector may be better treated, however: 'Rents certainly are a good example. With local authorities the government instantly try to stop the runaway train by putting a brick wall across the track. With us they first try the brakes, then try cutting back the fuel or changing the signalling, and only as a last resort do they shunt us into the sidings' (OLBHA).

Fair versus assured rents

As the new system of housing association finance was introduced, two kinds of tenant were created: 'secure' tenants, in place before January 1989, entitled to 'fair' rents set by the local rent officer; and more recent 'assured' tenants, whose rents are set by the association. Assured rents are generally higher than fair rents, although some associations have more recently put pressure on rent officers to increase fair rents while restraining assured rents to achieve 'convergence':

The bottom line is that tenants are confused about the differences in rent levels and why they exist. (RSBHA)

We do have an estate built in the 1920s without grant that is mostly fair rent, but there is, in its midst, new build which is not. This means that there are extreme rent differences very close to one another. (USSHA)

There is a difference between the two types of tenancy, which is hard to explain when we have next-door neighbours paying very different rents. On new build we don't have that problem. (UNSHA)

But this is not necessarily seen as a major issue:

Rent convergence isn't a big concern. (ILBHA)

We don't lose sleep over these differences, but in an ideal world I would rather have less fair rents than more. . . . the whole idea [of fair rents] seems so dated now. (OLBHA)

Affordability

In setting rents for assured tenants, the results are supposed to be 'affordable' to low-paid tenants in work. What this means has never been officially specified, although the Housing Corporation based some of its grant-setting on the basis of rents taking no more than one-third of income, after allowing for housing benefit. However, 'grant competition' in the mid-1990s led to strong upward pressure on rents as associations tried to secure new capital allocations. Only in the late 1990s did the brakes begin to go on:

Since 1995 the perverse results of this system have been officially accepted: pushing up rents led to a higher housing benefit bill, causing a poverty trap, and problems with the social mix of RSL tenants. . . . [But] when push comes to shove, politicians of all colours will also choose low capital bids over lower rents. Their concern, like that of most associations, is to ensure that rents do not become embarrassingly high. (HC)

Associations have varied in their view of high rents:

We've tried to get non-affordable rents down, with a huge related national cost, but I would favour lower rents even at cost of development. (USBHA)

We know that we are creating a benefit trap, but the corporation still shows 70 per cent of occupants going into housing association property are on housing benefit. (TFRLA)

No one has ever said what an affordable rent is. (TFRHA)

We get told very clearly that our rents are too high in this region. I don't think we are too bad, but we could do very little even if we thought otherwise. . . . Of course we are concerned with the poverty trap, just as we don't want to see our projects becoming social ghettos. . . . I do not think we are to blame for this type of problem. (UNBHA)

It's more important to provide good quality housing than bad homes for cheap rents. (UNSHA)

London associations, in particular, were reluctant to see rents as the problem:

Demand is high and supply limited. Rents reflect our costs, especially of land and construction. I think it's only fair. (OLBHA)

Housing benefit causes a poverty trap where it's not worth working. I don't think rents are the real problem in that system. (OLSHA)

Equity: Capital Allocations and the HNI

Many more of the opinions we were given related to questions around capital allocations, perhaps confirming the extent to which the concerns of associations are still, for many, 'development led'. In these allocations, the impact and use of the Housing Needs Index (HNI) is central. This index is used to distribute allocations for new development both between regions, and at subregional level between developments in each local authority area (subject to a discretionary variation up or down by 20 per cent at the discretion of the Housing Corporation regional office). This system was criticized by respondents across the country and by corporation officials, particularly on grounds of inflexibility:

HNI is a historic-based indicator, whereas [this southern region] faces problems of what is going to happen in the future. There is no future need element incorporated into the formula. . . . We end up making lots of small capital allocations to local authorities . . . There is a belief that HNI spreads it too thin, because everyone gets something. There is no zero HNI rating, so the government avoids too many complaints. (HCRO3)

An intellectual construct from beginning would assume that multiple deprivation should be rewarded . . . we have equally deprived areas and estates in this region [to Liverpool and London] but other patches in those local authority areas then raise the poor ones up when averaged out. . . . HNI is concerned with geographic equity, but the 20 per cent penalty/reward is not sufficient to enable equity of treatment in reality . . . Authorities are guaranteed in reality 85–115 per cent of their score. There is little variance in reality. (HCRO1)

Although, by contrast: 'The variance between authorities is getting lower because things are getting better . . . We must question whether we should punish an intermediate body if an area still has clear housing needs.' (HCRO2) From an association point of view, the origins of the HNI were strikingly obscure:

The HNI is steeped in politics and in mystery . . . If I were not involved in one of the National Housing Federation committees I would not get the national picture at all. (RSBHA)

I don't think anybody outside the corporation's staff could tell you how HNI is constructed. (UNBHA)

Most people say that HNI is meaningless and is set by politicians [but] if you came up with something new it may be politically unacceptable. (USSHA)

I know that the HNI is an indicator of need, and most of the indicators that go into it. But changes aren't explained, and we are supposed to trust that allocating resources by HNI is an accurate reflection of need. (UNSHA)

Southern associations were critical of the way resources were spread around the country:

HNI ends up giving new provision money in areas that don't need housing and does not take into account demand and supply. (USSHA)

There is serious housing need in the South and Midlands. In the North it is a problem of stock condition. (USBHA)

HNI also fails to reflect the cost of developing projects in inner London. (ILBHA)

Strictly speaking we have severe need whereas they don't. But it wouldn't be acceptable to see the North getting nothing, so we construct a formula which creates need where there are already enough houses. (OLBHA)

By contrast, northern associations pointed to other factors:

We clearly need money for housing, although nobody up here would suggest that we have the same demand problem that colleagues face down south. (UNBHA)

My problem with HNI is how it penalizes areas that need serious renovation. . . . Vacant properties are a problem, not a solution. HNI assumes that people will move into empty properties, which is obviously not the case. (UNSHA)

Some pointed to the way in which allocations to *associations* in an area were reduced if the *local authority* was judged by the regional office to be inefficient or to have the wrong priorities:

I can see why they want to do that, but I'm not sure an area should suffer at the discretion of an official, even if the local authority is useless. (UNBHA)

This is supposed to be an objective basis for local allocations, but it justifies favouritism. (OLSHA)

Before the [20 per cent variation] incentives it was a valid process . . . I would regard anything departing from need as heinous—including the introduction of incentives. (USBHA)

As with other parts of the system, most respondents fatalistically regarded the system as a given within which they had to live:

Battles were always lost. . . . [Lobbying about HNI] is a complete waste of time. (USBHA)

What would we replace it with? I can't see anything better being proposed. It's easy to criticize, but a lot harder to come up with something concrete in its place. (ILSHA)

We don't make a song and dance about HNI because there's not much we can practically do about it. (UNSHA)

Efficiency: Current Spending

Incentives before rent-bidding

While equity concerns appeared far less salient to social landlords than to actors in the other sectors we examined, efficiency loomed much larger in people's responses. For housing associations this reflected the way in which the reforms of the late 1980s had as one of their explicit aims to improve efficiency, particularly on the capital side, by removing the open-ended nature of what was then housing association grant (HAG). Up to the reforms of the late 1980s extra capital spending could simply mean higher grant, and the reforms ended this. However, at the same time rent controls on associations (through the fair rent system) were lifted, leaving them to set their own rents. This removed what had previously been a 'hard budget constraint' on associations' current spending. Through the first half of the 1990s, capital grant levels were cut back, and rents rose rapidly. This gathered pace when 'grant bidding' changed the allocation system so that associations could bid to carry out developments with lower grant, with the lowest bidders winning the allocations.

. . . the Treasury squeezed surpluses as tight as they could. The unintentional incentive of this was to raise rents. Rent increases above the rate of inflation were encouraged, until the rent scares of the mid-90s. . . . There were complaints from the government side [to the rent officers] that rents were not rising fast enough. So fair rents did rise quickly—well above the rate of inflation. (NHF)

Everything was concentrated on capital grants, with little or no interest shown in rents. . . . This was in the context of the late 1980s policy of pushing up rents in the belief that they had previously been too low. Rents were allowed to take the strain. (HC)

Associations agreed that there were initially few restraints on rising rents:

They took their eye off the ball as far as rents were concerned . . . Initially rents did not rise quickly because the grant system was generous enough to keep them low. But slowly rents did take the strain as grant levels decreased. There was no consideration of what this was doing to housing benefit. (USSHA)

It's true that there weren't many dissenting voices because most of our tenants were on HB—so someone else was picking up the tab—and the Housing Corporation were only looking at the grant rate. The bottom line was that more houses were being built for less grant. (ILBHA)

All the political pressure was to make grant competition a success. Nobody really cared about how that was achieved. (ILSHA)

I remember that it was a big decision for us to start multiplying rents in the way we did, but if we hadn't then we'd have lost out on development. (OLBHA)

Lots of the problems now stem from what many thought were the strengths of the system. I'm talking about falling grant rates, which led to the current rent policy. (OLSHA)

In retrospect I don't know how we thought we could have gotten away with the rent increases we were banking on. . . . nobody was stopping us. . . . Lenders' eyes were popping out of their sockets and the corporation were quite happy to join on the bandwagon. (OLBHA)

As with some other issues, northern associations saw things from a different perspective, especially as tenants have more option to move elsewhere:

It's too easy to say that we were implementing reckless rent policies and life was free and easy before rent-bidding. That may well be the case further south, but we have always faced the restraint of lower demand and rents in other sectors. (UNBHA)

There weren't really any severe pressures on cost while we could do what we wanted with rents. This doesn't mean we took advantage or abused this freedom. Higher rents did allow us to make lower grant bids, but it also allowed us to provide high quality services. (UNSHA)

In essence, associations had previously been in much the same position as schools and health authorities now are as far as their current spending was concerned: they had to live within a pretty well fixed budget given by management and maintenance allowances set by the Housing Corporation. The moves intended (in part) to increase efficiency on the capital side meant that this constraint went, and with it some of the passive incentives on the revenue side.

Incentives since rent-bidding

Much more recently, the government and corporation have introduced progressively tighter constraints on association rents. This was first through 'rent-bidding', under which competition for allocations depended not only on the grant requested, but also on the level of rents promised (with the implied future cost of housing benefit brought into the equation), and then through the 'RPI plus one' limit on associations' total rent income if they are to receive allocations. Most respondents could see the arguments for this, but differed as to what effect it was having.

Given the type of animals associations are, and [if] the signals are strong enough, then pulling the purse string really does work. (HC)

The current rent policy provides a far stronger incentive for us to lower costs. We are looking in particular at weaknesses in our organizational structure, and how our regional offices may be replicating services that could be centralized with a calling system. So the present environment is putting pressures on M&M costs that simply were not there a few years ago. (RSBHA)

The RPI plus one era has brought us back to earth with a bump. We do have to look at costs again and make a judgement on what level of M&M is appropriate. (ILBHA)

Others were more sceptical:

It is right that rents are controlled as part of the allocation of new resources, but it is too late to try to do so now—the horse has bolted six years ago, when we bumped up rents like there was no tomorrow. (USSHA)

Recent policy has made us look again at our expenditure, but it confirmed that we are good value. Savings could be made by centralizing further customer services, but that would have side effects in our relationship with tenants. . . . I can see why [rent-bidding] was done, but . . . it seems that RSLs are not trusted. The assumption behind the control is that we cannot behave ourselves. (UNBHA)

We haven't suddenly become more efficient because of rent bidding—incentives to cut costs have been there for years. . . . I can see why you ask that question, but the care of our tenants and quality of service we provide are non-negotiable. (UNSHA)

Others pointed to the way in which factors which were not directly related to the grant system put pressures on associations to run efficiently, such as 'benchmarking' comparisons with others:

There is a move from an aggressive rent ratcheting process to a more holistic approach where all costs are considered together with benchmarking. (HCRO3)

Performance indicators focus on comparisons: regulation plays as much a part as financial considerations. (TFRHA)

We feel pressure from other associations. We work closely with the regional office and the NHF who promote best practice. Pressure comes from them promoting all the latest techniques. (UNBHA)

The Housing Corporation agreed with this: 'There should be less concern about the detail of the formula in comparison with the messages sent by it down to the RSLs. It is the messages and impressions sent out that are really important' (HC).

But associations differed on the clarity of these 'messages and impressions':

The Corporation has become less subtle with their techniques of letting us know what they want. They are about as subtle as sledgehammers. (ILBHA)

Everything in this world is done through Chinese whispers. (UNBHA)

Efficiency: Capital Spending

Incentives before and after 1989

The key change in the system of capital finance for new housing association developments came in 1989, when grants stopped being a residual element after a calculation had been made of what loan an association could afford to service given the level of fair rents set for it. Instead, the percentage of capital cost covered by grant would be fixed, with part of the effect of any variation in costs covered by the association. For larger associations, the Housing Corporation encouraged a 'tariff' system, where grant was fixed, and all marginal cost variations were carried by (or benefited) the association. Later in the 1990s the system moved further towards competitive bidding, and actual grant rates fell further as associations were prepared to undercut one another to secure developments. As discussed above, higher rents took much of the strain of falling grant rates. However, one of the main justifications for the system had been that it would increase incentives for capital costs to be controlled. As the system took effect, capital costs did indeed fall, but our respondents disagreed on the extent to which the incentives in the new system and the general fall in building costs at the same time were responsible. More weight was put on the former from the centre:

Undoubtedly there have been efficiency gains under the new system above that which would have been achieved under the old formula. Figures have been helped by the depression in the construction industry, but the Housing Corporation does year on year analyses, which show costs falling since 1990 however you measure it. . . . the figures [have] come down more than all the other external factors related to the construction industry. There have been real efficiency gains in terms of cost and development lead times. (HC)

At regional level, the view was rather more qualified: 'The change in the late eighties was partly to do with development time, partly to do with pulling the purse strings. But the main effect and objective in this region concerned some esoteric concept of transferring risk. This did take place, and the change did alter behaviour' (HCRO1).

The balance of views amongst associations agreed that their had been some efficiency effects from the new system:

[It was] a very positive move to transfer risk—the total opposite of the risk-free environment of pre-1988. Pre-1988, good schemes that were expensive, faced a long time-scale and looked pretty, and were a nightmare to maintain were still built. Nobody really analysed the costs involved. Books would always be balanced in the end. (USSHA)

Costs did fall after 1988. It's unfair to suggest that rents took all the slack or that the slump was responsible for all the savings made. (ILSHA)

Grant system incentives did seem to be working in that less public money was being spent on each project, but major external factors also helped greatly—tumbling property prices and falling interest rates. (NHF)

There is an incentive for associations to lower costs, but this was not the immediate effect of the 1988 Act. . . . General costs were decreasing during the early-90s, and had little to do with government policy, but rather with the general conditions of the housing and construction markets. Moves towards 'design and build', for example, did not save that much but did help avoiding overruns, and lessened HA risk. (RSBHA)

This view was not universal, however:

There was a concern about costs in the old system—if you weren't reasonably efficient then you were affected. Capital costs did fall—but it's falling costs not remarkable efficiency from HAs that had the impact . . . [Parts of] the previous system created inefficiency—waiting for blocks of money from the Corporation. [It was] a nice piece of management by the Treasury—competition was inevitable. But it was mainly paid for by housing benefit. (USBHA)

It is difficult to say that we've become more efficient given that we got a lot of help from the economy. (OLSHA)

Planning for future repairs

A major change in the last decade has been the way in which funding for future major repairs has been withdrawn from associations, first for new developments since 1989, and now effectively for all association stock. In effect associations are now 'on their own' in thinking about the long-term cost of the housing they provide. This has both contributed to their higher rents and changed the way they operate:

What affected them was that there was no longer funding from the Housing Corporation for major repairs. The cost of repairs now dominates associations' thinking. (NHF)

We hadn't a clue about running a business ten years ago. We didn't need to think further than a year or two down the line. That all changed pretty quickly. We had to buck up our ideas or we would have lost out on the gold rush. (ILSHA)

We have to plan for the long term. . . . Without realistic projections, we wouldn't get the money. (OLSHA)

But long-term planning requires a stable environment:

We must also repeat the reasons why it is in associations' own interest to keep a close eye on stock condition and to plan ahead. . . . There is little planning of how the current system will affect things even in five years time because it is always changing. (HCRO1)

If they are serious about us planning for the future, they would give us some assurances that they aren't going to turn round in a couple of years and change all our predictions. (ILSHA)

Competition naturally costs associations money and it probably comes out of long-term repairs—it's something the corporation probably need to look at. (RSBHA)

The actual bill [for major repairs in the future] will be much higher than either associations' reserves or potential major repairs HAG would have been. . . . Whole life costs are beyond the means of most associations—but not this one. (USBHA)

Becoming more business-like

Overall, many respondents stressed the way in which the changes—including the involvement of private lenders in raising part of the capital they need—had made associations more business-like:

Costs did fall over the last decade. This was partly to do with the recession in the housing industry, but a lot to do with being more business-like in our attitude. It's very easy to forget how amateur we were [before] in all that we did. (ILSHA)

Whatever we would have liked to believe, associations before 1988 looked a lot like council housing departments today. We have had to speed development up, produce business plans and become far more like the private sector. It has wide-ranging implications in our attitude and professionalism. . . . The introduction of private finance forced us to draw up business plans and make forecasts . . . it is a very positive result from the change in system. (OLBHA)

The need to talk to private lenders was said to have had significant effects:

The private sector is a harder task-master than the Housing Corporation. We now make annual 30 year plans—it's the minimum requirement for our lenders. (ILSHA)

Having to work with lenders in the private sector made us realize how far we had to travel. . . . We were thrown in at the deep end, but we survived. (UNSHA)

Associations didn't have commercial input and couldn't see the pitfalls they were creating for themselves. . . . They had boards full of members who had never worked in the private sector. . . . Until 1988 no one had done a three year plan, let alone a 30 year projection. (USSHA)

The transfer association we spoke to stressed this feature as the main effect of transfer. As the council they left put it, 'After transfer they certainly sharpened their pencils' (TFRLA).

It's a completely different world, much more exciting, with much more independence and less bureaucracy than with the local authority context. [What takes] a lot of my time now are the financial issues of running the business (much more of a 'business' than with the council). In the council someone else did the finance. Now the buck stops with the finance director—there's much more feeling that the buck stops with someone. Before transfer I had the naïve view that I would be able to sit back—it was 'only housing'. In practice I have never worked so hard . . . We're much more conscious of resources being limited.' (TFRHA)

Grant levels and future development

Finally, given the context in which we were talking to associations in the course of 1998, with grants at lower levels than in the early 1990s and restrictions on rent increases, several of our respondents suggested that social housing grant no longer offered a strong enough incentive to continue to develop:

We find that associations are withdrawing from the system. . . . The corporation view the current system as being worth the pressure of a few associations withdrawing from the sector, but they should be worried about the signal that sends. (RSBHA)

We found that some large associations . . . hardly bid at all [in this region] last year. (HCRO1)

There is a real fear amongst friends in the sector that more and more are choosing not to develop . . . Of course the corporation can't see this danger because they just look at the competition for grant. (OLSHA)

Some stuff is worth going for, but there's a lot that isn't worth the effort. (UNBHA)

However, some Housing Corporation regional offices thought that this was just crying wolf:

The bid process is hugely over-subscribed . . . RSLs would not put much effort into this process due to costs and risks if the benefits weren't still significant. (HCRO3)

I don't believe them when they say there is nothing left to cut from construction costs. (HCRO2)

Interestingly, the language used by some was that new social housing was just one part of an association's overall 'business', and that other opportunities were now more interesting: 'There are other types of business opportunities for us—e.g. NHS trusts and health authorities, or PFI [Private Finance Initiative] for social housing. . . . HAG is now very poor value for associations and it would take millions of investment to make current rent levels viable' (RSBHA).

Conclusions

As the discussion in this chapter and the previous one has shown, funding for social housing raises very different issues from those involved in the other sectors we have examined. First, social landlords are trading bodies involved in raising money by charging for services (through rent) as well as receiving government grants. Second, capital assets are much more important than in the other sectors, raising difficult issues around subsidizing their cost and allocating funds for new construction or renewal. Third, the potential importance of rents is greatly reduced by the operation of the housing benefit system, which makes them largely irrelevant to the majority of tenants.

Our most striking finding was how alien—even baffling—the idea of an 'equity' objective was to local respondents. Funding systems for councils and associations simply were not seen in terms of an attempt to achieve fairness between tenants. Several said they had never seen an official statement of this kind. This is perhaps unsurprising, given the irrationality of the differences in rents between council and housing association tenants, and within the housing association sector, and given the way in which the principles underlying council rent guidelines have been obscured.

Almost as striking was how little respondents seemed to see the fairness or otherwise of the funding formulae for different tenants as an issue. Housing benefit, of course, wipes out the significance of most rent variations, and the rent variations for other tenants are seen—with at least partial justice—as caused by central policies. Councils seemed pleased their rents were not as high as associations, while associations were pleased to have the extra resources their higher rents allowed.

In strong contrast to the health sector, achieving an accepted 'scientific' basis for meeting differential needs for spending on different kinds of stock had proved difficult. For the centre, dealing with a relatively small number of local authorities, this was clearly made more difficult by the potential for 'gaming' behaviour by authorities: the history of housing subsidies in Britain summarized in Chapters 3 and 6 is littered with examples of incremental changes meaning that high spending or rents lead to a higher base in the next round. Actual past spending is therefore seen as an unreliable guide to spending needs, but this makes establishing acceptable allowances difficult.

Where equity was raised at local level it was mostly either in terms of the unfairness of the constraints on councils, preventing them raising money in the way associations could, or in terms of geographical equity in the allocation of new capital between areas. Indeed the issue of allocation between local authority areas was mentioned frequently—particularly the way in which the GNI and HNI systems appear devised to give 'something to everyone', and the issue of needs for new building in the North versus the South. It was surprising in the summer of 1998 to hear a northern authority arguing that allocating new housing to the North would be 'good value for money', just as the extent of over-supply in some areas relative to other parts of the country was becoming very clear (Power and Mumford 1999). On the other hand, central policy towards new housing association building had followed a similar 'numbers game' logic through most of the 1990s, so this view is perhaps not so unusual.

On the other hand, respondents were generally favourable to the Conservative reforms which had made social landlords more 'business-like'. For councils, this was the autonomy given to housing departments by 'ring-fencing' of the housing revenue account (HRA) in the late 1980s. For associations it was a much more radical transformation into businesses which set their own prices, raised private capital, and made trade-offs between short- and long-term costs, thinking in terms of long-term financial flows rather than just annual budgets. Although the higher rents accompanying this were regretted, few respondents wanted to go back to the 'old world' of association finance, and several council respondents would clearly have liked to have been in an equivalent environment, rather than trapped with annual current budgets and being supplicants to central government for credit approvals for major repairs funding.

In this sense, efficiency was an important concern. The balance of opinion was also that the associations' capital funding reforms (which removed the perverse incentive that capital spending was at the margin effectively free) had achieved *some* efficiency gains, although the state of the building market in the early 1990s was credited with much of the fall in unit costs. To this extent an efficiency objective of the reforms was realized. However, those reforms simultaneously decontrolled association rents for new tenants, and in the first half of the 1990s central government was content to see rents rise rapidly, apparently with some ill-defined idea that higher rents would in some way improve allocative efficiency (and paying little attention to the effects on housing benefit costs). But this meant that associations moved away from the productive efficiency pressures of a 'hard budget constraint' on their recurrent spending of the kind facing them before (or indeed facing schools under LMS funding or fundholding GPs). Given that—in most parts of the country—social rents are still below private ones, and that most tenants are on housing benefit, both councils and associations faced relatively soft budget constraints, and so attenuated efficiency pressures, through most of the 1990s. It was only very recently that a hard budget constraint was reintroduced through rent-capping for councils or, the 'RPI plus one' limit on rental income (although northern associations already faced much clearer pressures as their rents were not so far below the market).

In terms of the way the funding systems operate, views from

landlords were marked by fatalism. Funding was seen as political, random, and endlessly changing, in complete contrast to the NHS. This left an attitude that there was nothing which could be done about them, with little interest in negotiating about how they were set. It was the 'sledgehammer' of rent-capping which apparently had the clearest effect on behaviour rather than more subtle aspects of funding. However, the same sledgehammer raised new equity issues as the effective rent caps apply simply where rents happen to have got to for each landlord, rather than to any underlying principle.

PART IV

The Overall Pattern

12

Common Patterns

Three Services with a Common Approach?

Earlier chapters have examined the development of funding mechanisms, the ways in which they currently operate in England, and views about these mechanisms among both policy élites and those implementing services at the local level. One of the main reasons for undertaking this study was the development in recent years within health, education, and housing of two tiers of formula-based allocations from central government to an intermediary body and then from the intermediary body to the local level. In the past, there had only been a single formula for health and education, allocating money from the centre to local/health authorities.

The resources allocated from central government through intermediary bodies to local institutions take the form of *public* money. For health and education, most of the resources allocated are for revenue expenditure, although there have also been allocations of doctors and teachers through separate initatives. In the case of health, the money is derived from national taxpayers and cascades down the bureaucracy into the hands of trusts and GPs. In education, resources are allocated in a cascade which is very similar to health, except that local authorities add local taxation (about 25 per cent of the total) to money derived from national taxation (75 per cent of the total) before the resulting total is allocated to schools.

In housing, the position is significantly different. First, capital resources are a far larger proportion of the total than is the case for health and education and, second, for housing associations a substantial proportion of the resources devoted to capital spending is raised from the private sector. Therefore, the money allocated from Whitehall to housing associations is a smaller share of associations' overall resources than would be the case for, say, a health authority or school. The funding of housing for both local authorities and housing associations is profoundly affected by resources from housing benefit in a way that has no parallel for health or education.

Interviews in all three sectors sought to test how individuals involved at the centre, in intermediary bodies, and at the local level understood the processes of the funding arrangements outlined above. Interviewees were asked about their understanding of the objectives of the respective funding systems. They were also asked about the way in which these systems influenced their spending: were there incentives towards efficiency, for example?

One of the conclusions to emerge from the large amount of interviewing undertaken for this book project was the free-standing nature of the three funding systems. Although health, education, and social housing are key elements in the UK's welfare state, run by ministers and civil servants and funded predominantly by taxpayers' resources, the three systems exist with virtually no reference to each other. The project team organized two major seminars for the key individuals at the central and intermediary levels of the systems. Although the officials who attended these seminars were involved in similar services and working for various elements of 'the state', they had relatively little contact with each other.

Health, education, and housing funding systems are determined within Whitehall. In each case they cascade resources through intermediate bodies to local ones. Equity is a concern in all three services (though rather less so in housing) while efficiency is a universal policy-driver. There have been close philosophical parallels between the administrative devolution within the three services during the past decade or so (Glennerster *et al.* 1991). Yet their funding systems, though historically similar, are not so now. In some cases, individual civil servants or local authority officers have worked in more than one sector and can offer an overview. But there is no deliberate effort to operate to similar principles or to achieve consistent ends. Only one example of efforts to look across from one service to another emerged from the interviews: those responsible for the health formula had examined its interaction with the social services SSA.

Equity

Views from the centre

Interviews within the three services, at the national and local levels, produced startlingly different results. In health there was some surprise that anyone should ask about the equity aims of the formula. It was 'obvious—equal access for those in equal need'. The report of the Resources Allocation Working Party set out a definition of equity that was now recognized within the NHS as being of almost theological importance. By contrast, in education, one senior official commented 'it's interesting nobody talks about equity. Equity is rarely discussed and certainly does not have any kind of theological meaning. Fairness is far more likely to be the net sum of a political debate between councils.'

In housing, equity does not even appear to exist as an implicit requirement of the system (which it does, arguably, for education). In very broad terms, the structure of Housing Revenue Account Subsidy for local authorities can be seen as an attempt to achieve equal treatment for tenants in terms of the relative rents they pay for a standard level of service. But this definition for housing seems something of a *post hoc* rationalization of a system that is certainly not viewed on the ground as seeking 'equity'.

Within Whitehall, officials dealing with housing pointed to a vague notion of 'fair' rent relativities between regions, having made allowance for (as far as possible) scientific calculations of the costs of management and maintenance. This objective requires officials at both the national and regional level to manipulate subsidy and benefit systems so as to achieve a final impact on tenants (or, to be more precise, on the minority of tenants whose rents are not met by housing benefit). Housing Corporation officials were concerned with equitable housing outcomes. One regional office took the utilitarian view that 'fairness in a political sense is presumably happiness for the greatest number of providers'. Whether or not equitable outcomes for individual tenants mattered was not clear.

In health, equality of access has long been seen to be the driving force behind the NHS, though very recently a concern with equality of outcomes has developed. Fairness, in these terms would have been a healthcare system in which individuals had equal access to a system which treated them all in a similar way.

Under questioning, civil servants responsible for education readily accepted that equity and fairness underpinned their actions, though this was clearly an implicit rather than an explicit goal. All pupils should receive a similar education, though perhaps the continued (elected) local authority involvement in schools provision made it theoretically possible to envisage some variations from place to place. Education has in the past been described as a 'national service locally administered', whereas health provision (answerable to central government) is all part of a *national* health service.

Local opinions

Concern with the equity or fairness (or otherwise) of resource allocation within education was very strong within local government and at the school level. Indeed, the political interest in the Standard Spending Assessment (SSA) process had made local authority officers sceptical about the process and its outcomes. As one council officer put it, 'equity means each according to their need—but we don't have it, and we'd never all agree on the same outcome anyway'. SSA was widely seen as a grim inevitability and a mechanical process for central government to achieve a set level of local services and resources. Schools were generally far less critical of resource allocation than LEAs.

Regional and local NHS officials and local GPs shared the national view of equity. A district health authority official stated: 'The objective is equity. In access this is probably achieved, even if we still squabble over resource allocation . . .'. A GP was even more flattering: 'I do think that the allocation is generally fair, though of course I can point to areas where I think we get a rough deal.' These views were relatively typical.

Indeed, in both education and health there was broad acceptance at the most local level that resource allocation was relatively fair. Schools, trusts, and GPs appeared more willing to accept that the system was equitable than those in the intermediary bodies, particularly local authorities. Neighbouring schools, hospitals, and GPs were more likely to be used as comparators than those in other parts of the country.

In housing, there was no local expectation of a fair or equitable system. As one London housing administrator wearily put it, 'I have never heard anyone describe equity or even fairness of distribution as an objective . . . we just get on with coping with what we get'. No one within local authorities appeared to know of any statement about fairness or equity. More surprisingly, there was no real expectation that the funding system for local authority housing would be equitable.

There was no greater expectation of equity or fairness among housing associations than among local authorities. One large housing association in the North-East of England asked, 'Does equity mean geographic equity, or are we talking about rents between private, council and housing association rents within one area? How you define equity is going to have huge implications on policy . . .'. Generally, associations also believed the equity objectives of the housing sector had never been clearly defined.

The Quality of the Formulae

Resource allocation formulae must take account of objectively accepted needs indicators and data limitations while being informed by the existing research base and expertise within the service concerned. Formulae must also work within a framework of national and local politics. Interviews conducted within the three services suggested that the quality of the health formula is more widely accepted than those for schools or housing. There are good reasons for this difference. The modern health allocation formula has developed as a technocratic and relatively rigorous process. One of our civil servant interviewees, who had been at the Department of Health (or its predecessor) for almost thirty years described the creation of the modern funding formula as 'a wonderful story of the interaction between social scientists and politicians'. There had been a genuine sense of puzzlement (and a demand for inquiry) within government about the mismatch between expenditure levels within health authorities and the distribution of death rates, waiting lists, and so on. Economists published papers and a debate took place during the 1970s about the issue of resource distribution.

Eventually ministers, first Richard Crossman then David Owen, encouraged their officials to come forward with proposals for reforms. They, in turn, proposed the creation of a committee to inform the process of resource allocation. Thus was the Resources Allocation Working Party (RAWP) born. There was consensus within the NHS that something should be done. Even areas that lost as a result of RAWP accepted their fate on grounds of fairness, although the gradual nature of the losses and gains made it easier for politicians to envisage shifts in resources from one area to another. Also, there has been significant continuity within the Department of Health among the officials running the system: institutional memory is strong within health officials.

Of course, there were criticisms of the formula. GPs complained about such issues as inadequate measures of poverty, the loss of older industries, ethnicity, and the problems associated with rural areas. Virtually all of these complaints are very similar to ones made about the education SSA (and, in some cases, about LMS formulae). However, the level of discontent within the NHS is clearly less than in the education service. In the search for improvement, one of our interviewees pointed to the quality of data and research available in the United States about the determinants of health risk and morbidity. None of the interviewees in education or housing considered overseas models.

This rational approach within health was probably reinforced by the fact that members of local and regional health authorities have, since 1974, been appointed by the government. Members are accountable upwards to ministers rather than to a local electorate. Many have been appointed for their technical knowledge. For education, the opposite is true. Members of local education authorities are elected councillors and, therefore, more likely to be 'political' in a wide sense of the word. In particular, while appointed health members are appointed to the local or regional boards of a national service, council members are elected to serve the discrete interests of a geographically delineated group of electors. It is small wonder, therefore, that education authorities have taken a more challenging approach to the education SSA formula than health authority members have towards the more 'technically pure' health formula.

RAWP and its successor formulae (now the Weighted Capitation Formula) have been heavily based on objective research undertaken, in particular, by academics. The education SSA has seen a different approach, with significant quantities of research and lobbying material produced by local authority association officers, consultants, and academics. The officers and members of individual councils have also lobbied (and, in some cases, commissioned research) about the education SSA. Whereas the health formula is seen by people throughout the service as being objective, fair, and almost definitive, the education SSA is a matter for continuous negotiation, renegotiation, and argument. A widely held view is that the SSA 'doesn't recognize real spending needs'.

The age of data used within the education SSA was criticized, as was the ineffective measurement of poverty as a driver of the need to spend. The method used to calculate higher costs in the South-East was criticized heavily (by those outside the South-East). Unlike health, none of the education interviewees would have been prepared to argue for a change in SSA (or, indeed, the local schools formula) which would disadvantage their particular case. Methodological changes were thus viewed purely in terms of whether or not a particular council or school would win or lose.

Housing resources have been allocated according to a number of different systems (with different objectives variously affecting rents, subsidy levels, grants, efficiency, the cost of construction, and the benefit system) in recent years. Interviewees rarely mentioned research and methodological issues. There is no evidence that research plays much of a part in determining what would or would not be an appropriate change to the revenue or capital funding of social housing (apart from some limited work on local authority management and maintenance allowances). When decisions have been made to change elements within the housing funding system, the Department for the Environment, Transport, and the Regions (and its predecessors), the Housing Corporation, local authorities, and representative organizations such as the National Housing Federation have analysed the likely effect. But there is no body of academic (or other) research underpinning the logic of the resource allocation system for housing.

Perhaps the nearest housing gets to a researched formula is the Housing Need Index (HNI), which is used to distribute Housing Corporation resources for new development both between the regions and within regions to each local authority area. One housing association interviewee believed the HNI 'is steeped in politics and in mystery'. But there were few comments on the method used to construct the HNI beyond this observation. Other factors appear to be more important.

The use of objective, academic research varies significantly from service to service. The health formula uses academic research to the greatest extent and appears to achieve the greatest degree of acceptance within the service. A lack of territorial politics may assist in achieving such acceptance. The education SSA, by contrast, is riven with territorial arguments. Few local authorities (and few schools) believe the SSA is fair for them. With this concern about fairness come methodological criticisms. Research is used largely for lobbying purposes. Housing is the service least reliant on research as part of the process of determining the fairest or most appropriate way of allocating resources (this is not to say that research is not undertaken). Our interviewees did not seem concerned with methodological issues affecting the distribution of housing resources, rather they were interested in the distributional consequences of funding systems.

Complexity

It could be argued that there is a lack of concern with the methods used for allocation housing resources partly because they change so often and partly because they are fearfully complex. The charge of complexity was made against all three of the resource distribution systems under review, particularly by those lower down the system. One GP stated, 'The thing [i.e. the formula] is far too complicated. I do not know a single GP who could explain the national system with you' (USGP). Another believed, 'Only a few people at the top understand the whole process' (ILFH).

There were many other similar comments from GPs and some health administrators.

Even the process of negotiation and formula-setting appeared to be little understood by GPs, The more politically aware fundholding GPs were slightly better informed than non-fundholders. There are more locally available data about education funding than about the health service. However, this did not stop one local authority chief executive from describing SSAs as 'bonkers, time-consuming and futile'. Few elected members or school staff really understand the complexities of the education SSA.

Complexity in housing finance appears to be so great as to have stifled debate about just how difficult the system is to understand. Apart from the housing association officer quoted earlier—who claimed, 'The HNI is steeped in politics and mystery. . . . If I were not involved in the National Housing Federation committees I would not get the national picture at all'—there were few complaints about complexity. It is hard to believe that the lack of concern about complexity derives from an acceptance that the system is simple and comprehensible. Indeed, one local authority housing officer in Inner London was reduced to explaining the impact of rent increases on housing benefit subsidy in the following terms: 'We explained to members that it was like buying one pint of beer, but having to pay for three to do so.' This 'Ladybird books' method of explanation suggests the mechanisms within housing finance are so complex that most council members, in common with housing association staff and members, could not realistically be expected to come to terms with the complexity of the system. This is not new. Back in the 1930s Lady Astor commented on local government finance that 'I do not understand one quarter of it, but neither does anyone else. I do not understand electricity, but derive benefit from it.'

All three services have funding formulae and other financing arrangements which are sufficiently complicated and difficult to understand that intelligent people who do not study them for a living are unlikely to be able to grasp more than the most general of principles relating to funding. As a result, power is concentrated in the hands of central and local technocrats. Perhaps this concentration of power in the hands of full-time officials is inevitable in an age of computers, advanced economics and more sophisticated public expectations. There is a trade-off between simplicity and the capacity of a formula to measure a wide range of expenditure needs fairly in a country with a population as diverse as that in Britain. Complaints about complexity need to be addressed, but they are unlikely to go away entirely.

Politicization and Fairness of Treatment between Different Local Subsectors

The period from 1976 to 1999 has seen dramatic changes within British politics and political institutions. During the Thatcher years in particular there were a number of radical reforms that were accused at the time of being 'political', in the sense that particular authorities or groups of individuals gained financially (or in other ways) from the state at the expense of others. Health, education, and housing reforms were not immune from such accusations at the time.

Our interviewees were surprisingly relaxed about, for example, the allocation of resources. There were few claims that money was distributed between areas or institutions as a result of their politics. Interviewees within Whitehall, the Housing Corporation, housing associations, and local authorities did not generally believe that resource distribution had been affected by political considerations. Thus, although there were claims from housing associations that 'It's never been a level playing field' (OLBHA), and that 'the Housing Corporation has favourites' (TFRHA), the supposed favouritism was not tied to politics. Within local government, there were no accusations of political bias. Indeed, a typical view was expressed by an officer in a southern unitary authority who stated he did not 'know much about national distribution—we have enough problems dealing with our own HRA'. Thus lack of concern with the motives of distribution was typical.

Health funding allocations were also accepted to be politically neutral. There were no accusations of bias or unfairness resulting from politics. It was only within education that there were hints of the possibility that a political agenda might influence SSA distribution. But even within education, which is undoubtedly the most open of the three funding systems to political pressure, there was no suggestion that a party (it would have been the Conservatives for virtually all the time under consideration) used the SSA system for party advantage. This lack of complaint is the more remarkable given the more general accusations of unfairness that accompanied the original introduction of SSAs in 1990 (Butler *et al.* 1994). Chief executives interviewed within local government saw SSA as political only in the sense that they understood the government would annually choose the distribution of resources that would give them least political difficulty.

But there was another aspect of treatment by the government that drew accusations of unfairness in all three sectors during the period—generally during the late 1980s or early 1990s—when reforms were being made. Differences in resources allocated to GP fundholders as compared to non-fundholders, to grant-maintained schools compared to LEA institutions, and to housing associations compared to local authority housing departments, in each case drew accusations from the latter mentioned institutions about the relative generosity of the treatment of the former ones.

Our interviewees picked up a residual flavour of this earlier debate. Thus, one Inner London authority stated, 'It is not clear why there should be differences between associations and authorities . . . we believe Housing Corporation resources could be better spent'. A unitary authority in the south of England complained 'we are treated very differently to housing associations. They have total freedom to raise money, and their rents are allowed to go far higher.' Note these are concerns about freedom rather than the distribution of resources (though there were many complaints by councils about the relative generosity of funding for housing associations during the 1980s and early 1990s).

A GP claimed, 'the division between the funding of fundholders and other general practitioners left deep scars'. Local authority and school views can be summed up by the school that stated: 'There's been a lot of emotion surrounding the different funding regimes between local GM schools and us. I don't think funding was the main reason why they decided to opt out.'

Indeed, this view expressed by an individual school neatly summarized the wider feeling by the end of 1997 about fundholding, opting-out, and the split between local authority and housing association systems. According to our interviewees, political, local, and—in some cases—personal preferences seem to have been at least as important as funding advantages (real or imagined) in determining whether or not GPs or schools changed their status.

Efficiency and Incentives

After a period of considerable real-terms growth in expenditure during the 1950s, 1960s, and the early 1970s, health, housing, and education were subject to constraints during the later 1970s, the 1980s, and the 1990s. Although health and education expenditure continued to rise in real terms in most years (health rather more quickly than education), housing expenditure, in particular capital investment, was sharply cut back. Funding mechanisms adapted to the new environment, in particular rigid annual cash limits were imposed on virtually all parts of the services under consideration. Only housing benefit remained open-ended for virtually all of the period covered by this book.

The funding formulae used in health and education (both SSA and LMS) allocated resources to individual institutions as a simple cash input. Although there were some elements of grant that were tied to particular purposes, the overwhelming majority of resources flowed from the government (and, in the case of education, local authorities) through intermediary authorities into local institutions. The hospitals, GPs, and schools then used the resources as they saw fit. By contrast, the funding of housing was reformed on a number of occasions with particular incentive effects as the primary objective of the change. Thus, for example, funding was allocated at different times in such a way that rents would move in a particular direction, or housing benefit payments would fall, or the number of new housing units purchased for a given sum of money would increase, or the overall amount spent on public-sector housing would reduce. The finance of social housing was riddled with (often changing) concerns about incentives.

Not surprisingly, housing interviewees had a view about the way in which funding arrangements affected their behaviour. The ring-fencing of the housing revenue account was seen as having encouraged more rigour by one local authority: 'Ring-fencing was probably a good thing. . . . It made us more aware of what we were doing and how much we were spending.' Another council officer made the same observation: 'It [the ring-fencing of the HRA] was just another way of restricting our spending. . . . But it's not all negative. Thinking about our own costs and having to stand on our own two feet has made us feel stronger.'

The costs of housing benefit were a key element in the government's strategy according to an official at the Housing Corporation: 'The Department of Social Security were interested in fixing rent increases to RPI plus one because of its effects on the Housing Benefit bill, not on association behaviour.' An individual housing association officer waxed lyrical in describing the relative incentive systems in his own sector as compared with local government: 'Rents are a good example. With local authorities the government instantly try to stop the runaway train by putting a brick wall across the track. With us they first try the brakes, then try cutting back the fuel or changing the signalling, and only as a last resort do they shunt us into the sidings.'

It is clear that those working within housing are very aware of the incentive-laden nature of their funding systems. Chapters 10 and 11 include quotations from interviews which make this point again and again. Within health and education, there are few references to incentives as such. In the terminology of Chapter 7, it is the 'passive' incentives of fixed budgets which matter here, and these are less visible or contentious. The RAWP formula was designed (as, indeed was SSA) so as to make it impossible for those at the receiving end to change their behaviour so as to increase their allocations. As Chapter 8 made clear, none of our health interviewees could see perverse incentives within the current system (apart from for GPs to be less than diligent in pruning their list of patients). There was resistance among GPs to the use of resource allocation formulae to encourage certain kinds of behaviour. On the other hand, devolution of budgets to GPs (first fundholders and now primary care groups) has required some doctors to consider efficiency issues for the first time. As one GP put it, 'If anyone is to do the rationing implicit in a National Health Service we want to be part of it.' Primary care groups will also, it was believed, encourage GPs to co-operate in a way they did not in the past.

Within education, as in health, direct incentives to encourage efficiency are relatively few. It is true that SSA policy documents make it clear that the allocation of resources has objectives that include the restraint of expenditure. But incentives were not mentioned by local authority officers, whose councils receive grant (based on their total SSA) and then add it to their other income. The resulting total funds their budget, which is constrained more by local taxpayers (or capping) than by any incentives built into the grant system. The only reference made by education interviewees to the impact of an incentive was to the move (under LMS) to a per capita regime in which schools would receive more resources the more pupils they could attract (and, conversely, would lose resources if rolls fell).

The observation by officials within health that 'equity may not be enough' was part of a developing concern with the measurement of outcomes within government. Education funding—most notably the funding formula for further education—had made tentative steps towards incentive-based funding systems. A full-scale review of SSA was started in 1999 which could radically reform the grant system (including the possibility of outcome-linked grants). Housing funding, as observed, has long been concerned with efficiency and incentives. The committee responsible for health formulae had been told to consider how its allocations could help equalize health *outcomes*. This concern was mentioned in our interviews with senior civil servants before the government acted.

London

An issue mentioned by a number of health, education, and housing interviewees was the treatment of London within their funding systems. For example, a GP described the problems of being a practitioner close to the particular problems of London's mainline railway stations. Another GP believed, 'It did not take London long to dilute the impact of RAWP.' Similar sentiments were expressed in education. An interviewee in a northern authority believed London had a particularly generous education SSA. Yet interviewees in the capital believed their social needs were not properly assessed. Rapid population changes in London were issues for both education and health.

London was also mentioned by housing interviewees. A DETR official concluded, 'It is difficult to iron out the London effect', which leads to suspicion outside the capital. There is clearly some concern about the treatment of London throughout the rest of the country within all three services. RAWP managed to shift resources (relatively) out of the capital. SSA, by contrast, has worked in such a way as to preserve a large differential between the funding of schools in Inner London as compared with those in all other authorities. Housing finance has from time to time been manipulated so as to avoid a big impact on London tenants. The capital remains an issue.

Success or Failure of Devolution

In health, education, and housing there has been substantial devolution in recent years of resources to local institutions such as GPs, schools, and housing associations. These reforms were driven by a wider philosophical and political agenda. Nevertheless, such changes have had the effect of requiring new funding arrangements which, particularly in education, have opened up the system of funding to far greater levels of transparency. The devolution of resources to fundholding GPs had a similar effect.

None of our interviewees argued to return to the old system of funding where intermediary institutions allocated resources (often by unpublished means) between lower tier bodies. Even GPs, who—like schools—had been used to a system in which they were not required to make any decisions about the use of resources, appear to have relished the purchasing power that fundholding brought. LMS has been retained and strengthened by the post-1997 Labour government. Although GP fundholding has been abolished, an analogous system of primary care groups is being introduced in which GPs and other primary care professionals will make local decisions about the use of resources. Although very different funding regimes operate within social housing, there was no demand among interviewees for an end to 'ring-fencing' of local authority housing revenue accounts or for a shift to central control over housing associations by, say, local authorities. Indeed, the trend within housing remains towards smaller units of self-management with more financial autonomy.

Conclusion

The extensive interviews undertaken for this project, within different parts of central and local government, and among GPs, schools, and housing associations suggest there are a number of common themes which are identified within each service. What is perhaps more interesting is that these themes emerge quite separately as the result of three (or even eight) discrete systems of funding. Common strengths and weaknesses emerge, as do issues that affect all three services. It is the implications of these cross-cutting and common issues for future systems that will be considered in the Conclusion.

13

Where to Now?

Summary of Findings

In this chapter we discuss the main factors which are driving developments in funding formulae and suggest how they might develop in future. Before we do so, it is probably helpful to recap some of the main findings from our analysis of the systems and of our interviewees' perceptions of them. First, in terms of the main characteristics of the three services:

- Over the last twenty years, NHS funding has moved onto an increasingly sophisticated needs-related basis, applied to smaller and smaller sized areas. The last twenty years have reversed the position of the 1970s, when the health department was much less successful than education in equalizing resources between areas.
- Funding reaches most schools through a two-tier process. Since 1990 central government funding to LEAs has been fixed amounts, depending on their Standard Spending Assessments. Funding for schools is mostly dependent on fixed amounts per pupil (adjusted for items like numbers of lone parents, income support recipients, ethnicity, sparsity, and local costs). Most of the schools budget has to be delegated to schools, but LEAs can set their own distribution system between them.
- The two parts of social housing—council housing and housing associations—are funded in very different ways. This raises equity issues, as the rents paid by different kinds of tenant can vary considerably, even if in identical buildings and circumstances. The incentives built into the funding systems have also changed over time, and in opposite directions. The pressures on local authorities now look more like those on housing associations in the 1970s and 1980s, when they had to operate within pre-set allowances. Housing associations, meanwhile, became *less* constrained after they were allowed to set their own rents after 1989, as part of reforms designed to remove perverse capital spending incentives. Recent restrictions on rents designed to control housing benefit costs have

hardened budget constraints on both kinds of landlord, but the rent caps involved are unrelated to each other or to other parts of the funding systems.

Analysis of funding systems for the three services shows a number of common themes, such as the increasing stress put on geographical needs-based equity, including under Conservative governments in the 1980s and 1990s. There are also differences, such as the systems used to slow—or 'damp'—changes from year to year (where the system for NHS funding has been much more successful than that in housing in achieving convergence while leaving the underlying principles clear).

The systems vary in how they embody *positive* incentives for particular behaviour, *passive* incentives through the effects of a fixed budget constraint, or *perverse* incentives which may encourage undesired behaviour. All three services have moved away from positive incentives towards much more use of the passive incentives given by fixed budgets, particularly those devolved to provider units. Debate over housing subsidies has been much more dominated by worries about perverse incentives than the others.

The structures of the formulae reflect technical constraints, such as the number of observations of spending behaviour from which relative needs can be inferred. Health systems have been more successful in generating data and more sophisticated in using them. Another important difference comes from the involvement of local government in education and housing, strengthening political pressures for local allocations, rather than acceptance of 'national' equity objectives.

Comparing our interviews between the three services:

1. There was a strikingly shared view of what equity meant from top to bottom of the NHS: equal access to treatment for equal need. Lower down the system there was more scepticism and less understanding about the detail of the system, but overall trust in its aims. Differences between fundholding and non-fundholding GPs had breached equity principles, but the new primary care groups were popular with both groups, combining devolved budgets, but restoring a uniform system. We saw a national service with clear common values to which everyone we interviewed signed up, despite the deep divisions of the 1990s.
2. In our interviews with LEAs and schools there was virtually no questioning of the policy of devolving budgets from LEAs to schools, despite the criticism when it was first introduced. However, the distribution of funding was heavily questioned by

LEA staff, who found it hard to identify a clear equity objective. Most LEAs believed they should receive a larger share of the total, although they did not suggest that allocations are skewed on party-political grounds. The system was, however, seen as complex and confusing, even 'bonkers'. In schools, there appeared far greater acceptance of the funding system. The system we discussed in our interviews is unlikely to be radically reformed in the years ahead. There was certainly no evidence of pressure for such reform.

3. The idea of an 'equity' objective baffled local housing respondents, who had never seen an official statement relating to equity. However, they did not generally see the differences in treatment of different tenants as a major issue. They were favourable to the reforms which had made social landlords more 'business-like' (ring-fencing of council housing revenue accounts and increased financial autonomy and responsibility for associations). The balance of opinion was that the associations' 1989 capital funding reforms had achieved *some* efficiency gains. However, those reforms also decontrolled association rents for new tenants, which meant that associations lost the previous constraint on their recurrent spending. It was only very recently that a hard budget constraint had been reintroduced through rent-capping for councils or the 'RPI plus one' limit on rental income for associations.

Comparing these responses:

- The systems were free-standing, with little apparent official activity in drawing lessons between them.
- Equity objectives were seen as 'obvious' in health, but obscure in education and, particularly, housing.
- Debate over allocations between LEAs was highly politicized in terms of local interests, contrasting with local health services where greater needs elsewhere could be accepted. GPs and schools tended to see funding as fair, even if they did not understand it. Social landlords' responses were fatalistic.
- The technical quality of the systems varied greatly, with the NHS formula based on more detailed data, more sophisticated techniques, and more academic input.
- All the systems were seen as complex, which increases the power of the centre, but the pressures we have examined suggest that this complexity is unlikely to diminish.
- There were few accusations of party-political favouritism. There were complaints about the inequity of differential treatment

between different kinds of GPs and of schools (in capital allocations). Housing respondents were more relaxed about the differences in treatment, partly reflecting the effects of housing benefit (which makes gross rents of little immediate importance for most tenants).

- Efficiency and incentive concerns dominated housing funding far more than the others, reflecting the way in which health and education funding rely on the 'passive incentive' effects of fixed budgets.
- The treatment of London recurred as a concern, with accusations from outside that the cost adjustments favoured London providers.
- Despite controversy at the time, the Conservative reforms of the late 1980s which devolved budgetary responsibility to lower levels were welcomed and accepted: ring-fencing of local authority HRAs, local management of schools, and the parts of the GP fundholding system which have been built into the new primary care groups.

Back to Theory

The standard theories of local service funding we reviewed in Chapter 2 only take us some way to understanding these kinds of development. One of the classic papers, that by Tiebout (1956), only considers the case of local public goods. None of the services we have discussed in this book are public goods in the strict sense at all. They can be and are bought in the market-place. The other classic paper by Oates (1972) on fiscal federalism starts from the presumption of a federal constitution. The United Kingdom is a unitary state, despite devolution of powers to Scotland and Wales. Those powers were devolved by an all-powerful Westminster Parliament and can be revoked by the same.

To understand the story we have to have recourse to theories of political economy. The United Kingdom is not only a unitary state. It is also one that that has a highly centralized media and, for reasons of history, a strong national identity. Increasingly politics has become the politics of social policy. National UK elections are fought on primarily social issues. Nearly two-thirds of the national government budget is devoted to social-policy purposes. National politicians must deliver national policies in this field—otherwise they will be accused of failing the electorate. They have an overriding power to tax and to limit lower agencies' capacity to tax. That alone would be an unheard of, almost incomprehensible, idea in the United States and other federal systems. The consequence is that taxation powers have drifted steadily to the central government. By 1999 only 4 per cent of all UK taxation was being raised locally. This has left an essentially unstable political economy game. There are local electorates and local politicians whose existence dates from a time when they had far greater revenue-raising powers. There are also national politicians who now raise nearly all the tax and whose electorates demand results and hold national politicians to account for things they do not have direct control over. We are just beginning to see the next stage in the political economy game evolve.

In Chapter 2 we traced the origins of the idea that came to dominate thinking about social policy for much of the last century: the idea of the national minimum. Every citizen had the right to a minimum standard of life and access to a minimum standard of service for health, education, and other badges of national citizenship. These rights brought with them certain duties, such as the duty actively to seek work, but the state had the duty to see that all citizens had access to at least an agreed minimum standard of services.

As the century progressed, this standard minimum idea came to be extended to a rather more demanding notion of *equal* access to services of equal quality. The National Health Service was the pace-setter in this respect. That is not to say that this ideal has ever been achieved, but the articulation of the ideal and its elaboration in practical terms was taken furthest in the case of the NHS.

Later in the century and especially in the last twenty years, as growth in social budgets relative to the GDP ceased, so efficiency became governments' major concern. Equity took more of a back seat. However, even here, making sure that the shoe of spending restraint pinched in the least painful place meant more rather than less concern with spending in relation to 'need'.

We saw in Chapter 2 that theories of distributional equity, and efficient principal-agent relations between central and local government, suggest that lower level agencies should receive need-related budgets. Moreover, they suggest that these allocations should be as open and as visible as possible. Much of the political appeal of a service like the National Health Service in the UK, or of state education, is that all citizens in the country have equal access to it. The blatant breaching of that principle brings immediate popular displeasure. Hence the unpopularity of that aspect of GP fundholding, despite its other virtues, the pressure to take action against non-performing schools, to equalize class size, and many more recent examples.

Yet equal access entails unequal finance and provision. Some areas are in more need of some services than others. Areas with more schoolchildren or old people need more education or health spending. We have seen that this idea has been well understood since the turn of the century and increasingly sophisticated ways of measuring the relative needs of different areas have been devised in the past quarter of a century.

More recently, economists and organization theorists have argued that central governments or bureaucracies are ill-suited to managing services where quality depends on face-to-face contact between pupils and teacher, doctor and patient. Equity may require the central funding of these services—since local populations may not be in a position to afford adequate service levels—but efficiency requires local user involvement in their management and oversight. Moreover, the units to be overseen must be organizational units to which tenants or parents or patients can relate—not a large local authority, but a school or housing estate, or a general practice or group of general practices.

The user may be a parent or a tenant but can be an expert advocate like a GP. For these local agency watchdogs to do their job effectively they need expert advice and technical monitoring—hence such developments as the new National Institute for Clinical Excellence, the Housing Inspectorate, the National Curriculum, and OFSTED. Hood and colleagues (1999) describe this 'growing industry' of regulation within the public sector as 'itself largely unregulated'. For the most part that study was concerned with regulation in the form of inspection and performance measurement driven from the centre. The Conservative government also relied on competition as its preferred method of efficiency promotion. That required equal funding and funding that enabled local agencies to be fairly rewarded for the task they were set to perform. Consumers, or their representatives, could then choose the best provider making most efficient use of this central money. For a time, therefore, the old objective of formula funding—equal access—continued to be compatible with the new objective of creating an equal playing field for local competition.

However, the new Labour government elected in 1997 and the underlying problem of national funding for local provision began to unsettle a system that had evolved steadily in the ways we have described for over a century. Years of attempts to equalize access by making need-adjusted grants to local agencies had not succeeded in equalizing either access or outcomes. Health and educational inequalities remained. Indeed some research suggested they were even getting worse. For a

Labour government that had come to power saying it would do something about inequality this called for a rethink. It also reinforced the central dilemma. Central politicians take the blame for raising taxes but cannot get a handle on the distribution of the benefits or claim the credit if the taxes they raise are handed over to others to spend. Hence the growth of the regulatory state which Hood *et al.* (1999) describe. It was thus not surprising that, at the very end of our study in 1999, we saw the Labour government calling for a review of all the systems we have been considering. They wanted to use the formulae to advance the goals of equal outcomes more effectively. One likely result may be to reduce further the element of needs-based funding and replace it with more specific grants related to performance. Those health authorities that can demonstrate good or promising schemes to reduce health inequalities will get more money. The money will come from top-slicing the formula-funded element. That trend was already evident in the NHS settlements for 1999–2000. It led to considerable frustration for those on the ground though. The outcome of this tussle must await a later study!

Another reason to suspect the same trend is that in the new Treasury-driven world individual central departments have to prove that they have delivered on government targets before the Treasury will release them the money they have been voted by Parliament (HM Treasury 1998). This makes central departments even more concerned to gain more control over their lower agents. The days of untied formula-funded allocations may be passing. Perhaps we have seen the high tide of formula funding approaches that began at the end of last century. Nevertheless to go down that path would be dangerous. As the work we reviewed earlier suggests, the centre is not very good at deciding what local agencies should do. It does not possess the detailed information to make good judgements.

Smaller units like schools, GPs, and smaller housing associations, or tenant-run estates, do have the local knowledge. They have much more local knowledge than the local authorities and local health authorities that used to do the job. Our interviews suggested that this devolution of funding to them was now very popular. No one wanted to return to the old days of rule from county hall. What this suggests is that formula funding may indeed persist, if on a reduced scale, for the small units who deliver the service, while the rest is more related to performance indicators and special projects.

So long as central government goes on being the main, indeed almost the sole provider, of funds, the role of local government will look increasingly anomalous. It could find itself acting as a postal service for cheques which arrive from the centre with strict—and increasingly confident, if health formulae are anything to go by—instructions about how they are to be divided out between local providers. The temptation to bypass local government altogether may grow, not just in school-level education, but also in social housing, as its ownership is increasingly transferred to free-standing housing associations or companies. At the same time, the pressure for the centre to involve itself in local detail will become irresistible, but potentially unmanageable and inefficient.

The solutions may involve the reform of local government finance, a new role for local government much more clearly as a local monitor and inspector, and more genuine local input into the NHS—but that is another book. We have begun with some wide-ranging speculation, since as we write the systems we have been studying seemed destined for a significant overhaul. However, some more practical and detailed conclusions also emerge from our study. The increasing sophistication of the formulae has had both achievements and drawbacks.

Equal Access: Practical Issues

No service has achieved equal access or even equal opportunity of equal access which, perhaps, encapsulates the practical goal civil servants set themselves. The service which most nearly reached that goal was the National Health Service. It has now devised a national formula that can be applied to its smallest unit, the new primary care groups. Moreover, the formula itself is firmly based on evidence about the relative use of the NHS by different age and social groups. It is also based on studies of the relative cost of providing a service with equivalently qualified staff in different labour markets and in more or less populated parts of the country. Indeed, so sophisticated are these approaches that, given our present state of knowledge, diminishing returns may be setting in as far as improvements are concerned.

The system has generated a good deal of trust because it is evidence-based and relatively open to criticism and expert input. It has a well-understood goal: equal access for those in equal need. The means of achieving that goal are transparent, even if complex. That is not to say that the process is well understood. That did not prove to be the case as we moved down the hierarchy to the level of GPs in the new primary care groups. An education job remains to be done here. There is a natural tendency to respond to more and more detailed criticisms by special groups with more and more complexity. Over time there is a tendency for the 'barnacles' to obscure the system.

The NHS does have one key advantage over other services, it is national. Local authorities see their role as being to maximize resources for their area rather than to accept a system designed to match needs and resources, especially if they are the losers. Local authorities have locally elected representatives who see it as their job to fight for more. Lower level agents and less political ones, like schools, were more accepting of their allocations.

Even so, there are basic problems with allocations to any very small unit. The statistical relationships become much less robust. There will be special circumstances that do not average out. The smaller the unit, the more need for discretion, but the more the discretion, the less the transparency.

Designing and marketing a formula is made much easier if there is a great deal of information on relative costs and needs which can be used and externally validated. This is possible in the NHS because the level of analysis is that of individuals who are judged to be in need by professionals and referred for a service and treated. We have data on these outcomes and can relate them to the areas from which these patients come. With education or housing, the spending decisions are made by a few hundred authorities. The feedback from spending to funding can be perverse. Authorities could be tempted to spend on a group numerous in their area in the knowledge that this would affect the formula to their benefit. Avoiding this problem restricts the items that can be used to assess need. Moreover, the decisions to spend are affected by previous allocations to that authority. Authorities with more secondary pupils or sixth formers or pupils from ethnic minorities are given more in the allocations and tend to be high spenders as a result. Hence the findings become circular. The small-area statistics and the individualized data in the NHS formula tend to avoid that kind of self-perpetuating bias. The evidence basis for the education element in the revenue support grant is limited and at times counterfactual. Large sums are granted for each student from ethnic minority groups in the local population. These are not then reflected in allocations to each school. More to the point most children from ethnic minorities outperform white schoolchildren. There may be a strong case for supporting authorities with large numbers of refugees or pupils with difficulties of many kinds. The present measures do not do that. They are too crude and have no real evidence base.

Housing allocations are even further from the ideal. Public-sector and housing association housing is only a minority part of the housing market. Current spending is not cash-limited as it is with health or education grant levels. There are now limits on what maximum rent levels will be covered by housing benefit by central government, but up to those levels the full rent is met. That removes much of the consumer constraint on rent levels and on the budget. Levels of demand for social housing are affected by this relatively open-ended subsidy. Relative levels of demand are not good proxies for need, as they are in the case of health where judgements are made by professionals on an individual patient-by-patient basis. Judgements about relative capital needs are difficult to form and certainly seemed to be informed more by notions of 'a fair share' on a geographical basis than objective housing need.

The need for some kind of intermediate layer of governance at which some discretion can be applied, by health and education authorities for example, is more difficult at local authority level in the case of housing authorities who are housing providers themselves.

Finally, one of the clear impressions we formed in the course of our interviews was that, although they were controversial at the time, the Conservative reforms of the late 1980s which devolved budgets to lower levels of agency—schools, GPs, and ring-fenced housing accounts—were generally popular. They gave people a sense of ownership and control and had positive efficiency effects. The unpopular elements were those aspects of the changes that conflicted with the overall equity aims of the services: the separation between GP fundholders and the rest, and the favourable treatment of grant-maintained schools. The rather surprising acceptance of primary care groups in the NHS, which combine the fundholding principle of devolved budgeting with the fact that all GPs are now to be treated in the same way, is instructive.

In short, the principles and theories we outlined in Chapter 2 are to be found in the practical changes brought about in the past twenty-five years by governments of both parties. But there is some way to go before they are consistently applied.

Recommendations for Change

Evidence-based formulae on need

In so far as need remains the basis of resource allocation, as it will to some degree, there are practical issues in each service.

The NHS

Equal access. In seeking to meet the old objective of equal access for those in equal need there may be little further that the health service can go with its hospital and community services formula on the basis of existing information. However, the allocation of general practitioners through the country is regulated on an extremely crude basis. The same logic that applies to the main part of the health service budget should apply to the allocation of GPs. Logically the formula should be evidence-based and apply to the primary care budget as a whole. In practice this is extremely difficult to do, given GPs' independent status. In theory, the capitation funding of primary care should be needs-based. If more than an average number of GPs moved to an area of average needs their income would fall below average. The way to earn above average would be to move into a needy area.

However, it is in the other two services where the evidence basis of the funding arrangements needs to be strengthened.

Equal health. Clearly this new objective that ministers have given for review of NHS funding poses far more difficult challenge. Most of the factors that affect an individual's health are not directly the health service's concern, or not its prime responsibility. Income distribution, family policy, housing policy, food production, and tobacco advertising are not things that can be taken into account in an NHS formula. It remains important that services are allocated in such a way that all citizens have an equal chance of accessing them, wherever they live. What is needed is something in addition that facilitates those preventive and outreach services that will improve health and reduce health inequalities. There is no point in encouraging ineffective actions. It should be possible to distinguish preventive or health-promoting actions which primary care groups could undertake which have proven efficacy. These could be linked to populations at risk. The starting-point would be to identify variables that indicated 'avoidable deaths and morbidity'. There are such measures, but they would need to be able to be applied on a small-area basis and regularly updated. The next step would be to identify effective health improvement programmes that PCGs could undertake in relation to those at risk, and to give them cost weights. This health improvement formula could then be used as a top-up to the old formula. We shall have to see what results from this initiative. No such remit has been given to those working on the education formula.

Education: improvements to SSAs?

The existing research base for the education element in the local authority grant system—Standard Spending Assessments—is evidently less well-developed than that for health. The consistent programme of academic inputs into the health formula has ensured that it has been relatively rigorous. Data sources have been sufficient to allow the formula to work in such a way that it has not been seriously challenged of late.

The development of Grant Related Expenditure Assessments and, more recently, Standard Spending Assessments (SSAs) has taken place in a more political environment than health allocations. Moreover, the data underpinning the education SSA have been criticized. The research base appears to be weaker than for health.

As an example, the education SSA includes an additional education needs factor that is supposed—amongst other things—to take account of authorities' different needs to spend on children for whom English is not their first language. This additional allocation is based on the belief that children who do not speak English will require more teaching than English-speakers. Because no authority-by-authority figures exist for non-English-speakers, children of 'New Commonwealth' origin are used as a proxy.

Such a proxy may be the least-worst way of allowing for the additional costs of, say, teaching refugees. But statistics (Glennerster and Hills 1998) show that older children of a number of 'New Commonwealth' backgrounds now tend to outperform the average child. It is thus doubtful if a blanket allowance for 'New Commonwealth' is really appropriate, and certainly has no empirical basis. There are many refugee children who need, from common experience, far more attention than the average but are not 'New Commonwealth', and many white children who need extra help too. What is required is high-quality robust evidence about the extent to which language problems cause a higher requirement to spend on what kinds of child. There then need to be audited authority-by-authority data about the number of children with such problems, or better school-by-school data. At present the research base is weak and the data do not exist.

It would be possible to go further and undertake research about the resource inputs required to deliver a given curriculum and then to fund up to that level. Authorities would be left free to fund add-ons. But there are limits because of the high level of local political interest in education funding. The extent to which education needs assessments can ever be technically 'pure', as health needs assessments aim to be, is constrained.

On the other hand, given the recent development of official interest in performance indicators it should be possible to develop a needs-based SSA formula related to the achievement of particular objectives or curricular standards. Performance-linked resource allocation has been taking place in further education for some years (National Audit Office 1997). The Conservative government in its later years considered the possibility of performance-related funding for 16–19 year olds including sixth formers (DfEE 1996). Labour, in a review of the whole system of local government grants in 1999–2000, is moving further towards the idea of performance-related funding.

Whatever arrangements are made for education needs assessment and funding in the future, it might be possible to bring a greater degree of objectivity and trust into the process. This could be done by the adoption of an independent process of objectivity nearer to that for health, ACRA. This body advises government about health resourcing and oversees the development of research into needs assessment.

It is perhaps strange that the coming of a National Curriculum with clear targets of achievement for each school has not been reflected more in the way education budgets have been calculated. Doing so would also have the beneficial side effect of making governments think more about how much they can push into the National Curriculum without really considering the resource implications.

This would have another beneficial side effect. There would be a national recommended spending level by age in all schools necessary to achieve the national minimum required standards. This could then be used as the basis for funding each school. The LMS formula would be set nationally, just as the primary care group recommended formula is set nationally. The whole level of public debate would be raised, since every interested person would be able to follow the recommendations about spending levels and be able to see them applied to their local school.

To this could be added payments to cover children with special needs, as happens now, and extra for children from deprived homes, if a tariff could be produced from research findings. The method employed in the NHS could be adapted to weight the formula to take account of the home addresses of the students in the school and the postcode linked to the socio-economic characteristics of the area. This would have the double advantage of countering the incentives to cream-skimming. To take a child from a poor area would bring the school more money. It might be enough to discourage the school from excluding such a child, or at least to contribute towards alternative provision while a child is withdrawn from classes.

As we argued above, such a move—effectively towards direct funding of all schools—raises major issues about the future role of local education authorities, but it is simply a logical extension of what we have seen, and has proved popular, in the last decade.

Housing: towards a rational system?

Readers who have followed the detail of funding systems for social housing in Chapter 6 may have been struck—as were the authors not specializing in this area—by both the complexity and inconsistency of current arrangements. Depending on its past financial history, tenants of a local authority may have their rents determined in one of three different ways: a rent guideline related to capital values and regional earnings; a 'damped' guideline depending on rents in the late 1980s; or a 'rent cap' depending on rents as they were in March 1996. Housing association rents are determined in an entirely different way; differ between those who were tenants before and after 1989; and are now effectively capped at the level they reached two years ago, regardless of whether the association had previously charged high or low rents. As a result, it was not entirely surprising that the senior housing staff whose responses we report in Chapters 10 and 11 found it hard to identify the principles and objectives of the systems, although it was striking quite how unanimous they were in never having seen any statement of their equity aims.

Returning to the two strands of thought which have drive formula funding in the twentieth century, this matters for two reasons. In terms of equity, it means that some tenants may be receiving very different effective levels of subsidy, even if in similar properties and circumstances. In terms of efficiency, it means that, with no consistent relationship between rents and costs, there is no easy way of tenants, councillors, or indeed anyone else, judging whether a landlord is doing a good job or not.

In recent years the importance of these issues has been dulled by the operation of the housing benefit system, which has 'taken the strain' of variations in subsidies and has meant that they did not matter greatly for many tenants. However, this is already changing. First, the rent caps in both subsectors now set a hard budget constraint on their recurrent spending. But this limit is set by where rents happened to be 'when the music stopped' rather than in relation to costs and values. This determines the level of service to tenants, whether or not they receiving housing benefit. Second, the Labour government has been actively exploring ways in which the principles of the benefit system might be changed, including 'shopping incentives' under which more—or even all—tenants would pay at least a percentage of their rent (Kemp 1998). Asking very poor tenants to pay a percentage of rents which bore no relationship to each other or to the value of their accommodation would seem highly inequitable. Housing benefit reform would make the search for more rational rent and subsidy structures far more urgent.

A clearer and more consistent system for determining social rents would also help build more understanding of—and potentially support for—the system from housing providers. With organizations to some extent in competition it is unrealistic to expect the degree of solidarity we found in the NHS, but the position could clearly improve from what we heard in our interviews.

There is no space here to go into the details of such a system (see Hills 1991: 305–10, and Hills 2000 for some ideas). However, formulae could relate subsidies (whether recurrent or capital, or implicit in transfer terms) in a consistent way to the elements of the cost of providing housing: its current capital value; provision for depreciation or major repairs; and recurrent management and maintenance. Interestingly, reforms to accounting systems recently put forward by DETR (1998), as part of moves towards 'resource accounting' across the public sector, could lend themselves to a reform of local authority subsidies and their key 'rent guidelines' along such lines. Housing benefit rent caps would have to be brought into line with such principles, as would constraints on housing associations, if a fully consistent system was to be achieved.

The comparisons earlier in this book with systems elsewhere suggest two further lessons for housing subsidies. First, there is a case for 'damping' changes in subsidy from year to year, but the NHS system of clear targets for eventual allocations, with a single variable for the speed of 'movement to target', is much less confusing than the multiplicity of damping arrangements which have been used in local authority housing subsidies. Second, as discussed above, both education and housing seem to lag well behind the health sector in the research which has gone into establishing relative spending needs. In this case much better information could be collected to establish needs for management and maintenance spending and major repairs provision.

Putting Right Perverse Incentives

The NHS

The main problem of this kind with the NHS allocation is that it encourages cost-shifting between the NHS and the local authority personal social service departments. The sum the NHS receives for the care of elderly people, who are heavily cash-weighted, can be used to improve other services by minimizing the care elderly patients receive as they are shifted out of hospital and onto local authority budgets. The fragmentary nature of the service that results is exacerbated by the perverse incentives the funding arrangements produce. This is true especially of the long-term care of the elderly and the care of the mentally ill. It would make more sense for there to be one budget-holder for the whole range of services that related to one client group.

That budget-holder need not provide all the services—it could not in practice do so. But one agency would be the single source of funding and organizer of care. In the case of those needing long-term care the most obvious and best candidate for this role is the primary care group. They would hold the whole of the NHS budget, which would cover the hospital costs of an old person and the costs of community health services, when they came out of hospital. To add the social-care costs to this budget would mean that an unprejudiced judgement could be made of the best place to care for that person. The individual and their family would have a one-stop-shop service. Their local group practice or health centre would employ not just home nurses but a care manager who would help determine, with medical and other staff, what the person's needs were. The resulting care would then be financed from the cash-limited budget of the primary care group. Elderly people would pay for housing and food themselves, with the help of housing benefit and income support if necessary.

The Royal Commission on Long Term Care (1999) advocated the elements of this solution. The formula funding of primary care groups would, under this proposal, include an enhanced element for the very elderly which would cover the costs of personal care as well as their medical needs. The equivalent weighting would then be removed from the revenue support grant to local authorities for personal social services. This would not necessarily mean that local authorities would cease to provide meals on wheels or home helps, for example. The primary care groups could purchase those services from the local authority. This would remove one of the perverse incentives in the present system.

Education

The major perverse incentive of school choice and devolved budgets, taken together with league tables, is to encourage 'cream-skimming'. If we want to keep school choice, both for the incentives it brings to schools to keep on their toes, and because without it caring middle-class parents will probably leave the state system, then we have to find ways to discourage or even prevent schools creaming off the most able children. One route, as suggested above, would be using the formula to reward schools for taking particular groups of children. Weighting capitation payments in a way which favours schools taking pupils requiring more resources to deliver the National Curriculum—children with special needs or those from poor backgrounds or neighbourhoods—could achieve this. More radically, it could be done by a system of banding entry, and setting limits to the number of children that can be taken from any ability group. These are feasible, but are highly political decisions. Formula funding down to lower level units makes such choices and dilemmas more visible.

There have been other incentives, often unintentional, built into the system of school funding. The other side of the cream-skimming coin is the trend for increasing numbers of exclusions from schools, which has been linked to the need for schools to maintain their popularity and hence their units of funding. Although a school may receive significantly more resources for additional educational needs, it will lose resources if the overall number of pupils falls from year to year. The incentive to keep disruptive pupils and deal with them properly has to be big enough to counter the temptation to get rid of or avoid the difficult child. Sink schools and all that goes with them will be the result unless the formulae address this kind of issue.

Housing

The clearest incentive problems in social housing finance were the 100 per cent marginal subsidy on housing association capital costs, which was removed by the reforms of 1989, but also the removal of any strong restraint on associations' recurrent spending and rents by the same reforms, combined with open-ended housing benefit (see Chapter 11). The second problem has been dealt with through the 'RPI plus one' limits on rental income now being enforced by the Housing Corporation, but at the cost of the new equity problems described above. If central government is paying all of the bills at the margin, it is not unreasonable for it to impose limits of this kind, also with benefits in terms of 'passive incentives' for spending efficiency. However, as a corollary, those limits need to be consistent, and subsidy arrangements need to allow realistic recurrent spending and provision for major repairs.

That said, the current financial position of associations, which leaves them making trade-offs between short-run and long-run costs, has a lot to commend it. Local authorities have been in a very different position, dependent on obtaining credit approvals from central government for major refurbishments and repairs rather than being able to plan for them in the way associations can. Here again, recent 'resource accounting' proposals (DETR 1998) open up the possibility of local authority housing moving onto a more business-like basis, by allowing authorities to retain part of their rents corresponding to depreciation or accrual of major repairs needs and then deciding how and when to use the funds themselves.

Moves of this kind would help bring the two parts of social housing into a more similar financial environment. Indeed, they would increase the movement, started with 'ring-fencing' of local authority housing revenue accounts in 1990, towards separating off local authority landlord functions from the rest of councils' activities. Ultimately the result of this could be a system where all social housing was provided by single-purpose landlords (whether associations, transfer associations, or local authority-owned housing companies), while local authorities concentrated on their role of monitoring and 'enabling' activities.

Market forces factors

The simple proposition that individuals should be able to go to schools and hospitals of the same quality anywhere in the country of which they are a citizen is more difficult to achieve than it seems at first sight. Not only do individuals benefit to different degrees from the same sum of money spent on them, but also, all services also face the difficulty that a pound spent in London, say, will buy a less good service than a pound spent in Newcastle. The labour market is so much more competitive in London that, pound for pound, the quality of the labour hired is just not as good. That is what the 'market forces factors' or 'area costs adjustments' are meant to correct for. In practice, they do so only imperfectly.

What lie behind such calculations are attempts to see how far wages and salaries in some labour markets are higher than those in others by virtue of the shortages or differential demand and supply conditions that apply there. That works for general categories of labour and probably works rather well for those in general labour market situations in broad regions. What affects the attractiveness of a job in a school for a teacher, however, is something rather more distinctive. It is the attractiveness or difficulty of that job in that school. Difficult children from a very deprived area with little parental support may well face a teacher with less job satisfaction and more stress than teaching in a comfortable suburban school. Some young teachers may relish the task, but not many for very long. To get a teacher of an equivalent quality in front of a class means higher compensation is required in those areas. A true market forces factor would be measuring that. This is not unfair positive discrimination or making judgements about how much more teaching some children need than others. It is to seek to achieve the same goal as the NHS sets itself: equal access to equal quality staff wherever you live.

The NHS does not succeed either, for exactly the same reason. The job is less attractive and tougher in some hospitals and some GP practices than others. Much the same can be said of some housing estates, with the costs of maintenance and housing management costs. More work on rather more discrete cost differences needs to be done in all the services.

The education SSAs for inner-city areas have led to considerable criticism from less grant-favoured authorities about the fairness of the need assessment system. Inner London authorities in particular are said to have received SSAs that exaggerate the cost of provision in their areas. There is no doubt that the greatest schools needs assessments tend to be in authorities with the worst levels of educational achievement. Although this project has found no evidence that high assessed spending needs have actually provided a perverse incentive for poor school performance, it is obviously important to avoid systems where there is a danger of such feedbacks.

There is no doubt that the scale of London's education spending is different from other cities in England. It was in the times of the old LCC and of the ILEA that followed it. A national SSA formula which must work fairly for the average school is likely to be least accurate when dealing with London or other outliers. One way to cope with this would be to revert to a London-only formula of the kind used within the rate support grant during the 1970s. An overall London-based allocation based on political judgement could be made to London and then allocated within it. However, one of the consistent themes across the services, outside London, is the suspicion that London always does too well. Such an arrangement would only serve to increase that suspicion.

Attempting to avoid perverse feed-backs, and to produce defensible adjustments for higher costs in areas like London, again suggests that funding ought to be based on more fine-grained information about relative costs and needs than just the spending levels of a few hundred LEAs.

Outcomes and Access

At the end, however, we have to return to the conundrum we posed in Chapter 4 and again at the beginning of this chapter. Given the undoubted sophistication of the systems of resource allocation we have described, how come the outcomes in terms of health inequalities and pupil performance remain so unequal? The Acheson Report (DoH 1998) has shown how resistant health inequalities are to change. The same is revealed by the international comparisons on pupils' performance at school. The Plowden Committee (CACE 1967) noted that what distinguished the UK from most other advanced countries was the wide spread of attainment. The best did better than in most other countries. The low achievers did worse. Despite three decades of reduced inequalities in school resources that remains the case (see Glennerster 1998 for a review of the evidence). We are driven back to Tawney's caution noted in Chapter 2: 'equality of provision is not identity of provision'.

Equal resources in two areas do not necessarily give rise to equal use or use related to need. Here we need to move beyond the quantitative sophistication of multi-level modelling and try to understand better the factors that impact on differential use and differential effectiveness of services in meeting the needs of different groups, especially the least advantaged. We suspect that this will be the emerging agenda for formula makers and regulators in the next decade.

Another conclusion concerns the highly developed nature of funding formulae in Britain, and, indeed, the way in which such formulae seek to achieve equity and efficiency objectives. Although this study did not examine equivalent systems in other countries, we have seen little evidence that other countries have developed transparent, equity-seeking, national funding mechanisms on anything like the scale of those now operating within Britain. The top–down nature of British government, coupled with powerful media-fuelled demands for 'equal' treatment (both for individuals and areas of the country), has ensured that health, schools, housing, universities, colleges, and training services are funded through complex—and generally need-related—national funding formulae. 'Fair' treatment of individuals (whether this means equivalent waiting times for hospital treatment or similar chances of accessing a local college) is deeply ingrained in British political and cultural values. Given the right-of-centre nature of many of the country's governments during the twentieth century, this tendency to seek equality by the use of national funding systems is perhaps an unusual national preoccupation.

REFERENCES

Abel-Smith, B. (1964). *The Hospitals, 1800–1948: A Study in Social Administration in England and Wales*. London: Heinemann.

Akerlof, G. A. (1970). 'The Market for "Lemons": Quality Uncertainty and the Market Mechanism', *The Quarterly Journal of Economics*, 84(3): 488–500.

Balarajan, R. (1990). *Social Deprivation and Age Adjustment Ratios for South West Thames Region*. Guildford: Epidemiology and Public Health Research Unit, University of Surrey.

Barrow, M. (1998). 'Financing Schools: A National or Local Quasi-Market?', in Bartlett *et al.*, *A Revolution in Social Policy*. Bristol: The Policy Press.

Bartlett, W., and Le Grand, J. (1993). *Quasi-Markets and Social Policy*. Basingstoke: Macmillan.

Bartlett, W., Roberts, J. A., and Le Grand, J. (1998). *A Revolution in Social Policy*. Bristol: The Policy Press.

Birchenough, C. (1938). *History of Elementary Education in England and Wales from 1800 to the Present Day*. London: University Tutorial Press.

Bradley, S., Johnes, G., and Millington, J. (1999). *School Choice, Competition and the Efficiency of Secondary Schools in England*. Lancaster: Centre for Research in the Economies of Education, Lancaster University.

British Medical Association (1970). *Health Service Financing*. London: BMA.

Burchardt, T., Hills, J., and Propper, C. (1999). *Private Welfare and Public Policy*. York: Joseph Rowntree Foundation.

Burgess, R. L. (1997). 'Fiscal Reforms for Health and Education', in C. Colclough (ed.), *Marketizing Education and Health in Developing Countries*. Oxford: Oxford University Press.

Butler, D., Adonis, A., and Travers, A. (1994). *Failure in British Government: The Politics of the Poll Tax*. Oxford: Oxford University Press.

Butler, J. R. *et al.* (1975). *How Many Patients: A Study of List Sizes in General Practice.* Occasional Paper in Social Administration, 64; London: Bedford Square Press.

Butts, M. (1986). 'Questioning Basic Assumptions', *Health Service Journal* (19 June): 826–7.

Buxton, M. J., and Klein, R. (1978). *Allocating Health Resources: A Commentary on the Report of the Resource Allocation Working Party*. Royal Commission on the National Health Service, Research Paper 3; London: HMSO.

Byrne, E. (1974). *Planning and Educational Inequality*. Slough: National Foundation for Educational Research.

Carr-Hill, R. A., Hardman, G., Martin, S., Peacock, S., Sheldon, T. A., and Smith, P. (1994). *A Formula for Distributing NHS Revenues Based on Small Area Use of Hospital Beds*. York: University of York.

——Maynard, A., and Slack, R. (1990). 'Morbidity Variation and RAWP', *Journal of Epidemiology and Community Health*, 44(4): 271–3.

Carstairs, V., and Morris, R. (1989). 'Deprivation and Mortality: An Alternative to Social Class?', *Community Medicine*, 11(3): 210–19.

Central Advisory Council for Education (England) (1967). *Children and their Primary Schools*. Plowden Report; London: HMSO.

Central Housing Advisory Committee (1961). *Homes for Today and Tomorrow*. Parker Morris Report; London: HMSO.

Chubb, J. E., and Moe, T. E. (1990). *Politics, Markets and America's Schools*. Washington, DC: Brookings Institution.

Coase, R. (1937). 'The Nature of the Firm', *Economica*, 4: 386–405.

Cooper, M. H., and Culyer, A. S. (1970). 'An Economic Assessment of Some of the Aspects of the National Health Service', in *British Medical Association Health Service Financing: A Report of the BMA Advisory Panel*, Chr. Dr I. M. Jones, Appendix A, Pt. IV. London: BMA.

Cremer, J., Estache, A., and Seabright, P. (1993). *The Decentralisation of Public Services: Lessons from the Theory of the Firm*. World Bank Seminar Paper, mimeo.; Washington, DC: World Bank.

Culyer, A. J., Lavers, R. J., and Williams, A. (1971). 'Social Indicators in Health', *Social Trends*, ii. London: HMSO.

Davies, B. (1968). *Social Needs and Resources in Local Services*. London: Michael Joseph.

Department for Education and Employment (1996). *Funding 16–19 Education and Training: Towards Convergence*. London: DfEE.

——(1999). *Departmental Report: The Government's Expenditure Plans 1999–00 to 2001–02*. Cm. 4202; London: The Stationery Office.

Department for Education and Science (1988). *Education Reform Act: Local Management of Schools*. Circular 71/88; London: DES.

——(1991). *Local Management of Schools: Further Guidance*. Circular 7/91; London: DES.

Department of Environment, Transport, and the Regions (1998). *A New Financial Regime for Local Authority Housing: Resource Accounting in the Housing Revenue Account*. London: DETR.

Department of Health (1989). *Working for Patients*. London: HMSO.

——(1997). *The New NHS: Modern, Dependable*. Cm. 3807; London: HMSO.

——(1998). *Independent Inquiry into Inequalities in Health Report*. Acheson Report; London: The Stationery Office.

Department of Health and Social Security (1981). *Primary Health Care in Inner London*. Acheson Report; London: HMSO.

——(1986). *Review of the Resource Allocation Working Party Formula*. Interim report by the NHS Management Board. London: HMSO.

Department of Health and Social Security (1988). *Review of the Resource Allocation Working Party Formula*. Final report. London: HMSO.

Department of the Environment (1976). *Local Government Finance: Report of the Committee of Enquiry*. Layfield Committee, Cmnd. 6453; London: HMSO.

——(1987). *Finance for Housing Associations: The Government's Proposals*. London: DoE.

——(1988). *New Financial Regime for Local Authority Housing in England and Wales: A Consultative Paper*. London: DoE.

——(1989). *Housing and Construction Statistics 1978–1988 Great Britain*. London: HMSO.

——(1994). *Fundamental Review of the Generalised Needs Index (GNI) and the Housing Needs Index (HNI)*. London: DoE.

——(1996). *Standard Spending Assessments: Guide to Methodology 1996/97*. London: DoE.

——(1997*a*). *Education Sub-group Report*. London: DoE.

——(1997*b*). *Housing Revenue Manual*, i and ii (Mar. 1997, with earlier edns.). London: DoE.

Doyal, L., and Gough, I. (1991). *A Theory of Human Need*. London: Macmillan.

Dunleavy, P. (1981). *The Politics of Mass Housing in Britain 1945–1975*. Oxford: Clarendon Press.

——(1991). *Democracy, Bureaucracy and Public Choice*. London: Harvester.

Ellison, N. (1994). *Egalitarian Thought and the Labour Politics*. London: Routledge.

Epple, D., Filimon, R., and Romer, T. (1984). 'Equilibrium among local jurisdictions: Toward an Integrated Treatment of Voting and Residential Choice', *Journal of Public Economics*, 24: 281–308.

Evans, M. (1998). 'Social Security: Dismantling the Pyramids?', in H. Glennerster and J. Hills (eds.), *The State of Welfare: The Economics of Social Spending*. Oxford: Oxford University Press.

Forsyth, G. (1966). *Doctors and State Medicine: A Study of the British Health Service*. London: Pitman.

Foster, C. D., Jackman, R., and Perlman, M. (1980). *Local Government Finance in a Unitary State*. London: Allen & Unwin.

Gerwitz, S., Ball, S., and Bowe, R. (1995). *Markets, Choice and Equity in Education*. Milton Keynes: Open University Press.

Glennerster, H. (1974). *Social Service Budgets and Local Policy*. London: Allen & Unwin.

——(1991). 'Quasi-Markets in Education', *Economic Journal*, 101: 1268–76.

——(1996). *Paying for Welfare: Towards 2000*, 3rd edn. Hemel Hempstead: Prentice Hall.

——(1998). 'Education: Reaping the Harvest?', in H. Glennerster and J. Hills (eds.), *The State of Welfare: The Economics of Social Spending*. Oxford: Oxford University Press.

——and Hills, J. (eds.) (1998). *The State of Welfare: The Economics of Social Spending*, 2nd ed. Oxford: Oxford University Press.

——Cohen, A., and Bovell, V. (1998). 'Alternatives to Fundholding', *International Journal of Health Services*, 28(1): 47–66.

——Matsaganis, M., Owens, P., and Hancock, S. (1994). *Implementing GP Fundholding*. Milton Keynes: Open University Press.

——Power, A., and Travers, A. (1991). 'A New Era for Social Policy: A New Enlightenment or a New Leviathan?', *Journal of Social Policy*, 20(3): 389–414.

Goldstrom, J. M. (1972). *Education: Elementary Education 1780–1900*. Newton Abbot: David & Charles.

Gosden, P. H. (1966). *The Development of Educational Administration*. Oxford: Blackwell.

Gough, I. (1994). 'Economic Institutions and the Satisfaction of Human Needs', *Journal of Economic Issues*, 28(1).

Griffiths, J. A. G. (1966). *Central Departments and Local Authorities*. London: Allen & Unwin.

Groenewegen, P. (1990). 'Taxation and Decentralisation', in R. J. Bennett (ed.), *Decentralisation Local Governments and Markets: Towards a Post-Welfare Agenda*. Oxford: Oxford University Press.

Grossman, S. J., and Hart, O. D. (1986). 'The Costs and Benefits of Ownership: A Theory of Vertical and Lateral Integration', *Journal of Political Economy*, 94(4): 691–719.

Groves, T. (1973). 'Incentives in Teams', *Econometrics*, 31(6): 617–63.

Grumbach, K. (1998). 'Primary Care Physicians: Experience of Financial Incentives in Managed Care Systems', *The New England Journal of Medicine*, 339(21): 1516–21.

Hale, R., and Travers, A. (1993). *£36 billion and rising? A Study of Standard Spending Assessments (SSAs)*. London: Chartered Institute of Public Finance and Accountancy.

Harris, J. (1999). 'Ruskin and Social Reform', in *Ruskin and the Dawn of the Modern*. Oxford: Oxford University Press.

Hendry, R. (1998). *Fair Shares for All? The Development of Needs Based Government Funding in Education, Health and Housing*. CASEpaper, 18; London: London School of Economics.

Hills, J. (1991). *Unravelling Housing Finance: Subsidies, Benefits, and Taxation*. Oxford: Clarendon Press.

——(1997). 'The Distribution of Welfare', in P. Alcock, A. Erskine, and M. May (eds.), *The Student's Companion to Social Policy*. Oxford: Blackwell.

——(1998). 'Housing: A Decent Home within the Reach of Every Family?', in H. Glennerster and Hills (eds.), *The State of Welfare: The Economics of Social Spending*. Oxford: Oxford University Press.

——(2000). *Reinventing Social Housing Finance*. London: Institute for Public Policy Research.

Hirschman, A. O. (1970). *Exit, Voice and Loyalty: Responses to Decline in Forms, Organisations and States*. Cambridge, Mass.: Harvard University Press.

H. M. Treasury (1998). *Modern Public Services for Britain: Investing in Reform*. Comprehensive Spending Review, Cm. 4011; London: The Stationery Office.

Holmans, A. E. (1987). *Housing Policy in Britain: A History*. London: Croom Helm.

Hood, C., Scott, D., James, O., Jones, G., and Travers, T. (1999). *Regulation Inside Government: Waste-Watchers, Quality Police and Sleaze-Busters*. Oxford: Oxford University Press.

House of Commons (1993*a*). *Some Aspects of the Funding of Schools*. HoC Paper 419, Session 1992–93; London: HMSO.

——(1993*b*). *The Department for Education's Expenditure Plans 1993–94 to 1995–96*. HoC Paper 717, Session 1992–93; London: HMSO.

——(1994*a*). *The Disparity in Funding between Primary and Secondary Schools*, i. HoC Paper 45-I, Session 1993–94; London: HMSO.

——(1994*b*). *The Department for Education's Expenditure Plans 1994–95 to 1996–97*, HoC Paper 454, Session 1993–94; London: HMSO.

——(1994*c*). *A Common Funding Formula for Grant-Maintained Schools*. HoC Paper 255, Session 1993–94; London: HMSO.

Housing Corporation (1999). *Developing our Investment Strategy*. London: The Housing Corporation.

Hurst, J. W. (1997). 'The Impact of Health Economics on Health Policy in England, and the Impact of Health Policy on Health Economics, 1972–1997' (not published, but available from author at NHS Executive).

Jarman, B. (1984). 'Underprivileged Areas: Validation and Distribution of Scores', *British Medical Journal*, 284: 165–8.

Kemp, P. (1998). *Housing Benefit: Time for Reform*. York: Joseph Rowntree Foundation.

Kemp Committee (1914). *Report of Departmental Committee on Local Taxation*. Cd. 7315; London: HMSO.

King's Fund (1998). *The Health of Londoners: A Public Health Report for London*. London: King's Fund.

Klein, R. (1995). *The New Politics of the National Health Service*, 3rd edn. London: Longman.

Lawrence, B. (1972). *The Administration of Education in Britain*. London: Batsford.

Lee, T. (1997). *The Search For Equity: The Funding of Additional Educational Needs under LMS*. Aldershot: Avebury.

Le Grand, J. (1975). 'Fiscal Equity and Central Government Grants to Local Authorities', *Economic Journal*, 85: 531–7.

——and Vizard, P. (1998). 'The National Health Service: Crisis, Change or

Continuity?', in H. Glennerster and J. Hills (eds.), *The State of Welfare: The Economics of Social Spending*. Oxford: Oxford University Press.

——Mays, N., and Mulligan, J. (1998). *Learning from the NHS Internal Market*. London: Kings Fund.

——Winter, D., and Woolley, F. (1990). 'The National Health Service: Safe in Whose Hands?', in J. Hills (ed.), *The State of Welfare: The Welfare State in Britain since 1974*. Oxford: Clarendon Press.

Lewis, J., and Glennerster, H. (1996). *Implementing the New Community Care*. Buckingham: Open University Press.

Lindblom, C. E. (1965). *The Intelligence of Democracy*. New York: Free Press.

Ludbrook, A., and Maynard, A. (1988). 'The Funding of the National Health Service: What is the Problem and is Social Insurance the Answer?' Discussion Paper, 39, Centre for Health Economics, York: University of York.

McGuire, C. B., and Radner, R. (1986). *Decision and Organisation*. Minneapolis: University of Minnesota Press.

Macintyre, S. (1998). 'Social Inequalities in Health in the Contemporary World: Comparative Overview', in S. S. Strickland and P. S. Shetty (eds.), *Human Biology and Social Inequality*. Cambridge: Cambridge University Press.

Malpass, P. (1989). 'The Road from Clay Cross', *Roof* (Jan.–Feb.). 38–40.

——and Murie, A. (1987). *Housing Policy and Practice*, 2nd edn. Basingstoke: Macmillan Education.

Marx, K. (1875). 'Critique of the Gotha Programme', in *The First International and After*. Harmondsworth: Penguin.

Mays, N. (1989). 'NHS Resource Allocation after the 1989 White Paper: A Critique of the Research for the RAWP Review', *Community Medicine*, 11(3): 137–86.

——(1995). 'Geographical Resource Allocation in the English National Health Service 1971–1994: The Tension between Normative and Empirical Approaches', *International Journal of Epidemiology*, 24(3).

——and Bevan, G. (1987). *Resource Allocation in the Health Service: A Review of the Methods of the Resource Allocation Working Party*. Occasional Papers on Social Administration, 81; London: Bedford Square Press/NCVO.

Merrett, S. (1979). *State Housing in Britain*. London: Routledge & Kegan Paul.

Milner, P., and Nichol, J. (1988). 'Revising RAWP', *The Lancet*, p. 1195.

Ministry of Health (1956). *Report of the Committee of Enquiry into the Cost of the National Health Service*. Guillebaud Committee, Cmd. 9663; London: HMSO.

Ministry of Housing and Local Government (1958). *The General Grant Distribution Order 1958*. HoC Paper 15, Session 1958–59; London: HMSO.

——(1966). *The Rate Support Grant Order 1966*. HoC Paper 252, Session 1966–67; London: HMSO.

Morgan, M., Mays, N., and Holland, W. (1987). 'Can Hospital Use be a Measure of Need for Health Care?', *Journal of Epidemiology and Community Health*, 41(4): 269–74.

Morris, B. (1983). 'Education and the Heresy of Specific Grant', *Local Government Policy Making*, 10(3).

Mueller, D. C. (1989). *Public Choice II*. Cambridge: Cambridge University Press.

National Audit Office (1997). *Further Education Funding Council for England*. HoC 223, Session 1996–97. London: The Stationery Office.

National Health Service Executive (1997). *NCHS Revenue Allocation to Health Authorities: Weighed Capitation Formulas*. Leeds: National Health Executive.

Newhouse, J. P. (1989). 'Adjusting Capitation Rates Using Objective Health Measures and Prior Utilisation', *Health Care Financing Review*, 10(3): 41–54.

Niner, P. (1998). *Housing Needs Measurement: A Critical Assessment*. London: National Housing Federation.

Oates, W. (1972). *Fiscal Federalism*. New York: Harcourt Brace Jovanovitch.

Osborne, D., and Gaebler, E. (1992). *Reinventing Government: How the Entrepreneurial Spirit is Transforming the Public Sector*. New York: Plume.

Peacock, A., and Smith, P. (1995). *The Resource Allocation Consequences of the New NHS Allocation Formula*. Discussion Paper, 134, Centre for Health Economics; York. University of York.

Peters, T. S., and Waterman, R. H. (1982). *In Search of Excellence: Lessons from America's Best Run Companies*. New York: Harper & Row.

Plant, R. (1985). 'Welfare and the Value of Liberty', *Government and Opposition*, 20(3): 297–314.

Power, A. (1987). *Property Before People*. London: Allen & Unwin.

—— and Mumford, K. (1999). *The Slow Death of Great Cities? Urban Abandonment or Urban Renaissance?* York: Joseph Rowntree Foundation.

Regan, D. (1977). *Local Government and Education*. London: Allen & Unwin.

Rhodes, P. (1976). *The Value of Medicine*. London: Allen & Unwin.

Royal Commission on Local Taxation (1901). *Final Report*. Chairman Lord Balfour of Burleigh, Cd. 638; London: HMSO.

Royal Commission on Long Term Care (1999). *With Respect to Old Age*. Cm 4192; London: The Stationery Office.

Sanderson, I. (1995). *Current Issues in Local Government Finance*. London: Commission for Local Democracy.

Seeley, R. B. (1843). *The Perils of the Nation*. London: no publ.

Sefton, T. (1997). *The Changing Distribution of the Social Wage*. STICERD Occasional Paper, 21; London: LSE.

Shaw, E. (1996). *The Labour Party since 1945: Old Labour*. Oxford: Blackwell.

Sheldon, T. A. (1990). 'The Problems of Using Multiple Regression for Modelling the Demand Supply and Use of Health Services', *Journal of Public Health Medicine*, 12(3/4): 213–15.

—— (1997). 'Formula Fever: Allocating Resources in the NHS', *British Medical Journal*, 315: 964.

—— and Carr-Hill, R. A. (1992). 'Resource Allocation by Regression in the NHS: A Statistical Critique of the RAWP Review', *Journal of the Royal Statistical Society* (Series A), 155(3): 403–20.

Smith, G. (1980). *Social Need*. London: Routledge & Kegan Paul.

Stevens, R. (1966). *Medical Practice in Modern England*. New York: Yale University Press.

Stewart, F. (1985). *Planning to Meet Basic Needs*. London: Macmillan.

Sutherland, G. (1971). *Elementary Education in the Nineteenth Century*. London: Historical Association.

Tiebout, C. (1956). 'A Pure Theory of Local Tax Expenditures', *Journal of Political Economy*, 64: 416–24.

Timmins, N. (1995). *The Five Giants: A Biography of the Welfare State*. London: Harper Collins.

Titmuss, R. M. (1958). *Essays on the Welfare State*. London: Allen & Unwin.

Townsend, P., and Bosanquet, N. (1972). *Labour and Inequality*. London: Fabian Society.

——Phillimore, P., and Beattie, A. (1987). *Health and Deprivation: Inequality and the North*. London: Croom Helm.

Travers, A. (1986). *The Politics of Local Government Finance*. London: Allen & Unwin.

——(1993). 'Memorandum', pp. 1–7, in *The Department for Education's Expenditure Plans 1993–94 to 1995–96*. Third Report from the Education Committee, HoC paper 717, Session 1994–95; London: HMSO.

——(1994). 'Memorandum', pp. 32–5, in *The Department for Education's Expenditure Plans 1994–95 to 1996–97*. Fourth Report from the Education Committee, HoC paper 454, Session 1995–96; London: HMSO.

Tudor-Hart, J. (1971). 'The Inverse Care Law', *The Lancet* (27 Feb.): 405–12.

Tudor Walters Committee (1918). *Building Construction: Report of a Committee Appointed to Consider Questions of Building Construction in Connection with the Provision of Dwellings for the Working Classes*. Cd. 9191; London: HMSO.

Vaizey, J., and Sheehan, J. (1968). *Resources for Education: An Economic Study of Education in the United Kingdom, 1920–1965*. London: Allen & Unwin.

Vandenberghe, V. (1998). 'Educational Quasi-Markets: The Belgian Experience', in W. Bartlett *et al.*, *A Revolution in Social Policy*. Bristol: The Policy Press.

Wallace, G. (1992). *Local Management of Schools: Research and Experience*. Clevedon: Multilingual Matters.

Ware, A., and Goodin, R. E. (1990). *Needs and Welfare*. London: Sage.

Weale, A. (1978). *Equality and Social Policy*. London: Routledge & Kegan Paul.

Webb, S. (1911). *The Necessary Basis of Society*. Fabian Tracts, 159; London: Fabian Society.

——(1920). *Grants in Aid: A Criticism and a Proposal*, 2nd edn. London: Longmans, Green.

——and Webb, B. (1897). *Industrial Democracy*. London: Longmans Green & Co.

Webster, C. (1988). *The Health Services since the War*, i. *Problems of Health Care: The National Health Service before 1957*. London: HMSO.

West, A., and Pennell, H. (1995). *Evaluation of the New Early Years Admissions Policy in Tower Hamlets*. London: Centre for Economic Research.

West, A., and Pennell, H. (forthcoming). 'Publishing School Examination Results in England: Incentives and Consequences.' *Educational Studies*.

West, E. G. (1975). *Education and the Industrial Revolution*. London: Batsford.

Wilcox, S. (1998). *Housing Finance Review 1998/99*. York: Joseph Rowntree Foundation.

Wildavsky, A. (1975). *Budgeting: A Comparative Theory of Budgetary Processes*. Boston: Little Brown.

Williamson, O. E. (1975). *Markets and Hierarchies: Analysis and Anti-Trust Implications*. New York: Free Press.

INDEX

References in **bold** refer to figures, and those in *italic* to tables.